W9-AMT-777

PICTURES IN A MINUTE

THIRD EDITION

PICTURES IN A MINUTE

BY JOHN WOLBARST

Third Edition

Library of Congress Catalog
Card number: 60-7303

Printed in U.S.A. by Blanchard Press
New York, N. Y.

Printings:
First Edition
February, 1956
June, 1956
February, 1957
Second Edition
April, 1958
February, 1959
Third Edition
January, 1960

CONTINUED

About the illustrations: Every one of the full page display pictures in this book was made with a standard Polaroid Land camera, and the engraving was made directly from the Polaroid Land print.

All pictures intended to show the abilities of the Polaroid Land camera were made with standard models of that camera, using Polaroid Land films.

In order to get the widest possible variety of "idea" pictures, it was necessary to include some which had been made with other types of cameras. However, in every case the picture is one which is easily within the capabilities of the Polaroid Land camera and film. J.W.

Pages 119-160: Picture taking and using ideas for more fun with the camera.

Pages 172-192: Special types of equipment and films; information for the technically minded.

Editor's note: This book covers the use of all Polaroid Land cameras on the market at the time it went to press. These include: Model 150 Polaroid Land Camera; Model 800 Polaroid Land Camera; Polaroid Speedliner Land Camera, Model 95B; Polaroid Highlander Land Camera, Model 80A; Polaroid Pathfinder Land Camera, Model 110A. It also covers the following discontinued models: Polaroid Speedliner Land Camera, Model 95A; Polaroid Highlander Land Camera, Model 80; Polaroid Pathfinder Land Camera, Model 110; Model 100 Polaroid Land Camera; THE 700 Polaroid Land Camera; Model 95 Polaroid Land Camera. Frequently throughout the book these cameras will be referred to by their short title, such as Model 150, Model 800, Speedliner (Models 95A, 95B), Highlander (Models 80, 80A) or Pathfinder (Models 110, 110A).

WHY PICTURES

THE POLAROID LAND camera is more than just a novel device which has made picture taking much simpler and surer. It does more than just give you the fun of seeing your picture in a minute.

This camera has smashed the barriers to creative photography for the average picture taker. It has eliminated the technical complications and mysterious jargon which have always stood between the desire to create truly beautiful pictures and the ability to do so. For it is a fact that in the past only the elite few, the accomplished technicians, could predict with reasonable certainty what would "come out" after hours of skilled darkroom labor. And if the truth were known, even they were frequently disappointed at the results, while the opportunity to reshoot the picture was far past.

Some people may hoot at the idea of doing creative photography with a camera as simple to operate as this one is. They

◁ CONTENTS

IN A MINUTE?

talk of limited shutter speeds, small lens openings, and other technicalities. No doubt the present camera mechanism has its limitations (all other cameras have theirs), but none of them is in the realm of creativity. In its way, this is the most creative camera of them all, and its simplicity of operation is the very thing that makes creative photography possible for everyone.

For the first time, an ordinary picture taker can photograph a scene, view the print on the spot, vary exposure if necessary, change angle if desirable, come closer or move to a greater distance, add or remove filters, improve the picture, polish it, work at it, until the desired result is achieved.

Have you ever had the satisfaction of thus creating a beautiful picture, one which you can show to your family and friends with pride? That's what this book is mainly about.

Only a small part of the text is devoted to telling which button to push. It tries to avoid all the overworked "helpful" tips that tell you not to have telephone poles growing out of your subjects' heads. It assumes that you have found in the picture-in-a-minute camera a rather intriguing instrument that whets your creative curiosity, and it further assumes that you want to get the most out of it.

If this book makes you discontented with the first picture you take of any scene, it will have made a good beginning. If it prompts you to study your friends, your family, your city, your daily experiences, with the piercing eye of the camera, working at each subject until the print expresses in black and white what *you* want it to say—then the book can be called a success.

Ambitious? Yes. Challenging? Certainly. But we have no doubts that you can do it, with pictures in a minute. J.W.

THE CAMERA

A quick look at what makes it different from any other kind of camera and why.

WITHIN ONE MINUTE after taking a picture with a Polaroid Land camera, it will deliver a dry, finished, excellent print of your subject. No other camera can do this.

The physical operations necessary to perform this amazing feat are so simple that anyone witnessing them for the first time is apt to register disbelief. You take the picture. You pull a paper tab to start the film developing process. After about a minute, you open the back door of the camera, remove the picture you just took. That's it. The system of photography that makes this possible is the invention of Dr. Edwin H. Land, president and director of research of Polaroid Corp., and that's how the camera got its name.

These two pages are intended to give you a quick look at the Polaroid Land camera and its controls. If you're not already acquainted with the camera, you'll know what we're talking about in the following chapters. If you're interested in technical matters, the chapter *How it Works* describes in considerable detail the principles of operation of the camera and film, explains what makes them function as they do, and gives you a broad background of information.

Simplicity is the word

The Polaroid Land camera was designed for people who want the flexibility and resources of a camera with all the necessary adjustable controls, but who have no desire to learn complicated technical facts in order to take good pictures. To that end, every function of the camera has been simplified to a remarkable degree. Its controls do not resemble those of any other camera on the market. Even the ordinary photographic language does not, in large measure, apply to this camera. Let's examine it.

The camera is designed to give you a print. Ordinarily, the Polaroid Land film negative exists only to produce the print; in the process, the negative becomes worthless, so it is discarded. The camera takes a special film consisting of two rolls—one of negative material, one of print paper—so it has two film chambers into which the rolls drop quickly and easily. The two rolls are joined to a strong paper leader; on it are printed full instructions for loading, which takes only a few seconds.

The easy-to-set controls

You want to take a picture—what's the correct exposure? No fractional seconds or f-numbers on this camera. Instead, a single dial with numbers from 10 to 17 (11 to 18 on the Highlander). Older model Polaroid Land cameras are numbered 1 to 8 and 2 to 9.

The exposure guide that comes with each roll of film tells you that the exposure control should be set to a certain number—16, for example. You twirl a little wheel until 16 comes up in a window on the shutter housing. Both lens opening and shutter speed have been set in this single operation. A simple-to-use exposure meter can give you even more accurate exposure information—you aim the meter, read one number, set it on the camera. (You can attach to your camera a novel accessory—a photoelectric shutter —which automatically selects the correct exposure under most outdoor snapshot conditions.)

Focusing is just as easy as setting the exposure control. Coupled rangefinders give you accurate distance settings. (On the non-rangefinder cameras you move a lever or turn part of the lens mount

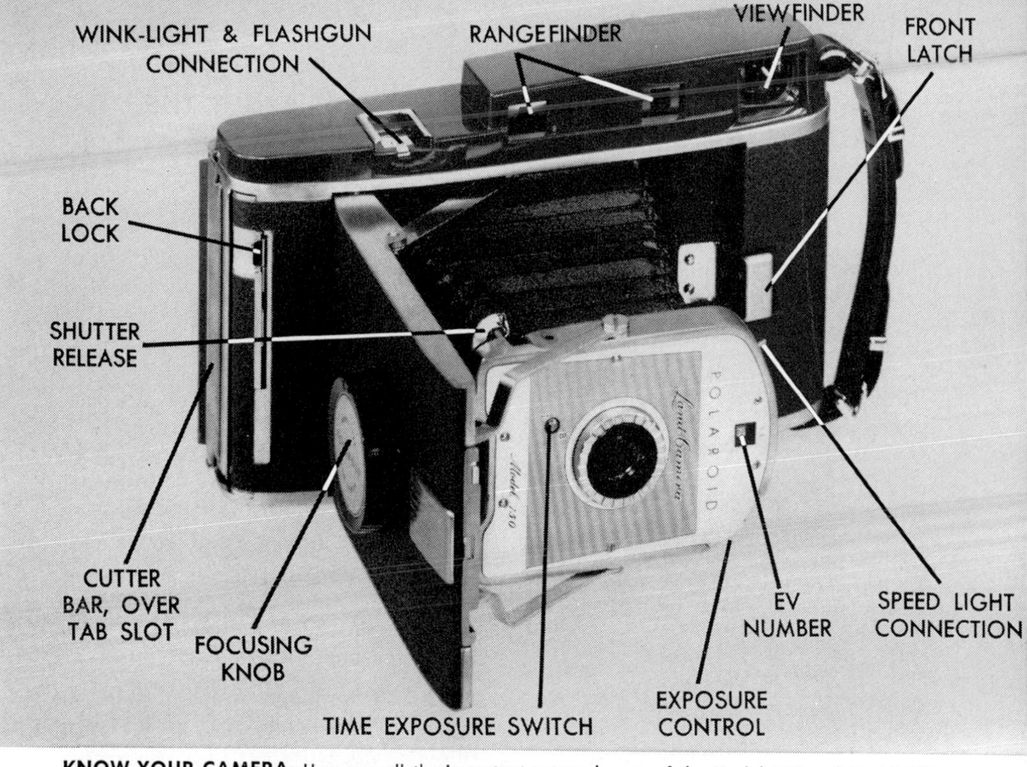

KNOW YOUR CAMERA: Here are all the important external parts of the Model 150 and Model 800 Polaroid Land cameras. Other models (next page) work on the same basic principles but vary in size and in the type and arrangement of the operating controls. Each of the "how to" chapters gives detailed operating instructions for the various models. For an inside view of the camera see *Loading.*

past a clearly marked distance scale.) The design of the lens absorbs slight distance setting errors, and when using the photoelectric shutter everything from 3½ ft. to as far as you can see is in sharp focus in your photograph.

Making a picture in a minute

You press the shutter release, take the picture. Within one minute you will know whether or not you like the results.

Now in two swift movements, you operate the film release and pull out the paper tab protruding from the camera back, thus drawing the exposed film into the developing compartment of the camera. (Be sure to pull the tab straight out, or the film may jam. Some important tips on this in *Let's Make a Picture.*)

Now the developing process is going on. After about a minute, open the back door of the camera, with a fingernail lift up a triangular bit of paper, carefully separate the print from the rest of the paper strip. There is the picture. You have just finished performing a photographic miracle.

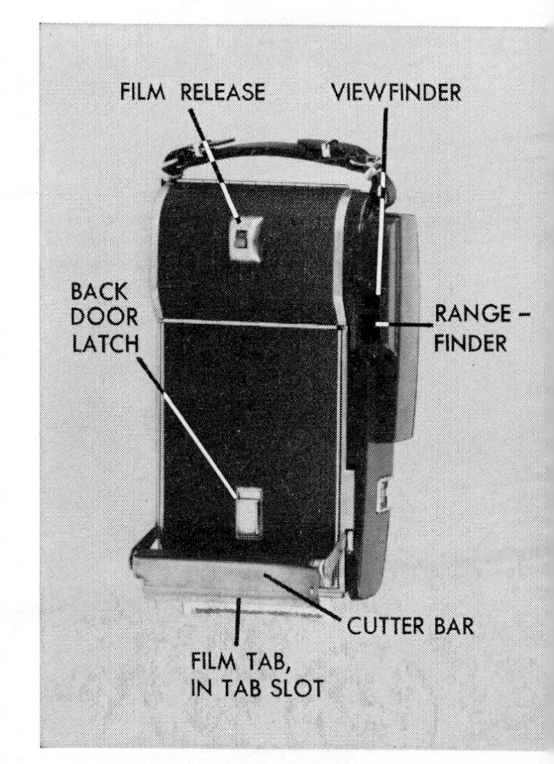

OTHER CURRENT MODELS OF THE LAND CAMERA

MODEL 95B SPEEDLINER: Mechanically similar to the Models 150 and 800, except that it has a different type of viewfinder and is focused manually instead of with a rangefinder. Also, the flashgun and the wink-light are connected by a wire, not through the accessory shoe as in Models 150 and 800.

MODEL 110A PATHFINDER: Same as the Models 150 and 800, but has a more complex and expensive lens/shutter system designed for press and professional use. This is fully described in the chapter *Using the Pathfinders.*

MODEL 80A HIGHLANDER: Smallest, lowest priced Land camera, it makes prints 2½ x 3¼ in. The exposure control system is similar to that on the Models 150, 800, and 95B.

FACTS ABOUT THE DISCONTINUED MODELS

All Polaroid Land cameras are basically alike in the manner in which they produce pictures in a minute, and no matter what the age of the camera, films currently manufactured fit it.

However, there are differences in the operating controls of discontinued and current models. Here are some identifying characteristics of earlier models.

Model 95A Speedliner: Same as the Model 95B, except that the exposure control is numbered from 1 to 8 instead of from 10 to 17. Discontinued in 1957.

Model 100: Similar to the Model 95A, but with specially selected lenses and shutters and some heavy duty modifications for business and industrial use. Discontinued in 1957.

Model 700: Similar to the Model 95A, but has a non-coupled rangefinder. Discontinued in 1957.

Model 95: The original model of the Polaroid Land camera. Differs from the Speedliner series by having: a shutter with top speed of only 1/60 sec., instead of 1/100 sec.; a lens with aperture range from f/11 to f/45, instead of from f/8.8 to f/35; "ball and mast" sighting point for viewfinder; no electronic flash synchronization; clips to hold the negative film spool in the film chamber. Discontinued in 1954. Can be factory converted to Model 95B.

Model 110 Pathfinder: Considerably different from the current Model 110A. It has a 127mm, f/4.5 Wollensak Raptar lens in a Wollensak shutter with speeds from 1 to 1/400 sec.; coupled Kalart rangefinder; separate folding optical and wire viewfinders; black finish; clips to hold the negative film spool in the film chamber (on earlier production models only). Discontinued in 1957.

Model 80 Highlander: Same as the current Model 80A, except that the exposure control is numbered from 2 to 9 instead of from 11 to 18. Discontinued in 1957.

The basic operating information for all of these models, current or discontinued, is included in this book.

THE FILMS

Names, types, development times, and how to pick the right one for the right job.

POLAROID LAND FILMS come in 8-exposure picture rolls, in two sizes. Those types in the "40" series fit all models except the Highlanders, and produce 3¼ x 4¼ in. prints. Those types in the "30" series are for the smaller Highlander, and make prints measuring 2½ x 3¼ in.

The package is a remarkably complete affair, as shown *below.* The box itself is designed to fold down into a handy pocket carrier for print protection.

Each picture roll consists of two parts: a light sensitive negative roll on a spool, and a larger roll of print material which is not light sensitive. How these produce a picture in a minute is fully explained in *How it Works.*

With the exception of some special purpose types, Polaroid Land films have the negative coated on a paper base. Once the print is removed, the paper negative which produced it is discarded, as it has no further usefulness. All the general purpose Polaroid Land films make pictures in a minute in the same manner. However, these films differ widely in their "speed" or degree of sensitivity to light.

To be able to pick the right film for your needs, you should know that the "speed" of a film is indicated by a number known as the exposure index. The higher the exposure index the "faster" the film, and the more capable it is of taking pictures where the light is dim. The exposure index for use in daylight is usually higher than that for use of the same film in tungsten light—that is, with household lamps or photofloods.

Polaroid Land films have always been somewhat faster than conventional snapshot films of the same era. This is still true today. Current Polaroid Land films are the fastest films ever offered to the general public for ordinary picture taking, and the high speed of these films makes it easy to produce pictures in a minute under conditions which would be hopeless for conventional snapshot cameras. And even when the light is good, the high film speeds help you make better, sharper pictures in a minute than would be possible if the films were slow.

All the current films are panchromatic —that is, sensitive to all colors, including red, which are recorded as varying shades of gray. The print images have a neutral black tone.

The general purpose films now available

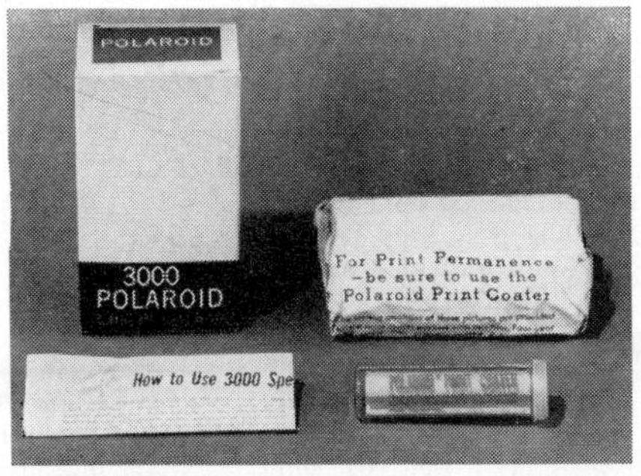

THE PACKAGE: It contains the hermetically sealed picture roll, a print coater in a glass tube, an instruction sheet, and a form for ordering copies and enlargements from Polaroid Corp.

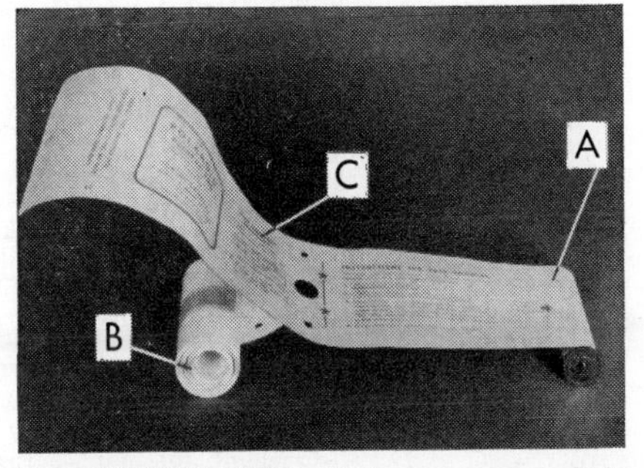

THE PICTURE ROLL: It's in two parts, a light sensitive negative on a spool (A) and a larger print roll (B which is not light sensitive. Both are firmly joined to a strong paper leader (C).

THIS IS THE FILM	THESE ARE THE USES TO WHICH IT IS BEST SUITED			
	People	Landscapes-Architecture	Flash	Special Uses
PolaPan 200 Type 42	Ideal, all 'round film—particularly good for outdoor scenes of moderate and high contrast			
High speed (200 daylight, 140 tungsten); Low contrast; Panchromatic; Wide latitude	Best for portraits of women and children. Good for *all* people with strong cross or back lighting.	For all moderate to high contrast scenes and buildings.	Best all 'round film for flash pictures. Fast enough to handle bounce flash in many situations.	Good for photomicrography and other scientific recordings where panchromatic effects are desired.
PolaPan 400 Type 32	Same as Type 42—but extra speed for dimly lit scenes and fast action pictures			
High speed (400 daylight, 140 tungsten); **PolaPan 400 Type 44** High speed (400 daylight, 280 tungsten); Low contrast; Panchromatic; Wide latitude	For sports events, where high shutter speeds are needed to stop action. Good for use with photofloods.	Same as 42 except extra speed permits deeper zone of sharp focus, especially when using darker filters.	Extra speed for bounce flash, action shots.	Extra speed useful for many scientific purposes, such as oscillography.
3000 Speed Types 47, 37	Fastest available film. Ideal for all indoor picture taking, by existing light, or with wink-light, house lamps, floods, bounce flash or speed light. Before attempting to use this film read *The 3000 Speed Film.*			
Ultra-high speed (3000 daylight, 2000 tungsten); Low contrast; Panchromatic; Wide latitude	Excellent for indoor portraits with all light sources. With #440 shutter, for bright sun portraits as close as 2 ft. without close-up lenses. With #440 shutter, in bright sun, speeds to 1/1000 sec. stop action.	With #440 shutter, sharp focus from 3½ ft. to infinity. For early morning, late afternoon, or night. Permits use of darkest filters for dramatic effects, with fast shutter speeds.	With wink-light, ends need for flashbulbs up to 8-10 ft. distance. For greater distances, tiny AG-1 flashbulbs give enough light. Increases range of bounce flash and speed light.	Makes possible many new applications of pictures in a minute in business, industry and science.
Projection Film Types 46, 46L	A specialized film which produces black and white positive transparencies for projection and a variety of other uses. High resolution film is of very high quality. Two minutes required for development time. Available in 3¼ x 4 ("lantern slide") size as Type 46-L and 2¼ x 2¼ size as Type 46. For details, see the chapter *Slides.*			
Very high speed (800 daylight, 600 tungsten); Medium contrast; Panchromatic; Wide latitude	Portraits show details sharply. Excellent for natural light shots indoors and outdoors.	Wide brightness range produces striking shots in sunlight.	Excellent quality for bounce as well as direct flash.	Many uses for science, industry visual aids, television, graphic arts, etc. For details see *Slides.*

fall into three speed groups, each of which offers certain picture taking advantages (see the chart on page 12).

Polaroid PolaPan 200, Type 42 (exposure index 200 for daylight, 140 for tungsten) is the ideal film for use outdoors with all model cameras except the Model 80A and 80 Highlanders. It is also good for flash pictures and is an all around first choice for top quality.

Polaroid PolaPan 400, Type 44 (exposure index 400 for daylight, 280 for tungsten) is similar to Type 42 except for its increased speed.

Polaroid PolaPan 400, Type 32 (exposure index 400 for daylight, 140 for tungsten is the all purpose film for use with the Model 80A and 80 cameras.

The 3000 Speed Polaroid Land Picture Roll, Types 47 and 37, is the world's fastest general purpose film. Its exposure index is 3000 for daylight, 2000 for tungsten. This film makes it possible to make pictures in a minute indoors, day or night, without the need for flashbulbs. It's a great film, but before attempting to use it please read carefully the important information in the chapter *The 3000 Speed Film.*

Beware of light fog

Although the high speeds of the films make the Polaroid Land camera versatile, they also introduce an increased danger of light fog. This is most likely to occur as a result of light leaking in the tab-pull slot when picture taking in very bright light. Here are some ways to avoid this difficulty.

Keep the cutter bar down and closed at all times. Let the cutter bar "ride" on the tab as you pull the tab to start development. Always pull the tab directly away from the sun or other light source, so the tab slot is shaded.

With the 3000 speed film the danger of light fog is increased greatly. Older model cameras must be fitted with certain light seals before they can be used with this film, and even with the newest cameras precautions are necessary. Be sure to read the chapter *The 3000 Speed Film.*

Development times

For all the general purpose films normal developing time is one minute for pictures with bright, contrasty lighting. However, pictures taken by soft, even light or of low contrast scenes, may appear slightly "flat" with normal development. These often can be given more "snap" by extending development to two minutes. Development for longer than two minutes may damage the print.

Rule to remember: For all film types, always follow the development times on the instruction sheet in the package.

As the temperature goes down, development times have to go up. At about 50°F develop for about two minutes. Polaroid Corp. recommends at least five minutes development when the mercury is near 32°F.

How to store films

Keep them in a cool, dry place. Excessive heat will damage unexposed film. Don't leave it in a closed car parked in the sun—don't leave it in the sun anytime. Remember, the bottom of the closet is cooler than the top.

Note the expiration date

All films give best results when they are fresh—that goes for the Land films, or any other type. To ensure that you have fresh film, each package carries an expiration date—something like: "Use Before July 1960." Polaroid Land films are sold with relatively short expiration periods. This is because the film carries its own developing chemicals with it, and these can deteriorate with age.

When you buy packages of Land film, always note the expiration date. If it has already passed, don't buy the film. Insist on fresh materials. If you buy some film and have it around the house for a few months before using it all up, you may find that the expiration date is quite close, or may even have been passed. Don't worry much about this—there is a reasonable safety period even beyond the expiration date. Storage conditions have much effect on the life of the film.

If you buy a fresh film, use part and leave some unexposed film in the camera a short time past the expiration date, it will probably still be usable, depending on where the camera was stored.

Caution: Stay away from "bargain" sales of outdated film (for any camera). It's foolish, false economy to buy anything but fresh stock.

LOADING

No camera loads faster or easier. Here's a step-by-step explanation in pictures

YOU CAN LOAD a Polaroid Land camera in a few seconds. The next three pages show it in detail. Here are some general points worth remembering.

Always load film out of direct sunlight. At least turn your back to the sun. Don't tear up the film box—it's a handy print carrier. Instructions are on the box.

The picture rolls are hermetically sealed. Tear this foil wrapper wide open. The two rolls are wrapped in a paper leader sealed with tape. Open the tape, unwind the leader (see photo, page 11).

Each roll is sealed with a sturdy plastic tape. *Don't break those seals!*

Only the negative (spooled) roll is affected by light. But the larger print roll carries the developer pods, which are easily damaged by crushing. *So don't squeeze hard while handling the film.*

Now let's load a film.

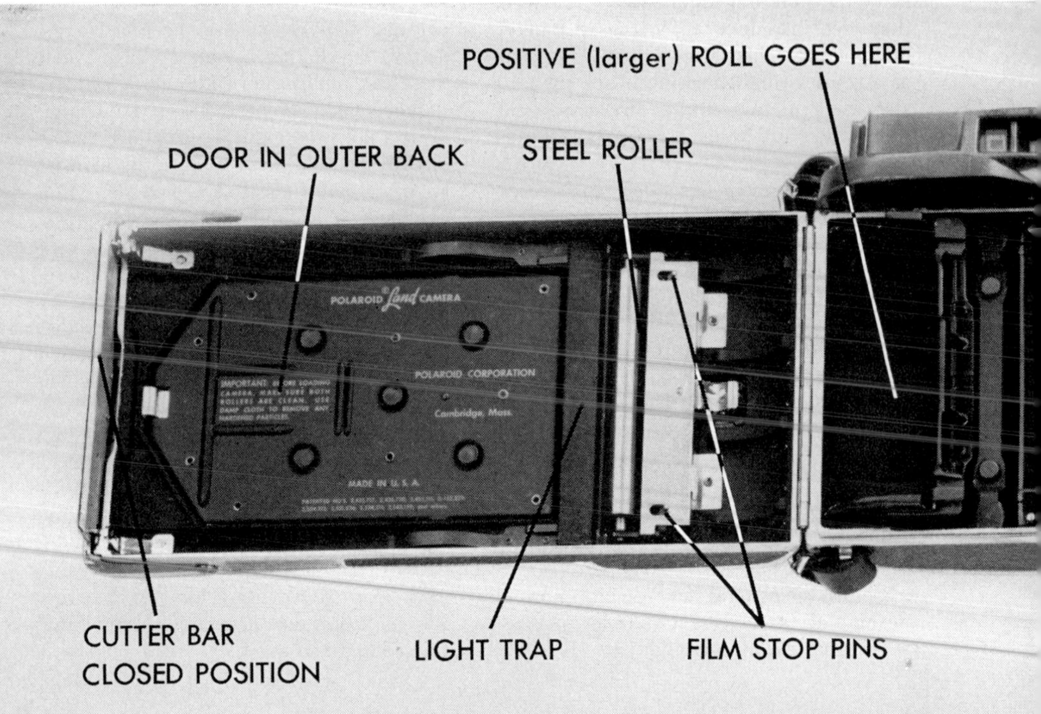

First item: open up the back of the camera.

ALL EXCEPT HIGHLANDER: Back lock lever is near tab slot. Flip it; back opens. Lay camera flat, open inner back.

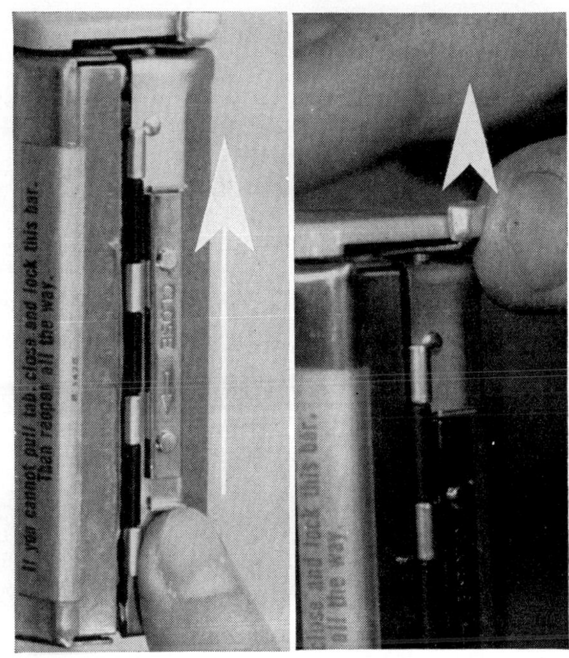

HIGHLANDER: Two steps. Slide lock to open position (left photo). Gripping camera so back can't open, lift cutter bar lever to disengage it from pin (in direction of arrow, right photo), swing it free. Open back. Lay camera flat, open inner back.

Follow the numbered steps and you can't go

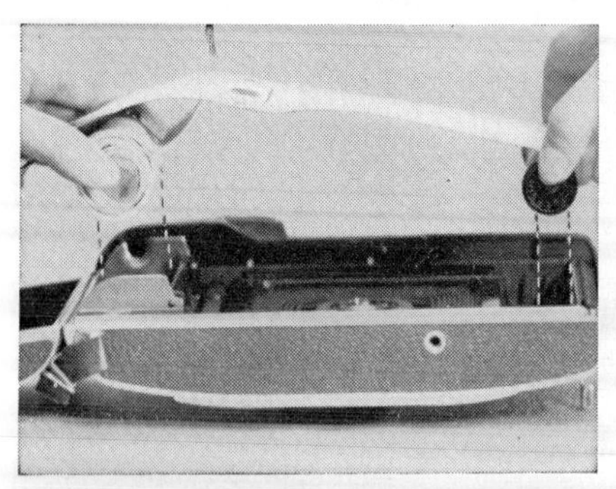

1. INSERT ROLLS: First set spooled negative in small chamber. Don't break seal (photo A, right). Fit print roll into large chamber. Avoid creasing shown in photo B, right. In some older models, negative spool snaps into clips on inner back; roll gets into chamber when inner back is closed.

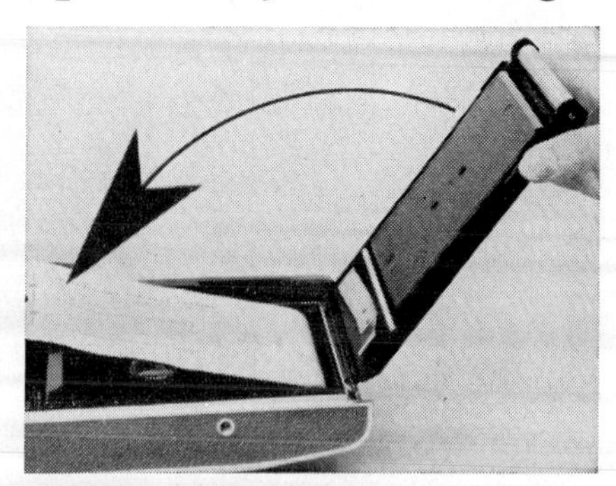

2. CLOSE INNER BACK: Guide paper leader straight to left, so it's over far side of camera (be careful not to break that negative seal by pulling too hard). Close inner back over paper. Leader should now protrude from under steel roller on inner back, as in photo 3.

4. REVERSE PAPER LEADER: Transfer leader from left side of camera to right side, so black paper shows, and spread it across inner back. It must go between two small metal guides (white squares in photo). Hold it in position and with left hand close outer back over leader.

5. CLOSE AND LOCK: Close outer back firmly over paper leader. Swing back lock lever to wide open position (it should click sharply), squeeze camera and swing lock lever closed (arrow). Check that both sides of camera back are engaged by latches and tightly closed. *Leave cutter bar open so you can pull leader.*

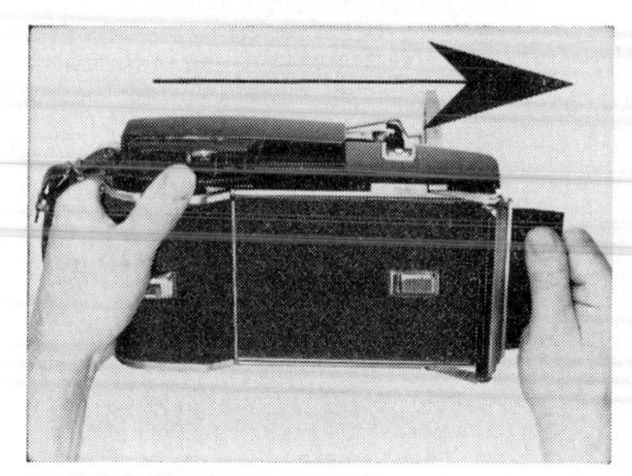

7. GET A GRIP: Hold camera in left hand. Grasp end of leader firmly, between full length of thumb and folded fingers (to avoid tearing). You're going to pull leader straight out, and there will be some resistance at first.

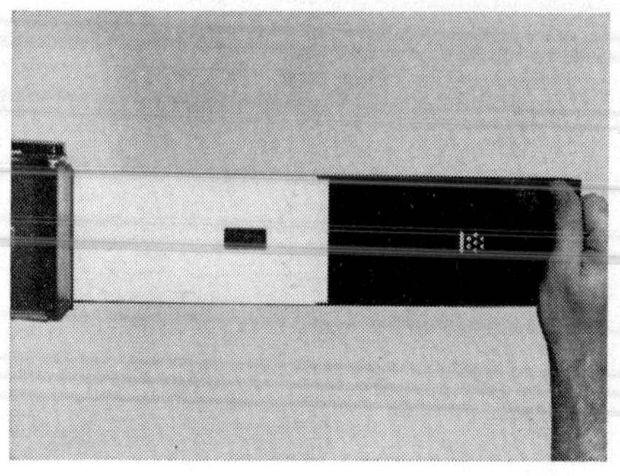

8. PULL IT STRAIGHT: Pull strongly to get it started (now you're breaking those seals you were so careful not to break earlier). Once it starts to move it will go easily. Pull out about 15 inches, until something clicks inside camera and movement comes to definite stop.

wrong loading film.

3. STOP AND LOOK: With inner back closed, steel roller should just clear two stars (arrow) on leader (Type 32 film has two arrows, not stars). If stars are still under roller, film is probably creased (photo B). Lift inner back and remove crease. Close inner back again.

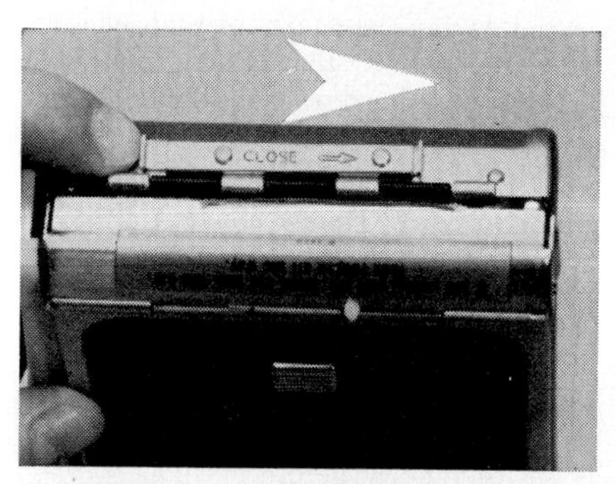

6. LOCKING HIGHLANDER: Close outer back, squeeze camera, slide lock to "close" position. *Don't latch cutter bar.* Leave it open so you can pull tab as shown in photo 7. Except for opening and locking, Highlander loading procedure is similar to that of other models.

9. CHECK IT: Lift cutter bar and examine paper leader. If you've pulled it far enough, you should see "Stop" sign and guide (arrow). If not, pull slowly until they come into view. Hold cutter bar closed (on Highlander close and lock cutter bar), and tear leader against cutter.

IMPORTANT LOADING DONT'S

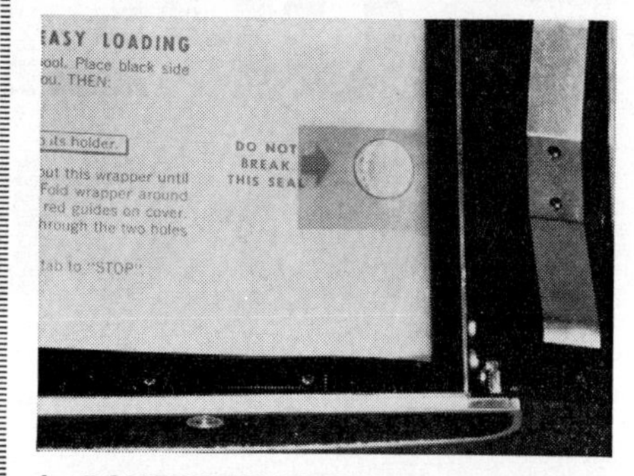

A. DON'T BREAK THIS SEAL: It keeps negative tightly rolled on spool. If seal breaks, negative may unroll and be light struck, causing big white streaks across prints. Also, film may get folded or jammed in camera and cause you to lose several pictures on that roll.

B. AVOID THIS CREASE: Result of tucking fold in print roll leader into film chamber when inserting print roll. If left creased, leader may rip when you pull it (photo 8), ruining roll. Lift inner back, remove fold from film chamber. Leader should run straight and smooth from print roll as shown in photos 4 and C.

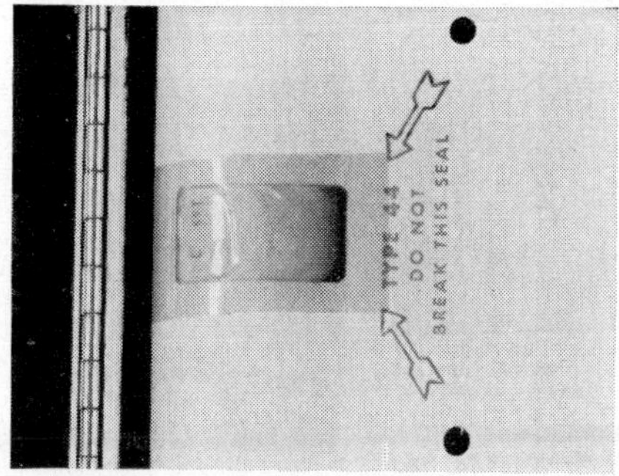

C. DON'T BREAK THIS SEAL, EITHER: This one holds print roll together. If broken, roll may unwind and expand, jam camera or tear. Or, prints may not match up properly with negative strip, so pictures will be ruined.

OPENING AND CLOSING

The steps are simple enough, but there are a few points that should be remembered.

LIKE ALL folding cameras, this one has a bellows which must be extended to its full length for picture taking and collapsed in order to close the camera.

The design of the Highlander cameras is such that all this happens automatically, as shown below.

With all the other camera models there are separate steps, shown in detail opposite. In connection with these, here are some important reminders.

Before taking *any* pictures, check that the bellows is fully extended and latched in place. If not, pictures will be out of focus. It's possible for the latch to be jarred during the course of snapshooting, with the result that the shutter/lens housing may be retracted slightly by the springiness of the bellows.

When the camera is focused for a distance closer than "infinity" the focusing track extends beyond the edge of the camera's front door. If the camera should be closed with the focusing track so extended, it will certainly jam the latch and you may have a gay time unjamming it. So, check that the camera is set to infinity before closing.

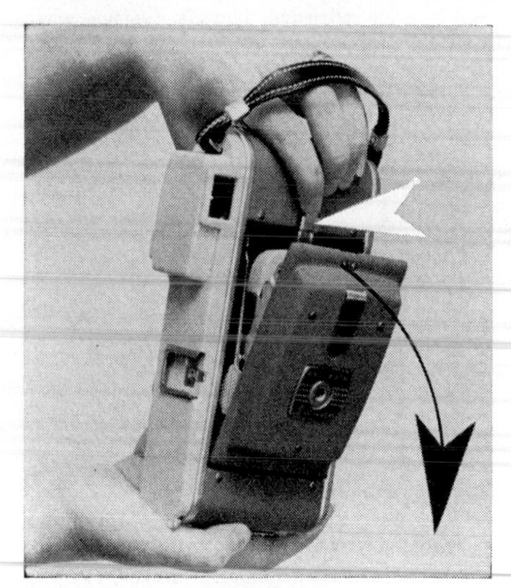

HIGHLANDER, OPENING: Press the front door latch and the front will pop open part way. Pull it down until the front braces snap into place and lock. That's all there is to it.

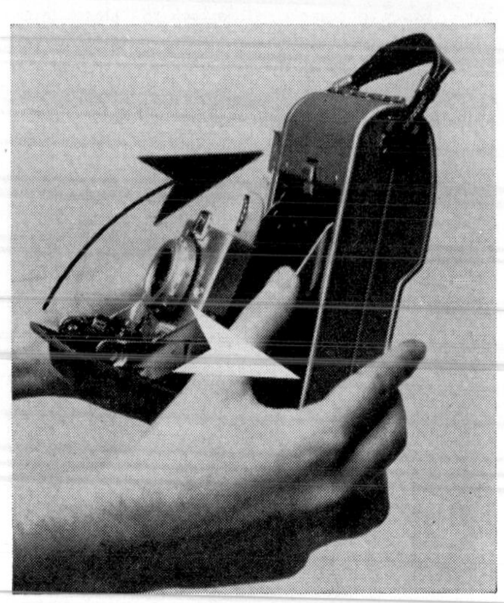

HIGHLANDER, CLOSING: Hold the camera upright, as shown, press in on the braces, close the front. Don't tilt the camera 'way back; the front may nip your fingers as it collapses.

How to do it: all models except Highlanders.

OPEN THE FRONT: Hold the camera as shown, press the front door latch. The front door will pop open part way. With your right hand pull the front door down until the braces lock it.

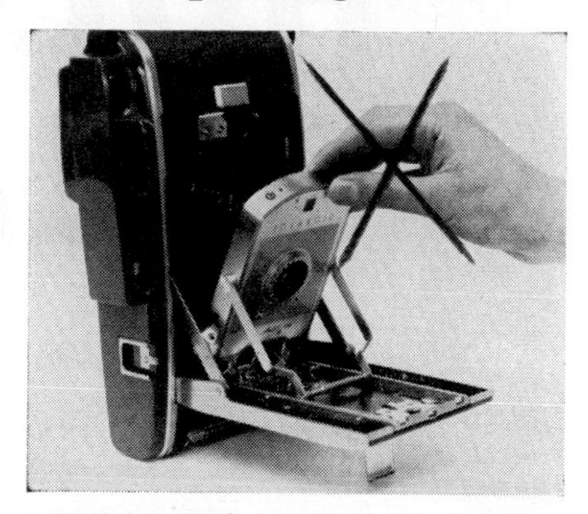

DON'T DO THIS: It's necessary to extend the bellows, but you won't get much accomplished by pulling on the shutter housing in this manner.

PULL IT OUT: Grasp the slide at the bottom of the shutter housing and pull it all the way forward along the bed tracks.

BE SURE IT LATCHES: If the bellows is not extended fully and locked in place all your pictures will be out of focus. Brace your fingers as shown and pull until the slide lock firmly engages.

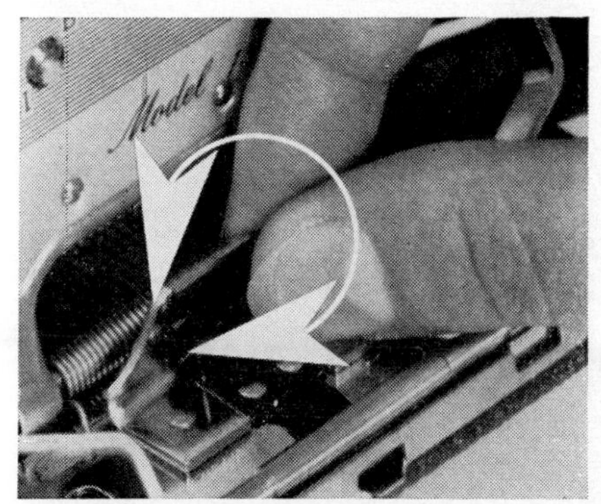

CLOSING, FIRST STEP: Squeeze the slide release (black piece) and push the slide all the way back into the camera body. *Caution:* If your camera has a wire viewfinder, close it first.

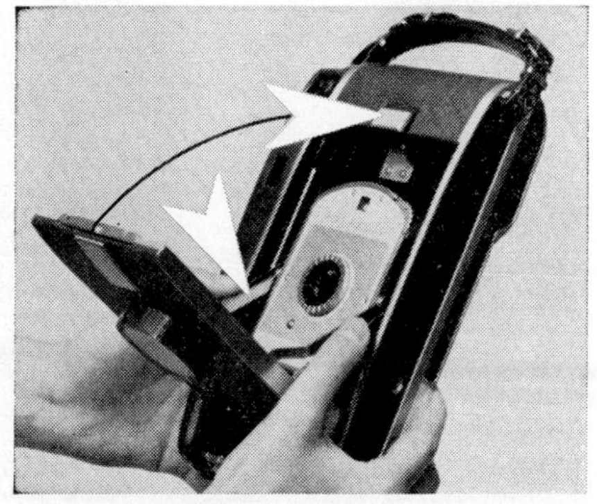

CLOSING, SECOND STEP: Check that the camera's distance scale is set to infinity. Press down on both front braces with your thumbs to unlock them; then push the front door closed.

ALWAYS SET THE DISTANCE SCALE TO INFINITY BEFORE CLOSING.

HOLD IT STEADY

Simple techniques borrowed from press photographers assure sharper pictures.

CAMERA SHAKE is one of the commonest causes of unsharp pictures. It happens most often at those settings with slow shutter speeds, such as EV 10 or 11, but it can occur at any shutter speed, with any camera, if you're not careful.

There are two sure ways to defeat camera shake: The first is to hold the camera properly. Some strong handed people can just hold the Polaroid Land camera in place with two hands without ever shaking. But the ladies aren't so successful at that, so here's a tested way to hold the camera for snapshots. Of course, for time exposures this won't do (see *Time Exposures*).

The second thing is to *squeeze* the shutter release until it clicks—jabbing at it shakes the camera at exactly the wrong time, so don't do *that*.

CAMERA SHAKE: Notice that everything in this picture is somewhat blurry. If everything but the girl was sharp, then the blurring would be due to subject movement. Very slight camera shake can produce results which are easily mistaken for incorrect focus or distance setting. Quite confusing.

THE GRIP: Grasp camera firmly in left hand, with your fingers under strap, wrapped around and into camera body. Hold it this way for all picture taking/making operations.

THE REST: Turn your body somewhat left, so your right shoulder points to subject. Set camera firmly on shoulder; turn head to right and look through range/viewfinder. Right hand is free to operate focusing knob.

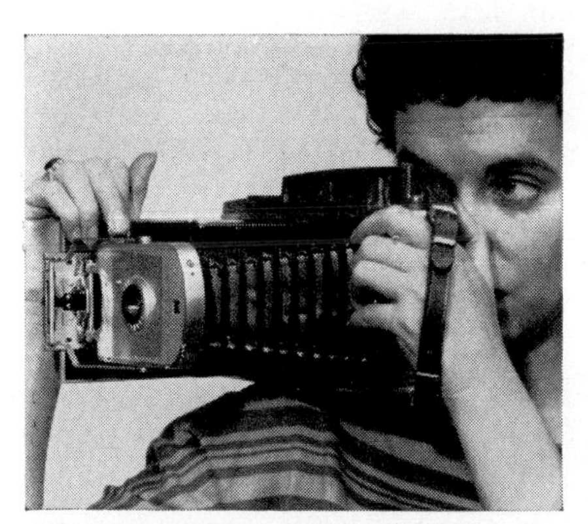

THE STEADIER: Right hand comes up and curls around camera bed (elbow should be high and pointing at subject). One finger engages shutter release; squeeze it gently—no jabbing.

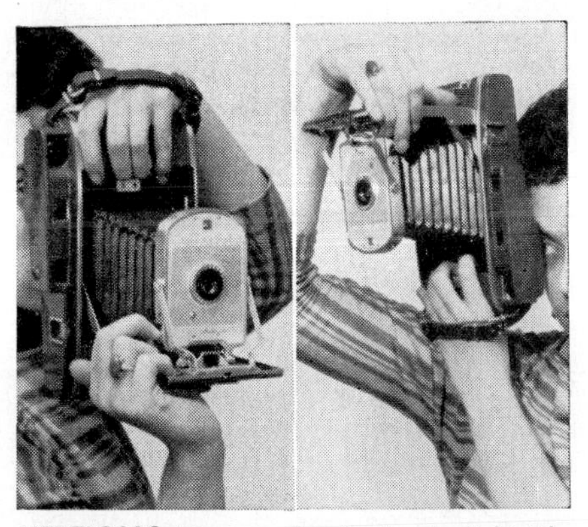

VERTICALS: Use same hand grips. In right side up stance, brace right elbow against side, rest camera on right palm. Upside down hold looks odd but is steady, comfortable. Camera and left hand are braced against shoulder.

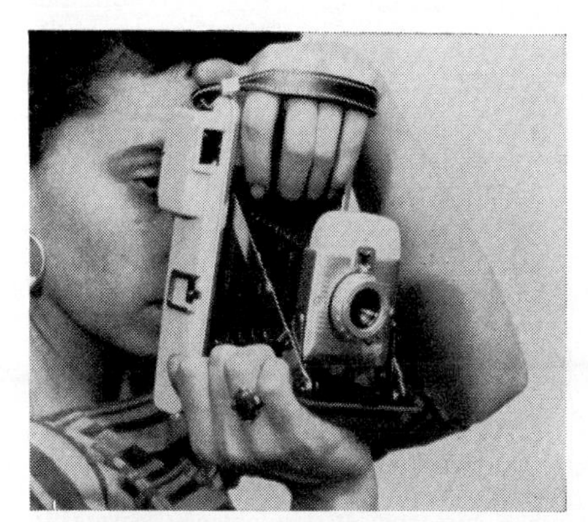

HIGHLANDER: It's easy to hold this little handful steady. Use same hand grips as *above*, but there's no need to support camera on shoulder. Just tuck your elbow into your ribs for steadiness.

GET THEM SHARP!

Whether your camera has a rangefinder or hand settings, well focused pictures are easy to get.

LOOK WELL at the chart opposite. You'll see how easy it is to get sharp pictures with the new coupled rangefinder Polaroid Land cameras, Models 150, 800, and 110A.

By "coupled" rangefinder we mean that this accurate distance measuring device is mechanically linked to the lens so that it automatically puts the lens in sharp focus on your subject—all you have to do is turn a knob.

The rangefinder is aided by the design of the Polaroid Land camera lenses. When set for any given distance, these lenses also record in sharp focus objects somewhat nearer and further than the exact point for which they are set. This is particularly true in bright light, or with flash, when the camera is set to high EV numbers, such as 16 and 17.

Thus, even models without rangefinders can consistently produce sharp pictures if you're careful in estimating the distance and setting the camera. (And, with the photoelectric shutter on your camera everything is in sharp focus from 3½ ft. to infinity. For details, see the chapter *Photoelectric Shutter #440.)*

This chapter shows in detail how to set all model Polaroid Land cameras for distance, and how to frame the subject accurately within the print area.

With the Highlander there are only two steps.

SET THE DISTANCE: Estimate carefully the distance in feet to your subject. Then rotate the lens mount until the mark for the desired distance comes under the peg near the EV number window. "INF" is for infinity (great distance); set the lens there for subjects beyond 50 ft.

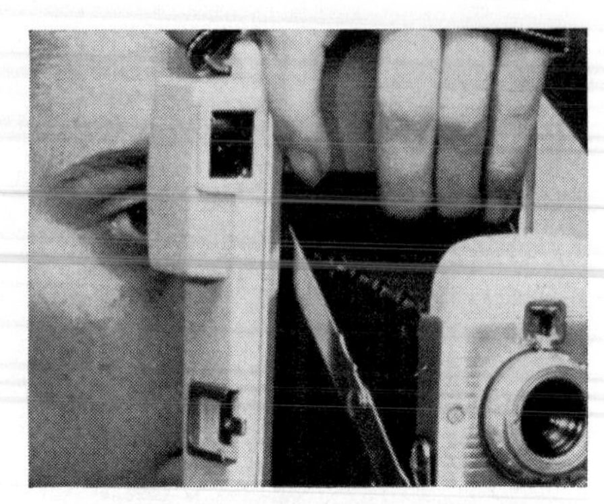

CENTER YOUR SUBJECT: Get your eye near to the viewfinder eyepiece; everything seen within the frame of the front window should be in your picture. Exception: At close distances leave extra space at the top and left edges of the frame to avoid chopping off a piece of the subject.

HOW THE RANGE/VIEWFINDER GETS YOU SHARP PICTURES.

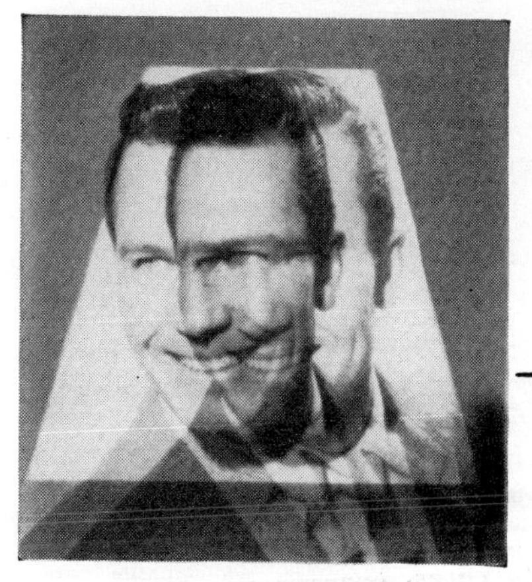

TURN THE KNOB

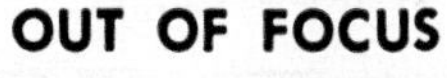

OUT OF FOCUS

IN SHARP FOCUS

◁ ***1. Focus sharply:*** Look through the rangefinder window. In the center is a pyramid-shaped brighter spot; get your subject in it. If you see two images (above, left), the lens is out of focus for that distance and pictures will be unsharp. Turn the focusing knob so the two images blend into one; that focuses the lens and pictures will be sharp.

◁ ***2. Shift eye to viewfinder:*** Center your subject. For distances from about 3½ ft. to infinity the viewfinder self-corrects for parallax error (explained on page 25), prevents chopped off heads. Don't use this viewfinder with close-up lenses; for how to aim then, see *Close-ups.*

▽ ***3. For flash, check distance:*** When the subject is sharply focused in the rangefinder (above) the footage scale (below) indicates the distance to the subject. You must know that distance to make correctly exposed flash pictures.

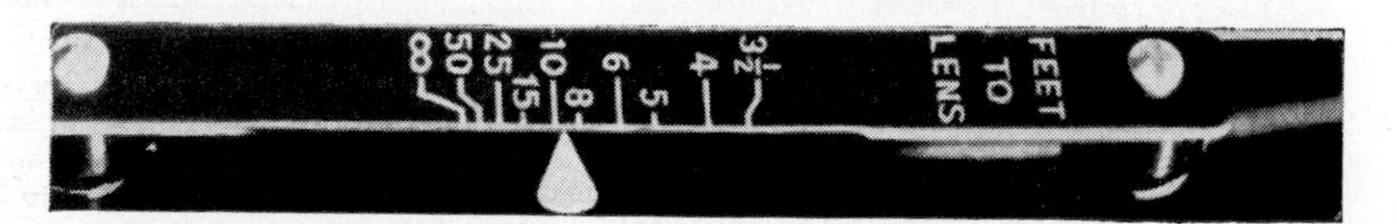

Other models have different systems.

1. FLIP UP THE FINDER: This is only the rear half of the viewing system; it's inaccurate if used alone. Keep your eye close to the finder but don't lean on it; the eyepiece is easily tilted by pressure, causing viewfinding errors.

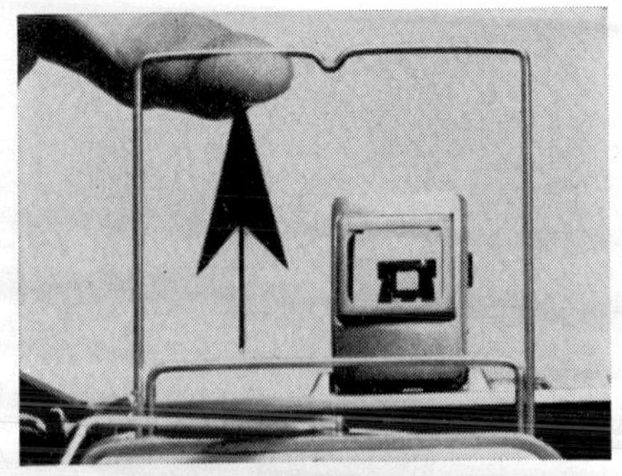

2. LIFT THE FRAME ALL THE WAY: This is the front half of the viewfinder system. You should see the complete wire frame through the rear finder. Everything within the wire should be in the picture. Exception: see opposite page.

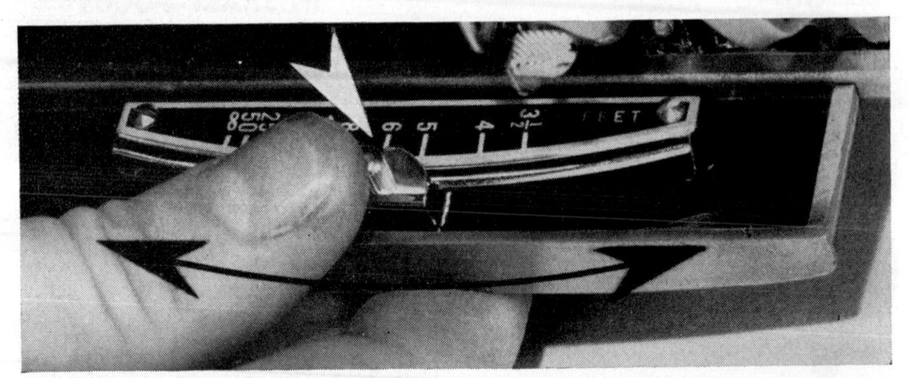

3. SET THE DISTANCE: Estimate the distance carefully, press the lever down, slide it until the notch (arrow) is opposite the estimated footage. Figure 8 on side, next to 50 ft. mark, is the symbol for infinity (great distance); set the lens there for subjects more than 50 ft. away. The viewing and range system described above applies to Models 95A, 95B, 100. Model 95 is similar but the front finder is a little mast with a ball on top; you center the ball in the field of view of the rear finder. For very accurate settings (close-ups, etc.) with all models, measure the distance from the subject to the front of the lens.

MODEL 110: Old Pathfinder has a lens-coupled rangefinder, similar in operation to that described on page 23. Eyepiece (arrow) is separated from the viewfinder system, which is like that shown in photos 1 and 2, above.

MODEL 700: It has a non-coupled rangefinder. You look through the eyepiece (arrow), turn the wheel at right until the rangefinder images blend, read the footage indicated on the wheel, set the distance manually as shown in photo 3.

Have you been cutting off parts of subjects?

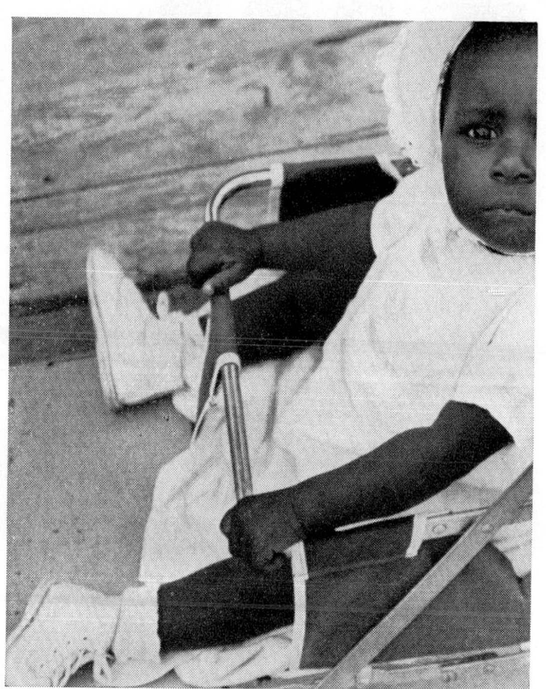

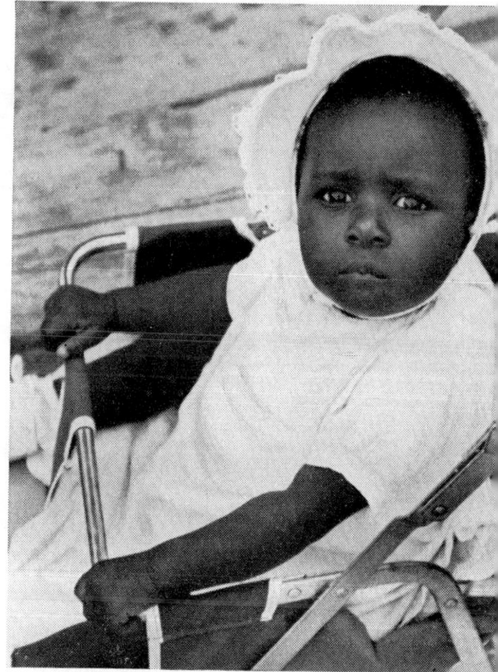

PARALLAX ERROR: This occurs because the line of sight of the viewfinder is several inches from the line of sight of the lens. This doesn't matter with mid-distant and far objects. But up close the lens doesn't "see" the same area you do through the finder. With a vertical picture (above) the right edge is cut off. Model 150, 800, and 110A viewfinders automatically correct for this at normal focusing distances.

Try this, to prevent that picture trouble.

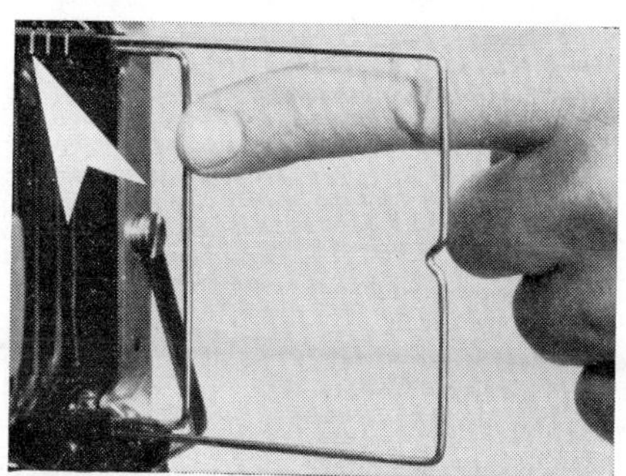

PARALLAX CORRECTION: All Land cameras with wire frame finders can be set to correct parallax error. There's a scale on the back of the shutter housing (on the Model 110, it's on the front) marked for INF., 8 ft., and 4 ft. Push the inner frame (not the outer one) to match the end of the wire (arrow) to the proper subject distance. This system does not apply when using closeup lenses; see *Close-ups* for proper aiming technique. With the Highlander, parallax error can be partially corrected (see page 22).

LET'S MAKE A PICTURE

THERE IS NOTHING complicated or in any way difficult about any of the steps in making a picture in a minute with a Polaroid Land camera. However, there are a number of steps, and the entire process is so unlike that used with any other camera that it must be learned from beginning to end as something brand new.

This chapter is in two main parts: the four steps involved in taking a picture, and the four steps concerned with developing the picture in a minute in the camera. There are far fewer steps than there are pictures in this chapter. However, since the various models of the camera differ in details of operation, if not in principle, it is necessary to show how each type works.

If you have attached the Polaroid Photoelectric Shutter #440 to your camera, the four picture taking steps listed below do not apply. When using that shutter refer to page 64. However, once the picture has been snapped, the picture is developed as explained in steps 5 through 8, below.

Much attention has been given to the steps known as "releasing the film" and "pulling the tab" as these are the points at which Polaroid Land camera users are most likely to get into difficulties, if at all. So please read this chapter with particular care, and then be sure to read the short chapter *Pulling the Tab*, which follows this one. It's one of the most important sections of the book.

THESE ARE THE FOUR PICTURE TAKING STEPS

1. Get the exposure (EV) number: A single number is all you need (except for the Pathfinders). Get it from an exposure guide or meter. For full details see *Correct Exposure.*

2. Set the exposure control: One control wheel sets both shutter speed and lens opening with a single movement. Pathfinder models have a different system. See *Using the Pathfinders.*

3. Set the camera for the right distance: If you don't, your pictures will be fuzzy because the camera is out of focus. For full information about aiming and focusing see *Get Them Sharp.*

4. Snap the picture: Hold the camera steady; squeeze the shutter release. Now you're ready to develop the picture in a minute, in the camera.

AND THIS IS HOW YOU DEVELOP THE PRINT

5. You must operate the film release: Just flip a little switch (page 28). On some models you move a lever or press a button. Now you can do the next step, pulling the tab.

6. Pull the tab and begin timing: This starts the developing process. If you don't pull the tab you won't get your picture in a minute or in a month. Pull it straight out, all the way. Pictures of how to do it and *important* information on page 29 and in the next chapter.

7. Wait a minute, then remove the print: When the time's up, open the back door and lift out the print as shown on page 30.

8. Coat the print: A simple but vital step (page 30) to protect pictures from fading and damage (see *Care of Prints* for complete instructions).

When using the photoelectric shutter the four picture taking

1. Use either way to get the exposure number.

...95, 95A, 100 and The 700.

SUN / SUBJECT	Bright	Hazy Soft Shadows	Cloudy No Shadow	Dull
AVERAGE: People, pets	16 or 15 / 7 or 6	14 / 5	13 / 4	12 / 3
BRIGHT: Beach, snow	17* / 8*	16 or 15 / 7 or 6	14 / 5	13 / 4
DARK: Shady spots	14 / 5	13 / 4	12 / 3	11 / 2

*Use filter over lens if picture is too light.

...o correct the exposure: If the picture is too light, use higher ...umber. If too dark, use lower number. Always set exact... ...umber, never between numbers.

EXPOSURE GUIDE: There's one on each film instruction sheet. Match subject and lighting columns; there's your exposure (EV) number. EV 10 to 18 are for current cameras; 1 to 9 for older types.

#625 EXPOSURE METER: Set film speed dial for film type in camera. Measure light reflected from subject. Rotate knob to match needle and pointer. Use EV number arrow points to.

2. Set exposure control to the right number.

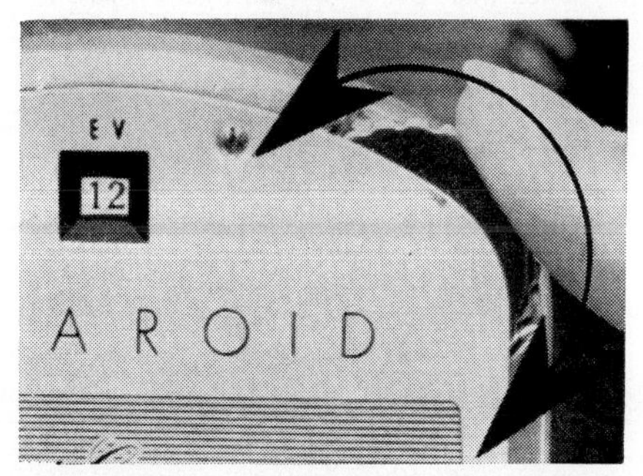

ALL EXCEPT PATHFINDERS: Turn the little wheel in the shutter housing, either way, until the EV window shows the exposure number recommended by the exposure guide or meter.

PATHFINDERS: These cameras have more complex exposure controls than those on the other models. How to set them is fully explained in the chapter *Using the Pathfinders.*

3. Set distance; see Get Them Sharp, page 22.

4. Now press the release to snap the picture.

ALL EXCEPT HIGHLANDER: Squeeze the lever gently; don't jab. It moves about ¼ in. before the shutter clicks. It's a self-setting shutter; press only once for each snapshot, then let go.

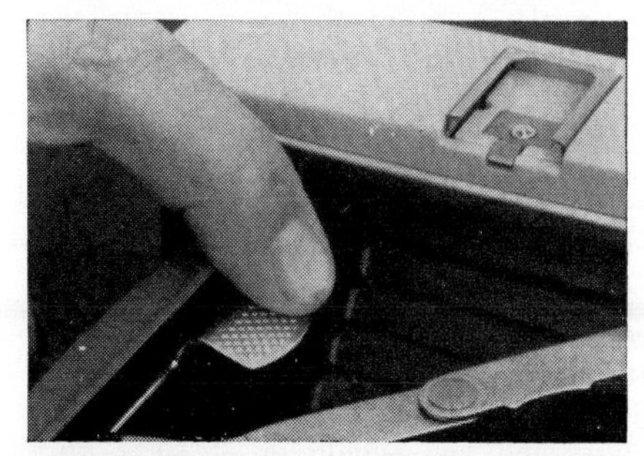

HIGHLANDER: Here you press in gently on a knurled plate. Be sure that the "B—I" switch on the front of the shutter housing is set to "I" which stands for "Instantaneous," or snapshot.

steps described here do not apply. See page 64 for details.

5. *You must release the film. This shows how.*

FLIP THE SWITCH: It's on the back of all current cameras except the Highlander. Snap it either way—once is enough, but if you repeat it will do no harm. Now you can pull the tab, as shown in the photos on the opposite page.

OLDER MODELS: They have a button on the back. Press it sharply, all the way (repeat if in doubt), and REMOVE YOUR FINGER. Now you can pull the tab, as shown at right, but don't press the button while pulling the tab (see text below).

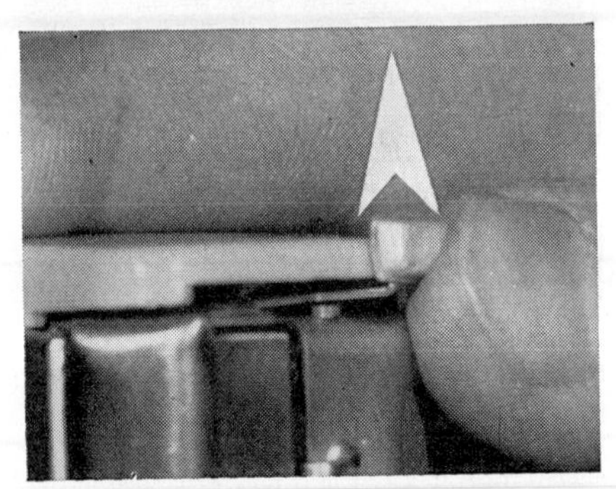

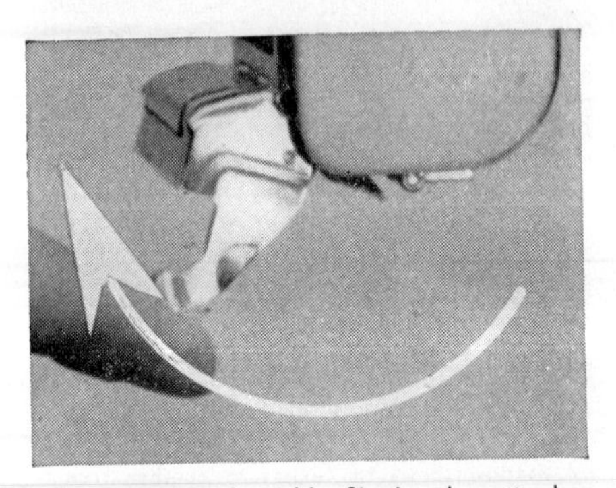

TWO STEPS FOR THE HIGHLANDER: On these cameras the film is released by flipping the cutter bar back as far as it will go. First you must disengage the lever from the pin (left) by pushing it slightly to the side (arrow). When the lever clears the pin, swing it back as far as it will go (right) until it hits the stop and there is a sharp click (repeat if in doubt). Then let go of the lever. Now you can pull the tab.

WHY IT'S SO IMPORTANT TO RELEASE THE FILM EACH TIME.

In the back of the camera are two metal stop pins (photo, page 14). When you load a film and pull out the leader (see *Loading*), these pins drop into special holes in the print paper to stop it at the right place for the first picture. However, before you can pull the tab to begin developing that print and to advance to the next one, the stop pins must first be disengaged from the holes in the paper. This is called *releasing the film*, and you should do it right after snapping the shutter. The photos above show how simple it is.

You must release the film before pulling the tab, or the stop pins will tear the print paper, spreading developer over the interior of the camera, and perhaps ruining a full roll of film.

Releasing the film doesn't start development—it just permits you to begin development by pulling the tab, as shown on the opposite page.

Caution: If your camera has a button type film release, don't hold it down while pulling the tab—you'll yank a yard or so of ruined film out of the camera. And if the whole film pulls out when you're not touching the button, the film release needs some repairs.

6. *Pull the tab as shown, and begin timing.*

GET A GOOD GRIP: Lift the cutter bar and grasp the tab firmly between the full length of your thumb and other fingers folded under it. A dainty fingertip pull won't do.

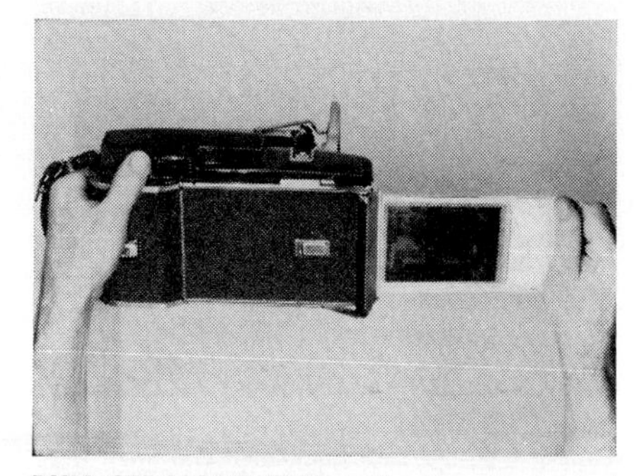

PULL STRAIGHT OUT: Pull swiftly, firmly, and without hesitation until film hits next stop. You should be able to see the full negative area, plus about ⅛ in. of the brown paper negative "mask" protruding beyond the cutter bar. Let the cutter bar "ride" the tab while pulling.

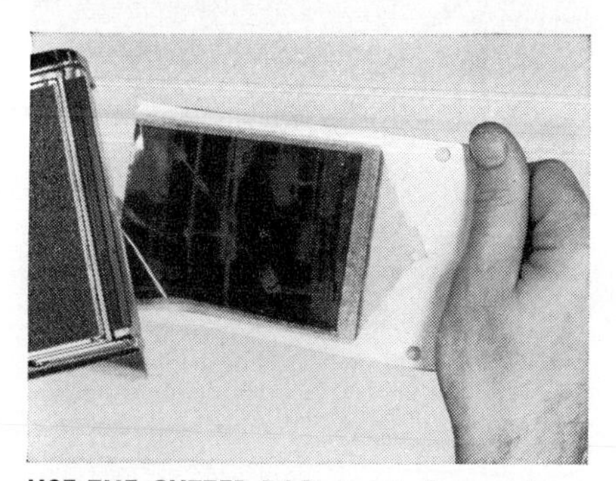

USE THE CUTTER BAR: Lock it down and tear the paper as shown. On older models, hold the cutter down firmly. Never tear the paper on the edge of the tab slot—always use the cutter.

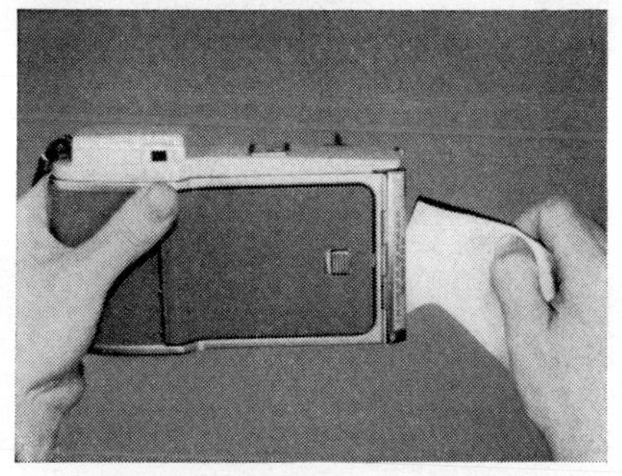

ON THE HIGHLANDER: Always close and lock the cutter bar after pulling the tab; this resets the stop pins so the film can be released next time the cutter is raised fully. Now tear the paper.

YOU'VE PULLED THE TAB; NOW WAIT A MINUTE. HERE'S WHY.

Pulling the tab is the most important single step in using the Polaroid Land camera, because that's what starts the development of the picture. *If you don't pull the tab, the picture will never develop.* Next to each picture space on the print roll is a foil pod filled with developer. When you pull the tab, the pod is squeezed between two rollers; the developer is forced out and spread evenly between the negative and the print paper. The picture now starts to develop. (The chapter *How it Works* explains this process in detail.)

You must wait at least a full minute after the tab is pulled for the developer to do its work.

Some people snap the picture, wait a minute, then pull the tab and immediately remove the print. All they have is a faint ghost of the picture which would have developed if the proper procedure had been followed.

Remember these steps: Snap the picture; release the film; pull the tab and wait a minute. Then remove the print.

That's tab pulling briefly; for more details of this most important operation be sure to read the short chapter *Pulling the Tab* which follows this one.

7. *Wait a full minute, and remove the print.*

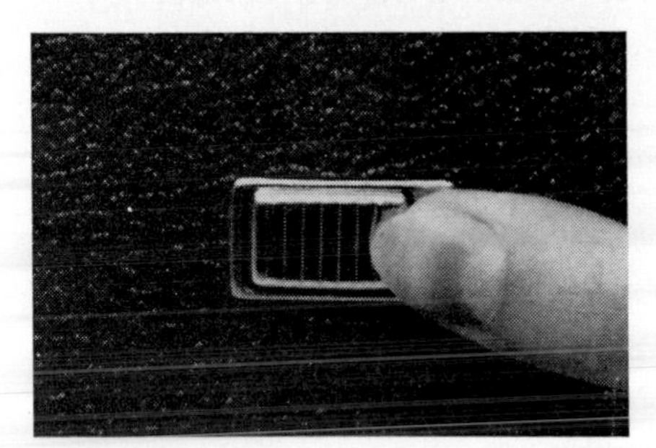

OPEN THE DOOR: About a minute after pulling the tab, slide the back door latch and open wide the door in the back of the camera.

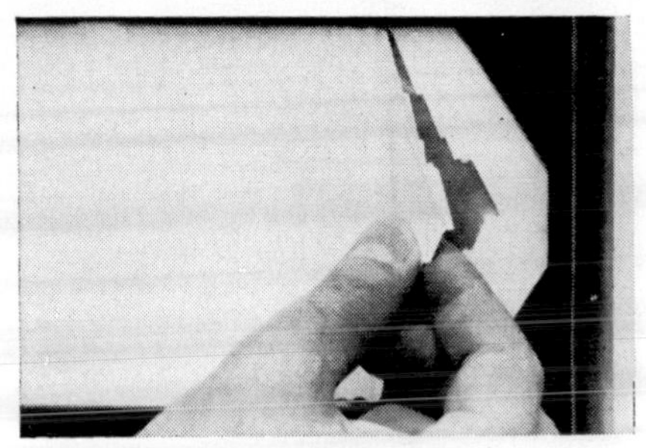

LIFT THE TRIANGLE: Get a fingernail into the slot at the point of the small triangular tab and lift the two slanting sides of the triangle loose from the rest of the paper.

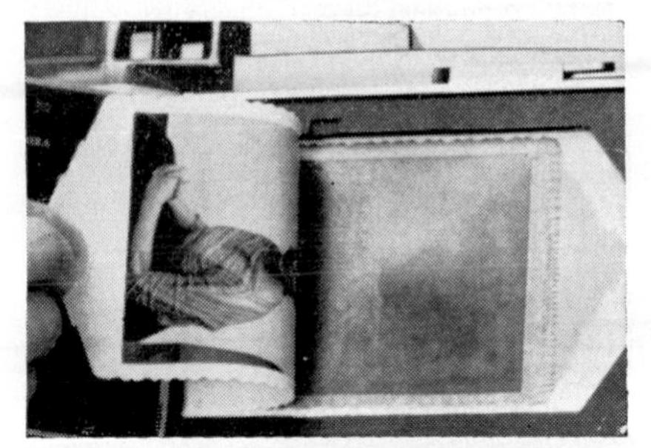

REMOVE THE PRINT: With one continuous motion pull the print away from the rest of the paper. Pull it straight, as shown, not at an angle. Once you've started to remove it don't hesitate, and don't let the print fall part way back onto the developer covered negative area.

DON'T DO THIS: Pulling at an angle is a good way to rip the print in half. Lift the print straight out as shown in the picture at left.

8. *Straighten the print, and coat it thoroughly.*

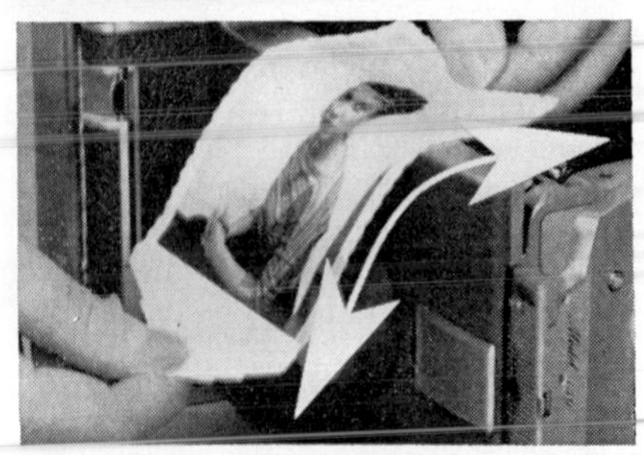

STRAIGHTEN THE PRINT: Take the curl out of the print by drawing the back across a straight edge on the camera, a table, or other object. Don't bend it more than about 45° and don't pull too hard. More helpful hints about print straightening in *The Care of Prints*.

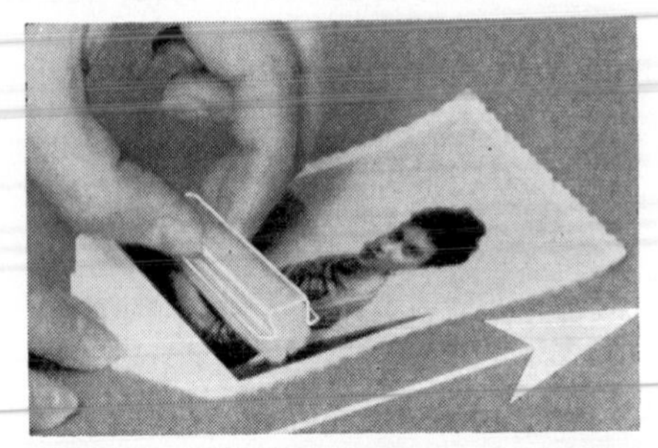

COAT ALL OF IT: There's a coater in each film package. Remove it from the tube, and spread the liquid over the ENTIRE print, including borders; it dries quickly. Careful coating protects prints from fading and damage. Be sure to read the film instruction sheet and *The Care of Prints.*

PULLING THE TAB

Now, a careful look at the most important step in making a picture in a minute.

PULLING THE TAB starts development of the picture you just snapped and moves the film up for the next exposure (page 29 explains exactly what happens). If the camera is working correctly and if you know how to use it, the tab should start easily (there is a slight resistance to overcome), pull smoothly, and stop firmly in the right place. If it doesn't, something is wrong. The following pages show some common tab pulling troubles.

Here are some tab pulling tips for all models except the Highlander—that one is discussed on page 32.

Before pulling the tab always release the film—flip the switch, or press the button (all the way, sharply, and remove your hand). To prevent light leaks, let the cutter bar "ride" the paper.

Pull all the way to the final stop. If not, the stop pins won't enter the holes in the paper until you try to pull the tab again—then you may think the film is jammed, but it can be freed by operating the film release again.

Ironclad rule: *Never force the tab!* If it won't pull, first operate the film release. If that's no help, open the back door—maybe it's stuck to a negative (see page 33). Finally, pull gently but steadily, while repeatedly operating the film release. If nothing helps, the film is hopelessly jammed–open the camera and load a new roll of film.

HOLD THE CAMERA CORRECTLY AND AVOID TAB HEADACHES.

HOLD IT THIS WAY: With the left hand through the strap and gripping the camera body, and the right hand pulling away from the camera, everything lines up, the tab comes straight out. Jamming and other difficulties are prevented.

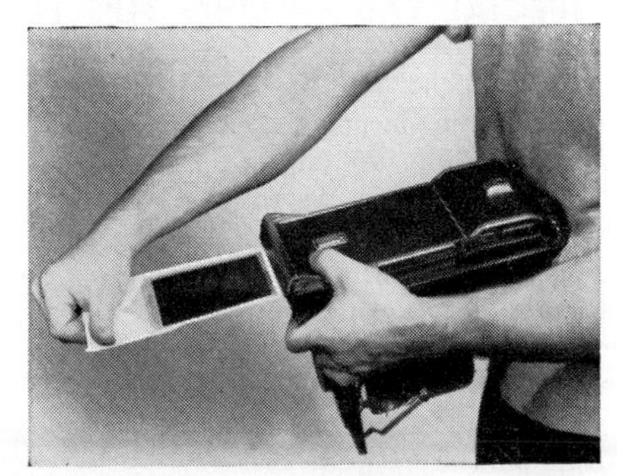

OR LIKE THIS IF NECESSARY: If you find it inconvenient to hold the camera in one hand, brace it as above (but flexibly) and push straight ahead — let the pull of the paper help line up the camera so the tab comes out straight.

Pull straight, with a swift, non-stop motion.

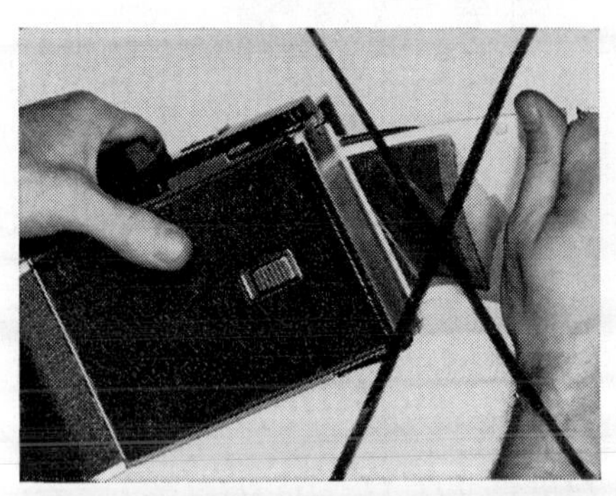

DON'T DO THIS: Such an unbalanced hold leads almost certainly to a crooked pull on the tab (results at right). Besides, there's a risk of dropping the camera in the process.

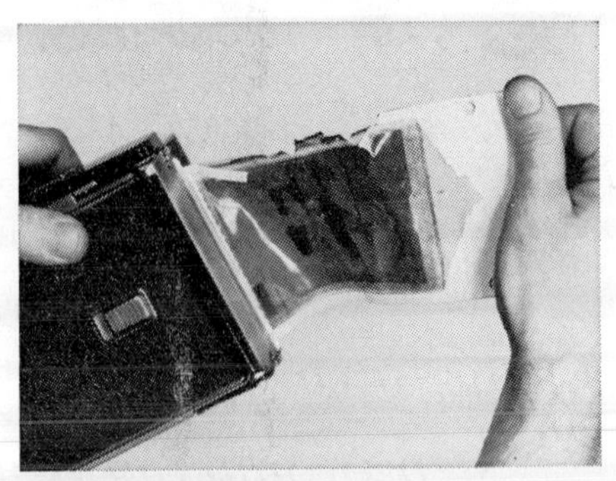

OR YOU'LL GET THIS: Ragged edges are a sure sign of pulling the tab at an angle. This can cause a jam in the camera. Pull too far off center and you may tear the paper in half.

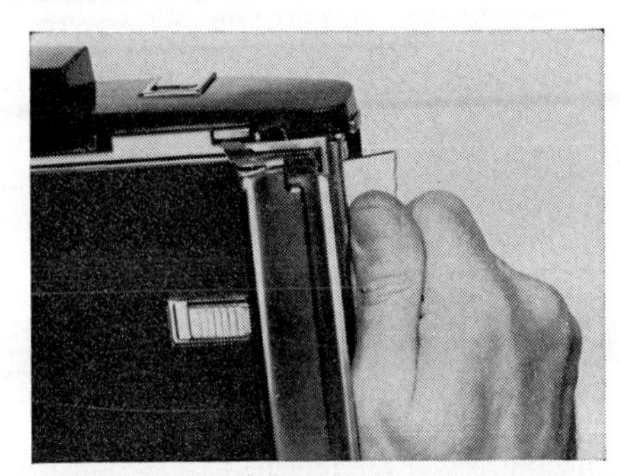

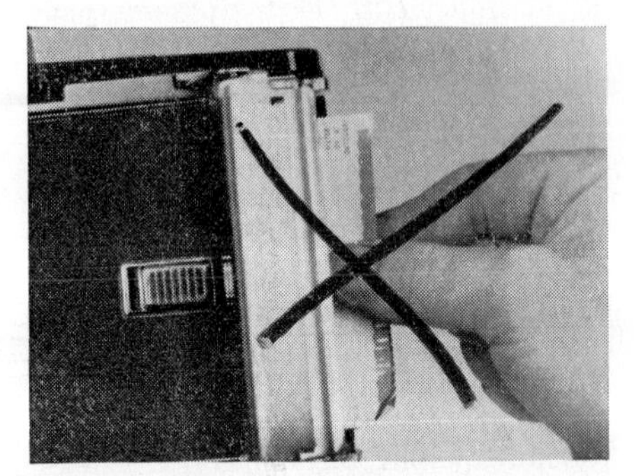

A GOOD GRIP IS A GOOD BEGINNING: To pull the tab you have to overcome a bit of resistance. You need a good hold on the paper. Lift the cutter bar and grasp the tab firmly between the whole length of your thumb and folded fingers (left, above). A dainty fingertip touch (right) won't do, and even if you hold tight enough there's a chance of tearing the paper. On the Highlander there's not quite as much room for fingers, but try to get the same general type of grip.

SPECIAL TAB PULLING TIPS FOR HIGHLANDER CAMERA USERS.

Pulling the tab on the Highlander starts development of the picture and moves the film up for the next shot. In those respects it's exactly like the other cameras. However, the film release mechanism is different (see page 28 for pictures and full details).

When releasing the film, be sure to raise the cutter bar as far as it will go. Hearing a click is no sign that the stop pins are out of the way.

Pull the tab all the way to the film stop—that last ⅛ in. is particularly important. But don't pull too far or too hard (see photo opposite for result).

Always close and *lock* the cutter bar after pulling the tab, and tear the paper while the cutter bar is locked.

Never force the tab! If the tab won't pull, close and *lock* the cutter bar, then open and lift it all the way back. Next, open the back door, which may be stuck to a negative (photo, opposite). As a last resort, pull steadily but gently on the tab and at the same time pump the cutter bar back and forth from closed and locked to as far back as it will go. If nothing helps, the film jam is hopeless—open the camera and load a new roll of film.

Tab pulling troubles: causes and remedies.

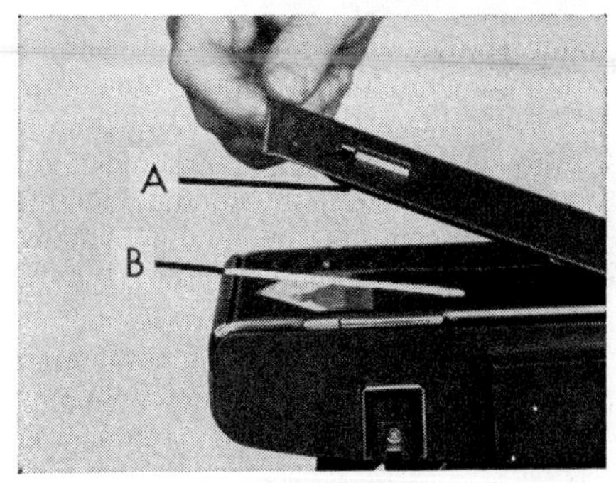

NEGATIVE STUCK TO DOOR: Sometimes the inside of the back door (A) sticks to old developer on the negative (B), makes it impossible to pull the tab. Open the door to separate them. Be sure to relock the door before pulling the tab.

HESITATION: Always pull with a single, swift, continuous motion until the film comes to the next stop. If you stop part way, then start again, the print will have a light streak across it. However, don't try to tear the film out of the camera.

NOT FAR ENOUGH: Black area at left or top of print shows the tab wasn't pulled all the way for the picture before this. However, if there's no black area but the white border at left or top is missing, or narrow, the tab wasn't pulled far enough for the print just developed.

PULLED TOO FAR, TOO HARD: Black area at right or bottom shows that previous picture was pulled too far. This usually rips the paper and may rupture a pod, causing developer to be spread around the inside of the camera. Don't yank it! You're not raising an anchor.

DIDN'T USE THE CUTTER BAR: The result of tearing the paper against the edge of the tab slot, instead of against the cutter bar, is that there's no tab to grasp the next time. Remedy: Operate the film release. Open the back door. Hold the cutter bar up with a finger and use both thumbs (on a dry part of the paper) to inch the tab out enough to get a grip on it. Always use the cutter bar.

PICTURE TROUBLES

Nineteen horrible examples of common and uncommon causes and how to avoid them.

IF ANY SINGLE Polaroid Land camera owner could look forward to turning out a picture collection like the one on these four pages the prospect would indeed be rather grim.

Fortunately such is not the case—we had to work hard to assemble this lot. However, all these pictures are actual samples of bits of ill luck which some Land camera owners have encountered at one time or another. So, it behooves us to know what each of these failures means and how to go about preventing its occurrence.

In almost every case the cause is disarmingly simple, and the means to prevent it consists of nothing more than following the normal camera operation instructions. And they're quite simple.

Causes of bad prints fall into some main categories: Picture taking (focus, exposure, shakiness); picture developing (failure to pull the tab properly); picture care (improper coating or storage); miscellaneous accidents.

Occasionally you may run into a series of bad prints, and this can be discouraging. *Don't throw them away!* And don't just put the camera away disheartened. Send the bad prints to Customer Service, Polaroid Corp., Cambridge 39, Mass. with a note explaining your trouble. You'll get a prompt explanation and in most cases a free roll of film for your efforts. Remember—in case of any kind of trouble, write to Customer Service.

PARTLY OUT OF FOCUS: Nobody moved, but nearby subject is blurred. Sharp background shows camera was set for wrong distance. This can be reversed, too, with distant subject blurred and unimportant foreground sharp. Remedy: Focus and aim as described in *Get Them Sharp.*

TOTAL LACK OF FOCUS: May be simply set for wrong distance, but most common cause is failure to extend camera bellows fully (except with Highlander models). Remedy: Pull front of camera all the way out until it locks securely, as shown in *Opening and Closing.*

OVEREXPOSED: Too much light has passed through lens and shutter. Remedy: Use higher number exposure setting—EV 17 instead of 15, for example. On Pathfinders, use higher f-number, such as f/16 instead of f/8. Follow exposure guide or meter recommendations. See *Correct Exposure* for full information.

UNDEREXPOSED: Not enough light has reached film. Remedy: Use lower number exposure setting, such as EV 12 instead of EV 14. On Pathfinders, use lower f-number—f/5.6 instead of f/11, for example. Follow exposure guide or meter recommendations. See *Correct Exposure* for full information.

CAMERA SHAKE: Usually occurs under conditions where slower shutter speeds are used, such as EV 10, 11, and 12, or 1/50 sec. and slower with the Pathfinders. Remedy: Handle camera as shown in *Hold it Steady*. Brace yourself or camera on solid object or use tripod. Always squeeze shutter release. Don't jab it!

FAILURE TO RELEASE FILM: Film tab was pulled so hard that stop pins tore developer pod and negative material, smearing developer every which way. Remedy: Always operate film release before pulling tab—it's most important. For full details, see *Let's Make a Picture*.

TAB PULLED PART WAY: Black area at end of print indicates no exposure there. Usually result of not pulling the tab as far as it should go when developing the print *before* the one with the black band. Remedy: Pull tab all the way, as described in *Pulling The Tab*.

HESITANT TAB PULLING: Streaks across print occur if you stop halfway during tab pulling operation and then start again. Remedy: Pull tab firmly, smoothly, in one continuous motion as described in *Pulling the Tab*.

To convert numbers on older model cameras to EV numbers add 9.

UNDERDEVELOPED: Print is gray and "flat" with very much less contrast than scene shows. Due to removing print too soon, or not allowing enough developing time in cold weather. Remedy: Follow development times listed on film instruction sheet in film package.

DIRTY ROLLERS: White spots, repeated regularly across print, indicate dirt or dried developer reagent on steel rollers. If debris is hard, scrape with fingernail, never with metal. Wipe clean with damp, lint free cloth, then dry.

FADING HIGHLIGHTS: Good print originally, but detail has disappeared in highlight areas. Due to failure to coat, improper coating, or bad storage conditions. Remedy: Follow recommendations in *The Care of Prints.*

STREAKY FADING: When new, this was an excellent print, but it was coated carelessly and has faded where the coating layer was not fully and properly applied. Remedy: Always coat prints thoroughly and as soon as possible. Follow recommendations in *The Care of Prints.*

EDGES FOGGED: Light has leaked in at edges of negative roll. Usually due to breaking transparent tape seal on negative roll, thus loosening roll; may be result of loading in bright sun. Remedy: Don't break seal in loading; never load the camera in bright sunlight.

STRAY LIGHT IN LENS: Result of aiming the camera too close to the sun or other light source, particularly when not using a lens shade. Remedy: Use a lens shade (see *Filters*) or if without one shield lens from direct rays with hand, hat, or piece of cardboard.

PARTIAL DEVELOPMENT: Usually caused by damage to pod containing developer, due to rough handling or crushing during shipment, carrying, or loading. May also occur with old, outdated film. Remedy: Handle films with care; always buy fresh film (check expiration date).

DEVELOPER SMEAR: Some developer sticks to print instead of to negative. May be due to hesitancy in removing print, or severe over- or under-development. If allowed to remain, developer causes brown stains and fading underneath spots. Remedy: Always remove print as shown in *Let's Make a Picture*. To remove spots, scrub them firmly with coater, towards edge of print. Then coat with fresh, uncontaminated coater. For free coaters write to Customer Service, Polaroid Corp.

TOTAL BLANK, BLACK: No light got to the film. Maybe you pulled the tab twice in a row, didn't push shutter release far enough, or failed to cock Pathfinder shutter. Flash sync may be inoperative or set wrong; shutter may be broken. Remedy: Check all your operations; check shutter functioning, without film if possible.

TOTAL BLANK, WHITE: Usually result of massive overexposure to light; could be badly damaged or ancient developer pod. Maybe camera was set for time exposure (B) when you wanted a snapshot (I). Camera back may have been open. Remedy: Check shutter setting; follow exposure guide or meter recommendations.

TAB SLOT LIGHT LEAK: Grid pattern appears at end of print nearest to film tab slot. Due to internal reflection of light entering slot. Remedy for older model cameras is shown at right. With ALL cameras, close cutter over slot in bright light, let it "ride" on paper as tab is pulled.

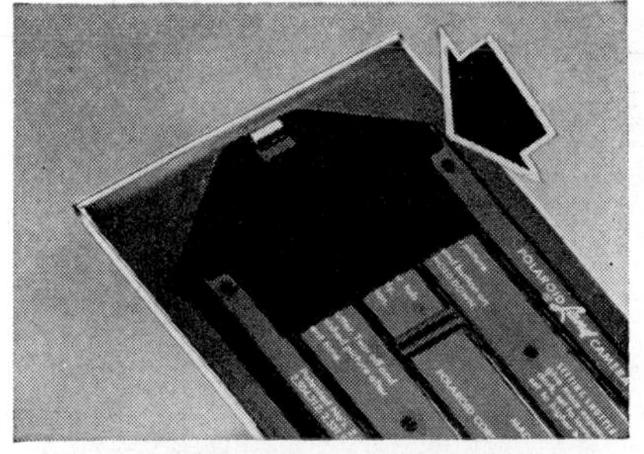

TAB SLOT LIGHT LEAK REMEDY: Older cameras have shiny raised ribs on inside of back door. Cover these with special tape obtainable free from Customer Service, Polaroid Corp., Cambridge 39, Mass. Tape helps to absorb stray light in tab slot and eliminate streaks.

To convert numbers on older model cameras to EV numbers add 9.

THE CARE OF PRINTS

What to do and not to do if you want those valuable pictures to last indefinitely.

EVERY PACKAGE of Polaroid Land film contains instructions about the care of prints, and they should be read and followed. Prints made in the Land camera will last as long and as well as conventional photos, *if properly handled*, and there's nothing complicated about taking care of them.

Keep this simple principle in mind: *Every picture must be coated* to protect it from fingerprints, dirt, abrasion, and the contamination that may come from chemical impurities found in some album paper, billfolds, glues, and other substances with which the print may come into contact. This can *only* be done by coating—and the sooner the coating is done, the better.

Remember, the first five minutes after the picture is taken are the most hazardous—everyone is excited at seeing the print and it gets passed around, collecting fingerprints and dirt in the process. Teach friends to hold the print by the tab before it's coated. If conditions are such that you can't coat the print immediately, make the film box into a print holder beforehand (directions on the box), and as you remove each print carefully put it into the folded box until you get to where they can be coated properly. For example, if dust clouds are flying, don't coat—unless you want a non-skid print.

Also excellent as temporary protectors are 4 x 5 in. Kodapak acetate sleeves (3¼ x 4¼ for Highlander prints).

STRAIGHTEN IT: Take out the curl by drawing the print over a smooth, straight edge. Straightening is important, but don't overdo it. If the print is bent too sharply the emulsion may crack. If you pull too hard the print can be torn.

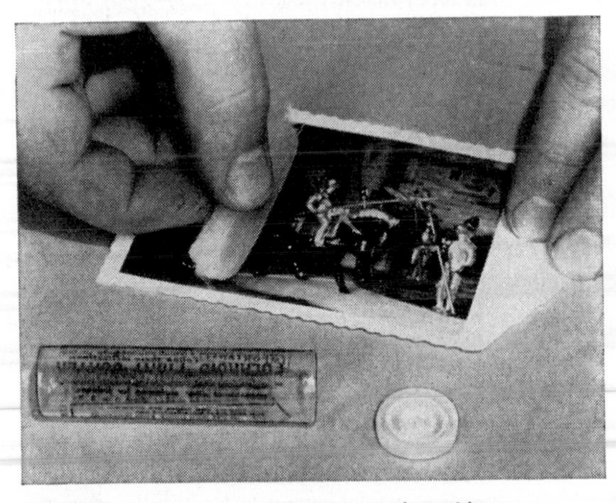

COAT IT: A few even, overlapping strokes with the coater will protect your Polaroid Land pictures from fingerprints, dirt, fading. Coat every part of the print, including the edges and the border. Text explains importance of coating.

These are made for use with color transparencies and are sold at camera stores.

Whatever temporary protector you use, don't delay getting the prints coated. Under conditions of high humidity, sunlight and/or heat, uncoated prints may start to fade in an hour.

Stick clear tape on each end of a Kodapak sleeve to keep the print in, and you have a fine permanent container for coated and *thoroughly dry* prints.

Using the print coater

Each package of film comes with a Polaroid Print Coater included—that's the glass tube containing a plastic soaked wad of cellulose in a special handle.

There are two steps to coating. First, take the curl out of the print by drawing it (back down) over the edge of a table, or similar surface. If outdoors, the edge of a car window is good. If there's nothing else handy, you can always use a straight part of the camera, as in the photos at right and at the end of the chapter *Let's Make a Picture*.

After straightening the print, hold it by the tab, and run the applicator down the length of the print with straight overlapping strokes and moderate pressure. Be certain to hold the applicator straight—don't let the edge of the handle scrape the print, or it will make a scratch. Be sure the entire surface is covered with the coating—edges and corners are just as important as the center of the print. (Don't use any other liquid, spray, or wax as a coating.)

If you should be doing this coating on your wife's best mahogany table, it's a good idea to work with the print on an old envelope or piece of paper to catch any excess liquid. Incidentally, any spill can usually be removed with water, if you get to it before the plastic dries hard. Once it dries, it will take a vinegar moistened rag to get it loose.

Keep the coater in the tube and capped when not actually using it. If left out in the open, the liquid will start to dry up.

How many strokes to coat a print? The tube containing the coater specifies six to eight. For the first two or three prints, when the coater is fresh and just bursting with liquid, moderate pressure will squeeze out the liquid plastic in

PRINT CARE HANDYTIPS

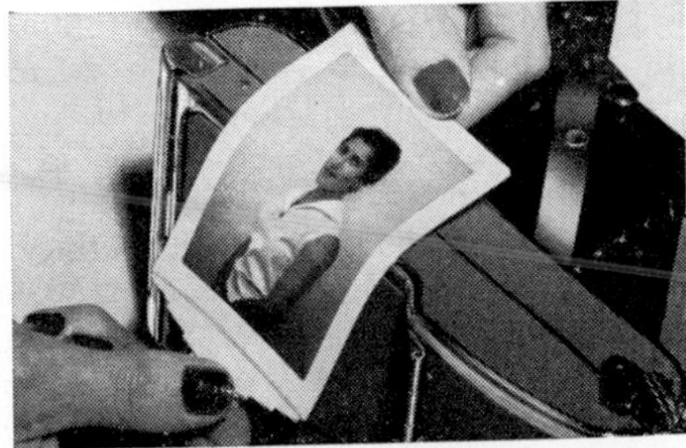

STRAIGHTENING ON CAMERA: On the Highlander models the straight edge of the back makes a good place to take the curl out of prints before coating. On all other models, use the side of the front door, as shown in the photo at the end of the chapter *Let's Make a Picture*.

CAR WINDOW: Many people use it. But be careful not to bend print more than about 45° angle (this one is bent just about the limit), or emulsion may be cracked. Don't pull too hard.

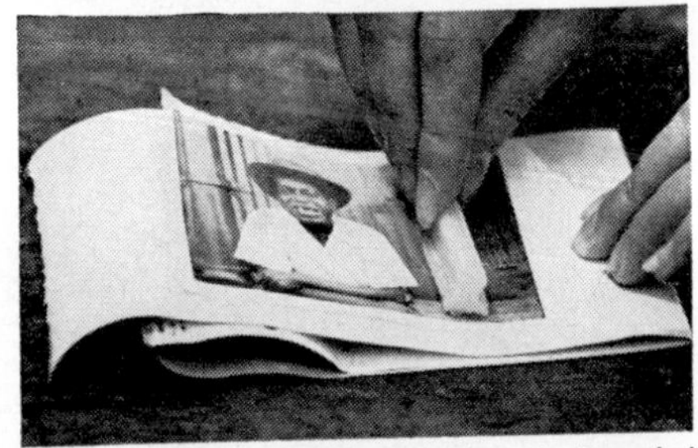

KEEP COATER CLEAN: Length of discarded negative paper is ideal surface for keeping coater and print grit free. Fold negatives under.

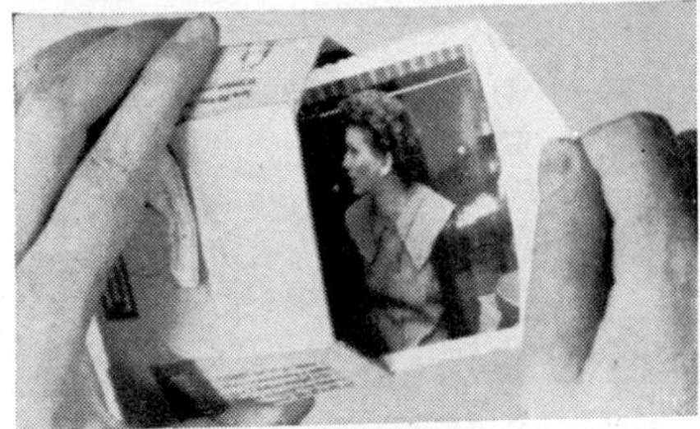

PRINT PROTECTOR: The film box converts to a handy carrier (directions on box). Squeeze edges slightly, so print goes in easily without scratching—very important if print is uncoated.

sufficient quantity. For later prints, it's a good idea to squeeze out more solution by pressing the coater down on the triangular tab before starting to coat.

The coating will usually dry in a minute or two—if it's very damp or humid it takes longer. If the coating is accidentally handled before it is thoroughly dry and gets fingerprinted, or if it looks rough and streaky, the first impulse is to coat it again, right then. Restrain yourself! Running the coater over the damp, sticky print surface may cause some of the image to lift off, ruining the picture. Let the print dry thoroughly, then recoat carefully as follows.

Take a fresh coater, or one that is still very juicy, and squeeze out a liberal amount of the liquid onto the white tab —*not onto the picture area.* With a light touch of the coater quickly spread the liquid over the print to form a layer. *Don't scrub the print when recoating.* Get the new layer on with as few strokes and as little friction as possible.

This procedure also applies to older prints which get cracked, fingerprinted, or smudged from handling.

Within a few minutes after application the coating is hard enough to handle and protect the print. However, if two recently coated prints come face to face under pressure and warmth, the coatings may stick the prints together. This has happened in shirt pockets. It's better to carry prints with all facing in the same direction—face to back.

In case two prints stick together, don't try to pull them apart—this is sure ruin for both. Instead soak the prints in a dish of plain white vinegar until they separate; wash a few minutes in cool water, let dry thoroughly, recoat.

Are extra print coaters available? Yes, if you need them, and at no charge. Ask your camera dealer if he has them. If not, write to Customer Service, Polaroid Corp., Cambridge, Mass, and they'll send the requested number of coaters promptly. It's handy to have a few extra ones around.

How not to handle prints

Don't bend, fold, or crease the pictures —aside from cracking the paper, it will crack the coating, letting air and moisture in, so the coating becomes worthless

POLAROID APPROVED ALBUMS: Specially selected papers are free of chemicals which might harm prints. Library Edition (top, $5.95) holds 96 pictures under acetate in a variety of arrangements. Portfolio Edition (right, $4.95) carries 90 prints, two in each sleeve. A novel index makes picture finding easy. Pocket album (left, 25 cents) holds 16 prints; no acetate sleeves. All are available in sizes for Series 40 or 30 prints at photo dealers or direct from Customer Service, Polaroid Corp.

and gives no protection to the print.

Don't attempt to flatten a curled *coated* print by setting the unabridged dictionary on it. More than likely it will stick to the book. If you draw it across a table edge, that may take the curl out, but it will certainly crack the coating and make it worthless, so recoat carefully if you do anything to damage the coating.

Don't write on the back of the picture itself—you will see everything you wrote on the image, too, only backwards. Confine any writing to the picture tab or to the white border. Don't write on an envelope if the prints are inside. Address envelopes *before* inserting prints.

Don't mail unprotected prints. The folded film box should always be used to protect prints from damage.

Don't carry unprotected prints in your pocket, wallet, purse, or hat. If you insist on carrying prints loose, place each one in an individual acetate sleeve.

How to store prints after coating

Some types of papers, mounting corners, glues, and pastes contain enough sulfiding agents to harm any photographic image. So, keep your Polaroid Land prints away from black paper snapshot albums and similar methods of keeping pictures for viewing.

Polaroid Corp. has tested and approved a variety of albums (photo, opposite) made of specially selected paper known to contain no damaging chemicals—ask for them at your photo dealer.

For large numbers of prints, economical binders can be made up of multi-ring loose leaf notebooks and individual acetate sleeves available at camera shops and large stationery stores. Caution—some of these have a black paper sheet inside each sleeve. Be sure to take it out before inserting the prints.

Such albums are also good where pictures are used for business records, promotion purposes, real estate listings, and so on. If prints are to be filed, or mounted on display boards, keep them in Kodapak sleeves as described previously. If they are to be affixed to file cards, use double sided transparent tape, or *transparent* mounting corners.

Whatever else you do, don't start pasting prints into black paper albums—that may be slow death for the images. And do not keep conventional prints in the same album unless separated by many pages. The residual hypo in conventional prints can contaminate Polaroid Land prints.

Remember, hot, humid or damp locations are bad for the storage of *any* photographic materials. The top of the closet, a hot attic, a damp cellar, the garage—all are bad places for print storage.

Do you need to laminate prints between plastic sheets to withstand heavy handling? Better write to Customer Service, Polaroid Corp., Cambridge 39, Mass. for correct technical procedures to be followed when laminating prints.

DO YOU KNOW THE SERIAL NUMBER?

It's a good idea to write down and file away safely the serial number of your Polaroid Land camera. You need to know the serial number if you wish to insure the camera. This is also vital information to have in case the camera should be lost or stolen. Without the number you have no way to identify the camera.

You'll find serial numbers in the following places: On all cameras except the Model 110, look under the little collapsible foot mounted on the outside of the folding front of the camera. On the Model 110 open the back door—the numbers are stamped into the frame of the camera body near the rangefinder.

COPIES AND BLOW-UPS

You can get good duplicates and enlargements of Polaroid Land prints, easily, inexpensively.

IT'S NO TROUBLE at all to get first-rate duplicate prints or enlargements from any of your pictures. They're made directly from the original print.

There are two main ways to get copies. Most people will find it convenient and inexpensive to make use of the Polaroid Corp. Copy Service. There's also the Polaroid Print Copier, a remarkable device which enables you to produce duplicate prints in your own camera. However, that's covered in a separate chapter, *The Print Copier*, so we won't go into it here. Now for the Copy Service.

Polaroid Corp. operates a fast reprint service which turns out work of amazingly good quality. It's all done by mail. You send in your original print; in a few days you get it back, together with your copies and/or enlargements.

In each package of Polaroid Land film there's a *Copy Service Order Blank*. It carries a list of the various copy services available: same size copies of prints from any Land camera; jumbo (enlarged a bit) copies of prints from the Highlander; 5 x 7 glossy and 5 x 7 deluxe enlargements; 8 x 10 custom prints; also the prices, which are quite reasonable (same size copies were two for 25 cents when this book went to press.)

Since prices and mailing information

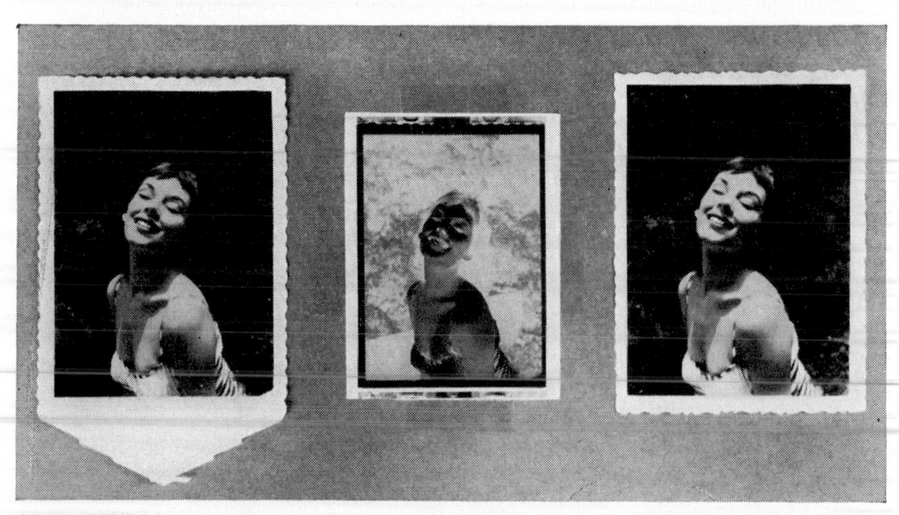

COPY METHOD: When you send your original print (left) to Polaroid Corp. for copying, first step is to make a copy negative (center). This is then used to make copy prints (right) or enlargements.

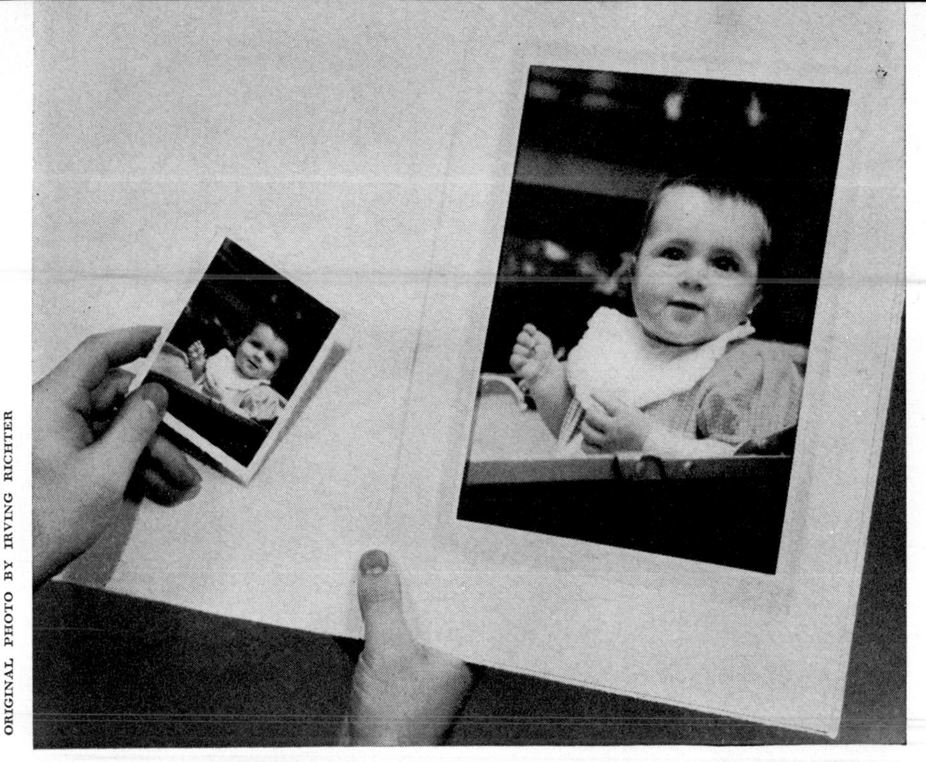

ORIGINAL PHOTO BY IRVING RICHTER

BEAUTIFUL CUSTOM PRINTS: Have you a particularly cherished Polaroid Land print of which you'd like to have a really fine enlargement? Here is one of the new 8 x 10 Polaroid Custom Prints, made from the original at left by skilled technicians. They crop your picture, if needed, for the most pleasing arrangement. Prints are spotted to remove slight blemishes, and are in strikingly handsome mounts. A custom print costs $3.00. *Important:* To enlarge this big satisfactorily, your original print must be clear and sharp. Muddy looking, fuzzy-focus images won't make good blow-ups.

can change, the best information is in your next package of Polaroid Land film.

The excellence and low cost of the copies are due to the method by which they are made. The copying materials are specially designed to record highlights, shadows, and middle tones in virtually the same ratio as they are in the original print. Exposure and processing are automatic, results consistent. While preparing this book, we had several hundred prints copied, and all were satisfactory.

If you request that a copy negative be sent to you (and we recommend that you do), you may have one for only 15 cents—a bargain, since it is of high quality.

The copy negative is sent to you in a glassine envelope—keep it there for protection. It's insurance, in case the original print gets damaged. Additional prints can be made from it locally (pick a camera store with a good photofinishing department). It's ideal for volume print orders, for personalized holiday greeting cards, for special enlargements (which you can make yourself, if you happen to be a darkroom fan). *However, don't send the copy negative back to Polaroid Corp. for more prints—they work only from original Polaroid Land prints.*

The secret of perfect copies

A copy can only be almost as good as the original. Any fuzziness or unsharpness, every bit of dirt, every fingerprint, smear, scratch, or other blemish in the original print will be in the copy negative and copy prints, and will be magnified in enlargements. So *protect your prints* as described in *The Care of Prints.*

If the coating of the original is badly scuffed or fingermarked, it may be desirable to try to recoat it. Careless recoating may cause damage to the print, so follow carefully the recoating technique suggested in *The Care of Prints.* Always mail between cardboards—the folded film box will do. Write only on the edges of the reverse side. Address the envelope *before* inserting the prints. *Follow to the letter the instructions on the Copy Service Order Blank when ordering copies.*

CORRECT EXPOSURE

A simple matter with this camera. Here's how to get it right every time, quickly, easily.

THERE IS no substitute for correct exposure. This is a basic principle in picture taking, with any camera. It's particularly true with the Polaroid Land camera, for there is no darkroom process to help make up for some of the deficiencies in an incorrectly exposed picture.

It's not difficult to make correctly exposed pictures in a minute. Each film package contains a useful exposure guide which helps you to make an educated estimate of the correct exposure. Also, Polaroid Corp. markets an excellent, easy-to-use exposure meter which takes all the guesswork out of exposure. This chapter explains how to use those two aids to correct exposure so as to get the most benefit from them.

In addition to the exposure meter there is a novel accessory—the photoelectric shutter—designed to fit over the lens of most Polaroid Land cameras, which automatically sets the correct exposure for bright light outdoor snapshots with the 3000 speed film. If you are using that device, this chapter does not apply. You'll find full details in *Photoelectric Shutter #440*, and *The 3000 Speed Film*.

Despite the fact that getting correct exposure is even more important with the Land process than in conventional photography, the camera has one outstanding advantage over all others—if

EXPOSURE PROBLEM: Before shooting any picture, ask yourself: What's the most important part of this scene? If the important detail is in the bright areas, set the camera so those areas are correctly exposed; if shadow details are more important, get them correctly exposed. It's easy to solve exposure problems when you can see your picture in a minute.

PHOTO BY HAROLD FEINSTEIN; 200 SPEED FILM

SUN / SUBJECT	Bright	Hazy Soft Shadows	Cloudy No Shadow	Dull
AVERAGE: People, pets	16 or 15 7 or 6	14 5	13 4	12 3
BRIGHT: Beach, snow	17* 8*	16 or 15 7 or 6	14 5	13 4
DARK: Shady spots	14 5	13 4	12 3	11 2

*Use filter over lens if picture is too light.

EXPOSURE GUIDE: There's one on the instruction sheet in each film package. This one is for Type 42. For other film types the information is different. Along the top of the guide are the lighting conditions; down the left side, the type of subject. Match up the two, set your camera to the exposure number recommended. The upper set of numbers is for EV numbered cameras; the lower set is for older models with Polaroid numbers.

#625 EXPOSURE METER: It's a sensitive, capable photoelectric device which gives accurate exposure information. A foot on the meter lets you attach it to the same accessory shoe which holds the wink-light, and it may be used while so mounted on the camera. However, it's preferable to use it as shown on pages 48 and 49.

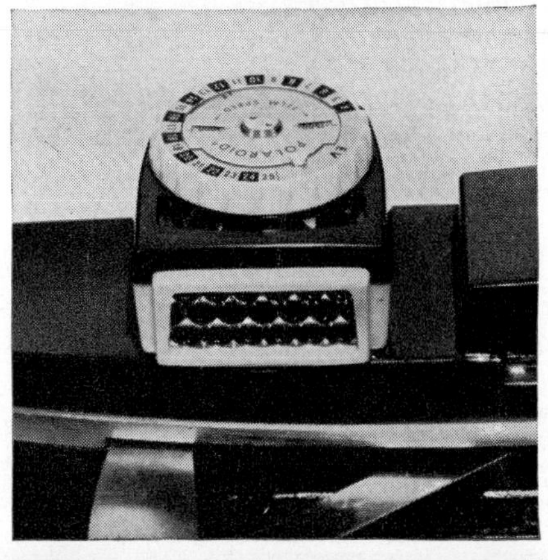

the exposure is wrong, you know it a minute later, when you see the picture, and can make a quick and easy correction according to a simple rule:

If the picture is too dark it is underexposed and needs more light to brighten it up; *move the exposure control to a lower number*—from EV 15 to EV 14, for example.

If the picture is too light it is overexposed and you must reduce the amount of light entering the camera; *move the exposure control to a higher number*—from EV 15 to 16, for example.

A film is "exposed" by allowing light to reach it for an instant. The amount of light reaching the film is controlled by the shutter speed and the size of the lens opening. In a conventional camera (other than a simple box type) there are separate fractional second and f-number controls to regulate the shutter speed and the size of the lens opening. The complications of learning to use these have discouraged many a picture taker.

In contrast to this, all Polaroid Land cameras (except the Pathfinders) have but a single exposure control wheel which sets shutter speed and lens opening simultaneously. And you need concern yourself only with a single number used to indicate the exposure setting.

What the EV numbers mean

The exposure control wheel protrudes from the top of the shutter housing (see photo, page 27). Rotate the wheel and a series of numbers appears in a small window above the lens. These are the exposure value or EV numbers. Each EV number is a sort of shorthand that stands for a specific, unchanging amount of exposure—a certain combination of shutter speed and lens opening. Fortunately, we need not concern ourselves with the technicalities that add up to a given EV number. Here's what we must know:

Low numbers (such as EV 10 and 11) are for use in dim light—they represent slow shutter speeds and wide lens openings used to let the maximum amount of light into the camera.

High numbers (such as EV 16 and 17) are for use in very bright light—they represent fast shutter speeds and small lens openings which cut down to usable proportions the brilliant light from sun or flashbulbs.

Turn the exposure control from a low number to the next higher one—you have cut the exposure in half. Turn it again to the next higher number—you have once more cut the exposure in half. And so it goes, all the way up to the highest EV number—the exposure is halved at each step upward.

Turn the exposure control from a high number to the next lower one—you have doubled the exposure. Turn it again to the next lower number—you have once more doubled the exposure. And so on, down to the lowest EV number—the exposure is doubled at each step down.

Caution: The exposure number must always be exactly centered in the little window. If the number is off to one side, the internal mechanism of the exposure control system will block the lens, ruining your picture.

Although all Polaroid Land cameras (except the Pathfinder) use this system, not all models carry exactly the same sets of numbers. Here's a summary:

Current large cameras (Models 95B, 150, 800) are numbered from EV 10 to EV 17. Current Highlander cameras (Model 80A) are numbered from EV 11 to EV 18. However, on all current cameras similar EV numbers stand for similar exposures. For example, EV 15 is the same exposure, whether it's on a Model 80A or a Model 150.

Older model cameras (discontinued in 1957) carried a different set of numbers. Models 95A, 100, and 700 were numbered from 1 to 8; the Model 80 Highlander was numbered from 2 to 9. The only difference in the exposure control systems of all these cameras is that the old exposure numbers started at 1 and 2, while the new EV numbers start at 10 and 11 (a change made for technical reasons which really don't concern us).

The original Polaroid Land camera, the Model 95, also had exposure numbers from 1 to 8. While each number represented the same effective exposure as the similar number on the Model 95A, the combinations of shutter speed and lens openings were quite different.

The Pathfinders, Models 110A and

 To convert numbers on older model cameras to EV numbers add 9.

110, are equipped with completely different types of exposure controls. How to set these is fully explained in the chapter *Using the Pathfinders.*

Some important exposure words

Before going any further, here are a few words which crop up in all discussions of films and exposure.

Speed: A film is "fast" if it is extremely sensitive to light, and can be used to take pictures under adverse lighting conditions. Just the opposite is a "slow" film, which requires very long exposures if used in dim light. Film speeds are indicated by numbers called *exposure indexes.* The higher the exposure index, the faster the film. You must know the film's speed (exposure index) in order to use an exposure meter correctly, because the first step in using a meter is to set it to the film's exposure index. How to do this is shown on page 48.

Polaroid Land films (and most conventional films) are faster in daylight than in tungsten light (household or flood lamps). So the film instruction sheet will specify two exposure indexes—one for daylight use, one for tungsten. Exception: For 3000 speed film, only a daylight exposure index—3000—is given. On the #625 exposure meter there is a special setting to be used with 3000 speed film in tungsten light. This is shown on page 51. If you're using 3000 speed film with a meter other than the #625, set the film speed dial to 2000 for tungsten light.

Latitude: The amount you can be "off" from correct exposure and still get an acceptable print is the latitude of a film. The latitude of Polaroid Land films is not as great as that of conventional films, but has been improved with each new film type marketed.

Latitude is greater for evenly lighted scenic subjects, in which you can't see distant shadow detail anyway, and less for pictures of people nearby in which shadow detail may be important.

Contrast: The difference in brightness between the darkest and lightest parts of the subject is called contrast. If the differences are great, as between black and white, then that is a high contrast subject. If the subject is made up of shades which will register on the print as mildly different grays, then it's a low contrast subject.

Films also have a contrast characteristic. Current Polaroid Land films are of moderate contrast—they handle easily the widest range of tones, softening too brilliant highlights and registering much shadow detail. They are excellent for use with harsh lighting. For softly lighted scenes one minute development may produce prints of too low contrast. You can often pep up contrast a bit by developing for two minutes.

What is correct exposure?

As pointed out before, a film is "exposed" by allowing light to reach it for a certain amount of time, which may vary from an instant for a snapshot to several seconds for a time exposure.

If *too much light* reaches the film it is *overexposed.* That is, all the important lighter areas of the subject will be too light, lack detail, perhaps even form a blank, white area.

If *too little light* reaches the film it is *underexposed.* All the important darker areas of the subject will be too dark, lack detail, perhaps even form a blank, black area. Only bright parts of the subject will appear in the print.

A photograph is *correctly exposed* if all the important subject areas, light, dark, or in between, are reproduced in the print with satisfactory detail.

Notice that the word "important" is included in each case. Even a very light picture, or a very dark picture, may be "correctly exposed" if that bit of important detail which puts across the picture idea is clear.

How to get correct exposure

To begin with, let's eliminate one method—guessing. It's too inaccurate, and much too expensive in terms of wasted film and lost picture opportunities.

If you don't have an exposure meter handy, the exposure guide printed on the film instruction sheet can help to guide you to correct exposure outdoors in bright light. However, your camera and films can make pictures in a minute under such a wide range of lighting conditions that no exposure guide could cover them.

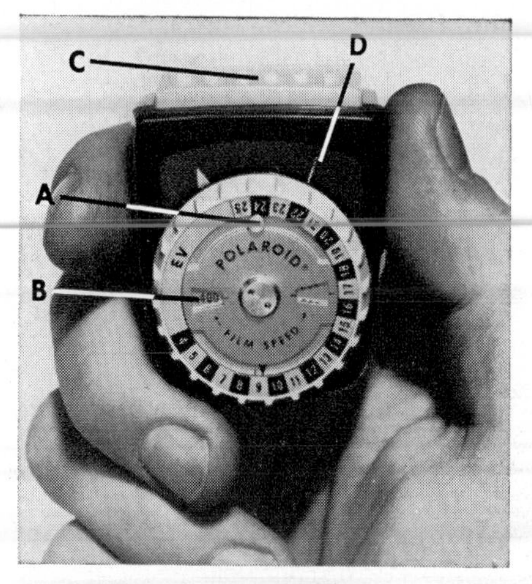

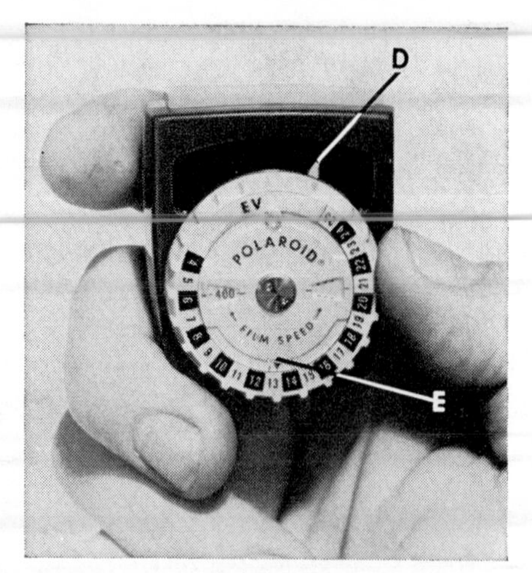

HOW TO USE #625 METER: First set film speed. Move knob (A) until film speed number (400, here) is centered in either opening (B). Aim meter cell (C) at subject, as shown below and at right. As light hits cell, needle (D) will move across window and stop. With thumb rotate knurled knob (right) until pointer covers needle (D). Now read EV number facing arrow (E). Set camera to that number (13, here). When using 3000 speed film with house lamps, technique is varied slightly, as shown on page 51.

To get correctly exposed pictures consistently, you need an accurate, highly sensitive exposure meter, and you must learn the few simple steps required to use it correctly. It's very easy to do.

The Polaroid exposure meter

There have been several Polaroid exposure meters for use with the Land camera. The current one is the #625. Previous meters were similar in principle but most were less sensitive than the #625 and cannot be used with some of the current films.

The exposure meter measures the brightness of light reflected from the subject. As this light enters the window in the front of the meter it strikes a *photocell*, which generates a tiny electric current. Wires carry the current to the movable coil of an ultra-sensitive ammeter, energizing the coil, causing it to pivot and swing a needle across a dial. The brighter the light, the more current the photocell generates, and the further the needle swings across the dial.

The #625 meter is designed to work with all Polaroid Land cameras and films. It comes with a scale calibrated in EV numbers, for use with current model cameras. In the box there is an additional scale, numbered from 1 to 9, for use with older model cameras. Instructions for installing the 1 to 9 scale, if necessary,

RIGHT: Come close enough so meter cell "sees" only your subject, is not affected by light or dark areas beyond, but don't cast hand shadow.

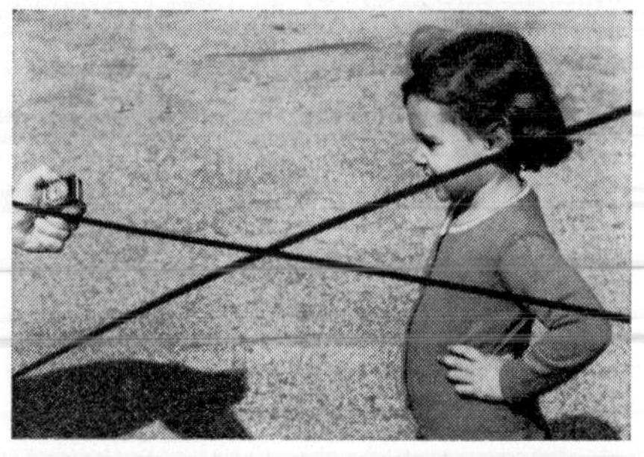

WRONG: Meter is too far from face; background light or darkness will affect it and cause it to give false reading, wrong exposure.

come with it. The meter has an interchangeable foot and can thus fit in the accessory shoe of all model cameras, if you care to carry it in that manner. It is a highly sensitive, extremely able meter.

How to use the meter

The first step is to set the film speed dial according to the exposure index of the film being used. Get the exposure index (daylight or tungsten, depending on where you are) from the film instruction sheet and set the meter as shown in the photos at left. Then "take a reading" of the subject, following the methods shown in the photos on these pages.

Note the number to which the meter arrow points and set your camera's exposure control to that number. *Important:* Read the dial while holding the meter aimed at the subject. If you move it away to get a better look at the needle and dial the reading will be inaccurate.

Most important: Remember that the meter measures light *reflected* from your subject. Therefore, be careful that the meter cell is aimed only at the particular area you are "reading." If you hold the meter close to a face, the photocell can "see" only that light reflected from the face, and indicates correct exposure for that face. But if you get too far away from the face, the meter "sees" light not only from the face, but also from the sky behind (or perhaps it's the open door to a big barn), and anything else within its angle of view. The unwanted light (or darkness) in the background causes the meter to give an incorrect reading.

Of course, if your hand is so placed that it casts a shadow on the face in front of the meter cell, the reading will also be inaccurate. So come close, but don't take readings of your shadow.

The discontinued meters

On the next page are shown four discontinued models of Polaroid exposure meters. Only the #620 is sufficiently sensitive to be used with 3000 speed film, under some conditions. Models PR-23A or 23B can be used outdoors with Polaroid PolaPan 200 and 400 films. The PR-22 and PR-23 are obsolete and should be retired as soon as possible.

FOR SCENICS, PROPER METER AIMING IS MOST IMPORTANT

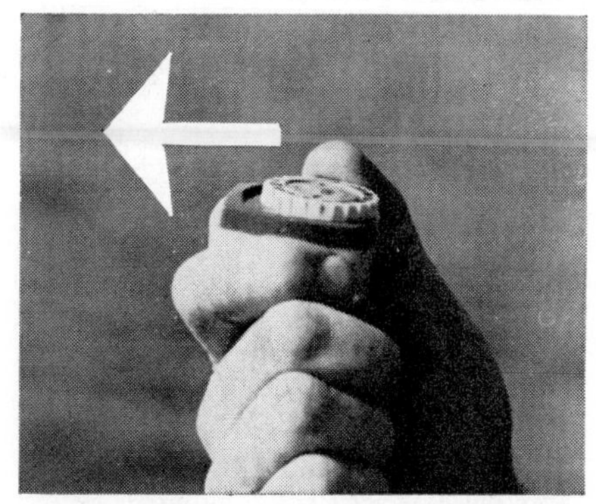

NEARBY SUBJECT, NO SKY: You're snapping building across the street, the side of a large ship, or something else that fills the picture area with little or no sky. Aim the meter straight at it.

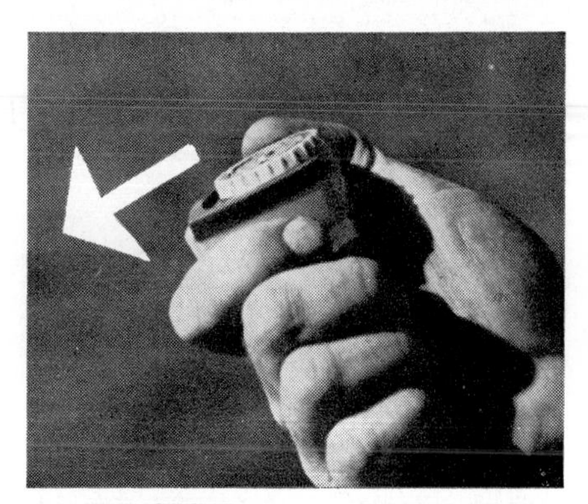

DISTANT SCENE: If you want the foreground shadow detail fully exposed aim the meter down as shown. Skies will be bald white. If the foreground is unimportant, aim the meter as at top, to get the background properly exposed. If the sky is important, aim as below.

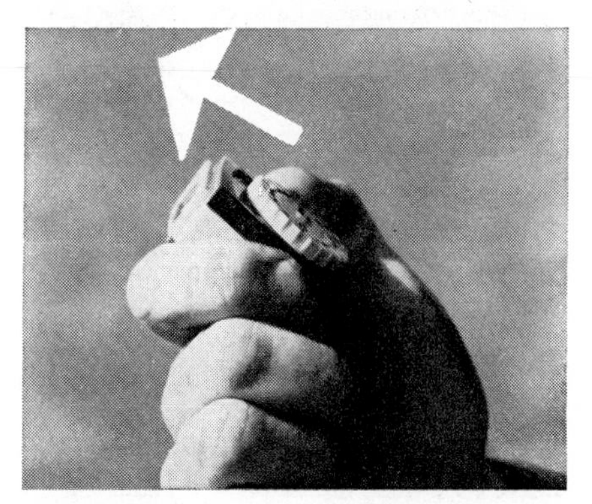

GET THAT SKY: Where beautiful clouds make the scene, expose correctly for them by aiming the meter up. Ground shadow detail may be dark, but the picture will have lots of punch.

To convert numbers on older model cameras to EV numbers add 9.

THE DISCONTINUED METERS

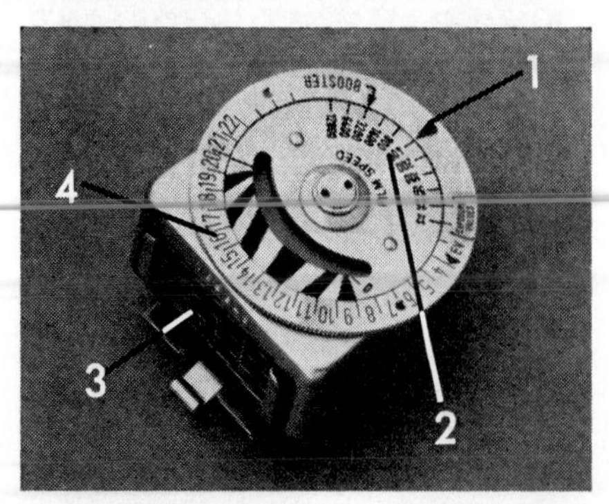

#620 METER: Let's use Type 44 film, exposure index 400. Turn outer ring so arrow (1) matches 400 film speed (2). Aim light cell (3) at subject to measure its brightness. Note number (4) to which needle points; here it's EV 16 (black and silver wedges guide eye from needle to numbers). Set camera's exposure control to EV 16. The #620 has a limited usefulness with 3000 speed film.

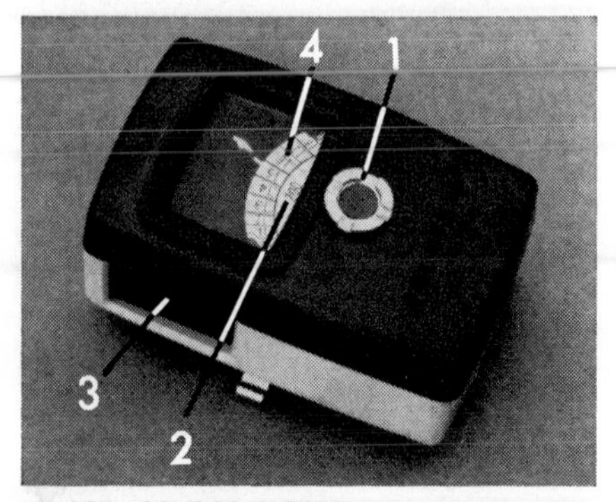

PR-23A OR 23B METER: Here we are using Type 42 film, exposure index 200. Turn film speed control (1) until 200 is visible (2). Aim light cell (3) at subject to measure its brightness, using meter handling techniques shown on pages 48 and 49. Note number (4) to which needle points. Here it's EV 15. Set camera's control to EV 15. PR-23A & 23B are suitable for use in bright light outdoors with PolaPan 200 and 400 films.

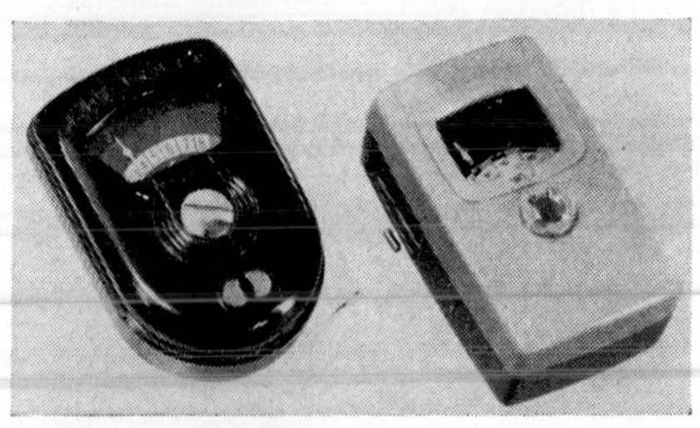

OBSOLETE METERS: PR-22, left, and PR-23 are calibrated only in Polaroid numbers. They are not recommended for use with current films. For information about them, write to Customer Service, Polaroid Corp., Cambridge 39, Mass.

Here are techniques to help you solve some common exposure problems.

1. When the light is too dim: If there is so little light reflected from the subject that the meter needle barely moves, use the methods shown in the chapter *Time Exposures.*

2. When the light is too bright: When using PolaPan 200 or 400 at the beach, over snow or water, or with other bright subjects, prints may be over-exposed even with the camera set to the highest EV number. Remedy: Slip an orange filter over the lens. This not only cuts down the light reaching the film but will improve the picture.

3. When you can't get close to the subject: For a medium distant subject, such as someone in the water, or maybe 10 ft. away, take a reading from your own hand, making sure it's lighted the same as your out-of-reach person is. Or, if the subject is something dark, such as an animal or inanimate object, take a substitute reading off clothing or any other surface which fairly well matches your subject for lighting and brightness. If nothing dark is available, take a hand reading, set to next lower exposure number.

If you are using 3000 speed film in the camera with a 4S light reducing filter over the lens, and wish to cut the light even more, you can add the orange filter *under* the 4S light reducer. With some cameras this may permit a light leak around the I-B switch, so try to protect the front of the camera from direct sun. (For details, see *The 3000 Speed Film.*)

4. When using a filter: A filter over the lens cuts down the light reaching the film. Usually, this is compensated for by increasing exposure (exception: 2, above). Each Polaroid filter has rim markings stating how many numbers lower to set the exposure control (see *Filters* for complete details).

5. For night scenes: Time exposure is usually necessary. Best time is at dusk, when there is still a little light in the sky to give outline and substance to trees, buildings, even people. If lights

 To convert numbers on older model cameras to EV numbers add 9.

THE "AVERAGE" READING: When one side of your subject is brightly lighted and the other is dark, as here, try an "average" reading. First get the EV number for correct exposure of the bright side (maybe EV 14), then for the dark side (perhaps EV 12). Set the camera's exposure control at the midpoint (EV 13).

TUNGSTEN LIGHT READING: When using the #625 meter with 3000 speed film, the film speed dial is set to 3000. When the light is from tungsten lamps, read the EV number facing the small marker alongside the arrow. Here the marker is pointing to EV 12. In daylight, read the EV number next to the arrow; here, EV 13.

are included in the picture, overexpose for them in order to get shadow detail. Best night scenes are made after rain or snow, which reflect the light. Use a tripod, or other support.

6. Shooting into the light: Best outdoor portraits are made in diffused light, not in direct sunlight. You can provide this light yourself, even in bright sun, by having the subject face away from the sun. Then the exposure is for a face in bright shade. Bring the meter very close; make sure direct sunlight isn't leaking around and getting to the meter's photocell.

Caution: If the sun is low in the sky be careful it doesn't shine into the lens. A lens shade will help, but even that's no good if you aim at the sun.

7. Where shadow detail is most important: In some subjects all the highlight areas are unimportant—the picture's story is all in the shaded parts. Take a meter reading of important shadow details and expose for them. Let the highlights be overexposed, thus emphasizing shadow detail.

8. Where highlight detail is most important: This is exactly the opposite of 7, above; all the important areas are brightly lighted, so expose for them and let the shadows go dark.

9. For a silhouette: You need a brilliant light source on the far side of the subject—by comparison, the near side should be almost dark, or at least well shaded. Your light source can be the sun itself (subject must block it out completely, of course), a bright sky, a window in a dark room, or even a powerful house lamp.

Whichever you use, take a reading for the bright part, get correct exposure for it. The subject will be very dark.

10. Shooting from shade to sun: You're on a porch, or other shaded spot, but your subject is brightly lighted. Forget what the light is where you are—expose for the subject.

11. Shooting from sun to shade: Now you're in the bright sun, your girl friend's in the car. Go over and take a meter reading in the shaded car,

THE 3000 SPEED FILM

It opens the door to a new world of photography, where "impossible" pictures become easy to take.

LOAD a Polaroid Land camera with 3000 speed film and you increase its picture taking abilities to a degree which is hard to imagine until you've done it yourself.

With this revolutionary product it is easy to make pictures in a minute under conditions which would otherwise present impossible obstacles. This chapter and the two which follow (*The Wink-Light* and *Photoelectric Shutter #440*) are intended to introduce you to this new world of photography, and to explain the uses (and limitations) of the 3000 speed film and the remarkable accessories designed to go with it. Please read all three chapters before using the 3000 speed film.

What 3000 speed means

The exposure index of a film is an indication of its "speed" or sensitivity to light. The higher the exposure index, the "faster" the film and the more able it is to take pictures where the light is dim. Polaroid PolaPan 200 and 400 are considered "fast" films, compared to conventional snapshot films. But an exposure index of 3000 can only be described as sensational. That's where the 3000 speed film gets its name—from an exposure index of approximately 3000 in daylight. In tungsten light (such as house lamps) the exposure index is 2000.

With such film speed it becomes easy to make snapshots indoors by window-light, or by house lamps in a room of ordinary brightness. Where the lighting is fairly even, this presents no problems. However, "available light" from lamps or windows is often highly directional, so that subjects are brightly lighted on one side, while the other is in shadow.

To fill in those shadows and add a little overall light to the scene, there is a novel, low-powered repeating flash called the Wink-Light. Under proper conditions its effect can be quite startling. And, where the available light is too dim for shooting, even with 3000 speed film, the wink-light can be used as a flashgun for fairly close subjects. All this is explained in detail in *The Wink-Light.*

3000 speed film in daylight

Oddly enough, the enormous film speed offers real advantages even in bright sunlight, where you might think it would be absolutely unnecessary, if not useless. However, in order to make use of it, you need the Photoelectric Shutter #440. This device fits over the front of the lens. In bright light it automatically sets the

AVAILABLE LIGHT: Here's a wonderful example of the kind of informal pictures which 3000 speed film makes possible. This was shot in a compartment of the USS Wasp, using the available light. For such work, try EV 10, 11, 12. These are slow shutter speeds, so hold the camera steady.

◁ GREG MASSEY

Older cameras need seals to stop light leaks.

1. CHECK SERIAL NUMBER: All cameras except Pathfinders which do not have "L" before serial number (arrow) need seals. Those with "L" have built-in light seals.

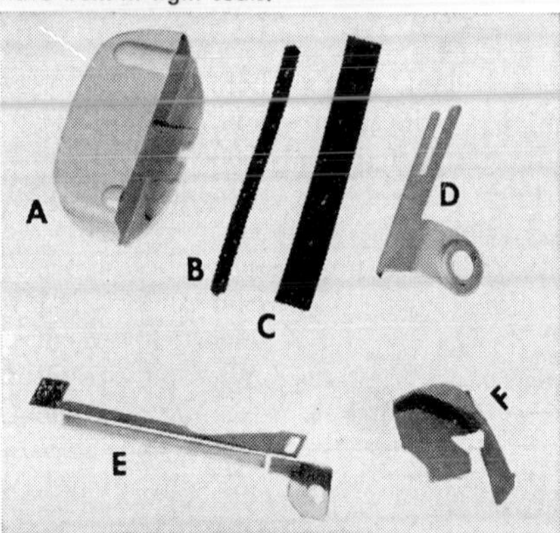

2. LIGHT SEALS: Package of light seals to fit all camera models comes with each wink-light and photoelectric shutter. A, B, C, D are for Highlanders; E, F are for large cameras.

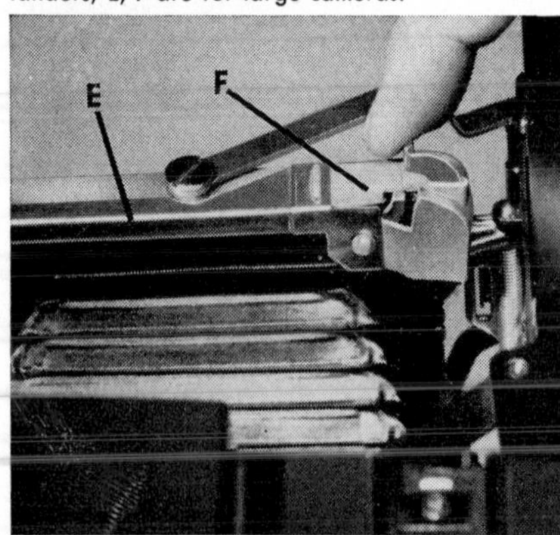

3. LARGE CAMERAS: Rubber fitting (F) covers openings around shutter lever, which goes through slit in rubber. Metal strip (E) sticks to shutter housing, retains rubber seal.

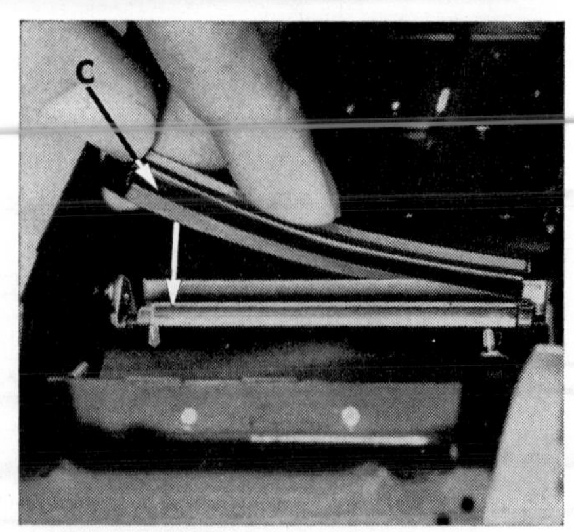

4. HIGHLANDER: Slotted plastic (C) covers bright metal strip in outer back.

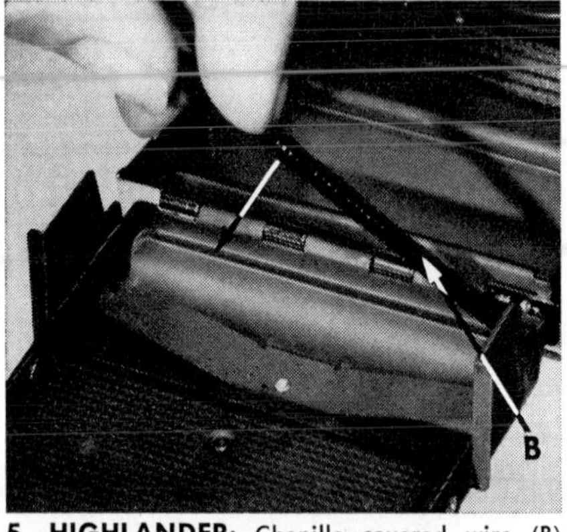

5. HIGHLANDER: Chenille covered wire (B) fits groove in inner back next to hinge. Be sure to seat it firmly in place.

6. HIGHLANDER: Remove cap (A) only to adjust exposure control. Strip (D) goes around I-B knob and under housing. Slot in (D) must fit around shutter actuator arm (DD).

correct exposure, provides high shutter speeds to stop fast action, puts everything from about 3½ ft. to infinity in focus, and has other advantages. It's described in *Photoelectric Shutter #440.*

What if you don't have the photoelectric shutter on the camera but it's loaded with 3000 speed film and you want to take a picture in bright daylight? For this situation you must place over the lens the 4S Light Reducer (see photos at right). That's a neutral density filter which cuts the light entering the camera the equivalent of four EV numbers, to the point where the 3000 speed film is, in effect, no faster than PolaPan 200. (With the Pathfinders it's possible to get the same result, with improved pictures, by placing deep colored filters over the lens. See *Filters* for details.) Without the light reducer or other heavy filters, 3000 speed film will be hopelessly overexposed in bright daylight, no matter how you set the exposure control on the camera.

A light reducer is supplied free of charge with each wink-light. One type fits all Polaroid Land cameras. The little pouch for it is designed to be carried attached to the camera's carrying strap or tripod socket. Try to avoid getting fingerprints on the filter—it's easier to smear it up than it is to clean it.

If you intend to do much shooting in bright daylight (and you don't have the photoelectric shutter) there's not much point in loading with 3000 speed film and then adding the light reducer—PolaPan 200 or 400 is a more logical choice. However, the 3000 speed film/light reducer combination makes sense when you're shooting in and out of deep shade, or at dusk or sunrise when other films are not fast enough. Keep the light reducer over the lens as long as your exposure meter (set to 200 film speed) indicates settings of EV 14 or higher (15 for the Highlanders). However, when the meter readings get below EV 14 (15 for Highlanders) remove the light reducer, set the meter's film speed dial to 3000, and make use of the full film speed.

Beware of light leaks

When a camera loaded with 3000 speed film is carried in daylight, special precautions must be taken to prevent light leaks

4S LIGHT REDUCER PREVENTS OVEREXPOSURE IN DAYLIGHT

ALL MODELS BUT 110, 110A, 80, 80A: Press filter over lens mount. Lip on rubber ring (arrow) must cover I-B switch.

PATHFINDERS: Remove filter from rubber ring, turn it over, replace in ring. Press outer edge of rubber ring over lens mount.

HIGHLANDERS: Remove rubber ring and fit filter right onto lens mount.

J. W.

LAURIE SEAMANS

SELECTIVE FOCUS: For available light pictures, slow shutter speeds and wide lens openings (EV 10, 11, 12) are needed. The zone of sharp focus is shallow, particularly for close subjects, and focusing must be accurate. If the camera had been focused for the man, the woman would have been out of focus.

EVEN LIGHTING: Available light shooting is easier with even illumination than when bright highlights and deep shadows are present. If the lighting is of high contrast, you may need the wink-light to lighten the shadows. These pictures were made with 3000 speed film.

through the camera body which will fog the film and ruin pictures.

Except for Pathfinder models, all cameras manufactured prior to mid-1959 must be fitted with the light seals shown on page 54. If your camera doesn't have an "L" before the serial number (photo 1, page 54) it needs light seals. A package of light seals to fit all camera models is included free of charge with each winklight and photo-electric shutter sold. The seals are easy to install, and full instructions are on the package. Those for the Models 95B, 150, 800 and other large cameras do not interfere with normal camera operations. For the Highlanders, however, there's a plastic hood which fits over the top of the shutter housing. This must be removed each time you want to set the exposure control. Be sure to replace it right away.

Light seals cannot be fitted to the original Model 95 cameras. However, owners of those cameras can have them converted to Model 95B cameras with built-in light seals. For information about this conversion service, write to Customer Service, Polaroid Corp., Cambridge 39, Mass.

Cameras with an "L" before the serial number have built-in light seals. Nevertheless, even with these cameras (and also those with seals added) certain precautions are necessary.

Don't forget the light reducer

The 4S Light Reducer should be kept on the lens at all times outdoors (not necessary with Pathfinders), especially when extending or collapsing the bellows while opening and closing the camera. All model cameras except the Pathfinders may be closed with the light reducer in place over the lens.

When pulling the tab, always turn away from the sun so your body casts a shadow over the camera, and let the cutter bar "ride" on the paper as you pull. Keep the cutter bar closed and locked except when actually pulling the tab.

Never leave the camera in the direct sun for any length of time, whether it's open or closed.

Did your camera come with an instruction card over the back door? This may cause a light leak. As soon as you are familiar with the operation of the camera, remove the instruction card. Always keep the back door closed and latched except when actually removing prints.

METER READING: When using the #625 meter with 3000 speed film, the film speed dial is set to 3000. In daylight, read the EV number facing the arrow. Here it would be EV 13. When the light is from tungsten lamps, read the EV number next to the small marker alongside the arrow. Here the marker is pointing to EV 12.

An exposure meter is a must

For best results with 3000 speed film (when you're not using the photoelectric shutter) an accurate, sensitive exposure meter is absolutely necessary. The Polaroid #625 meter is designed for use with this film. Be sure to set and handle the meter as shown in *Correct Exposure.*

For other Polaroid Land films, the instruction sheet lists separate exposure indexes for daylight and tungsten light. For example, Type 42 has an exposure index or "speed" of 200 in daylight and 140 in tungsten and you set the film speed dial of the meter according to the type of light. Not so with the 3000 speed film. Only the daylight speed (3000) is given, and the film speed dial of the #625 meter is always set to 3000, whether in daylight or tungsten illumination. However, the technique of using the meter is slightly different for tungsten light than for daylight readings (photo, above).

If you're using 3000 speed film with an exposure meter other than the #625, be sure to set the film speed dial to 2000 when the exposure is by tungsten light.

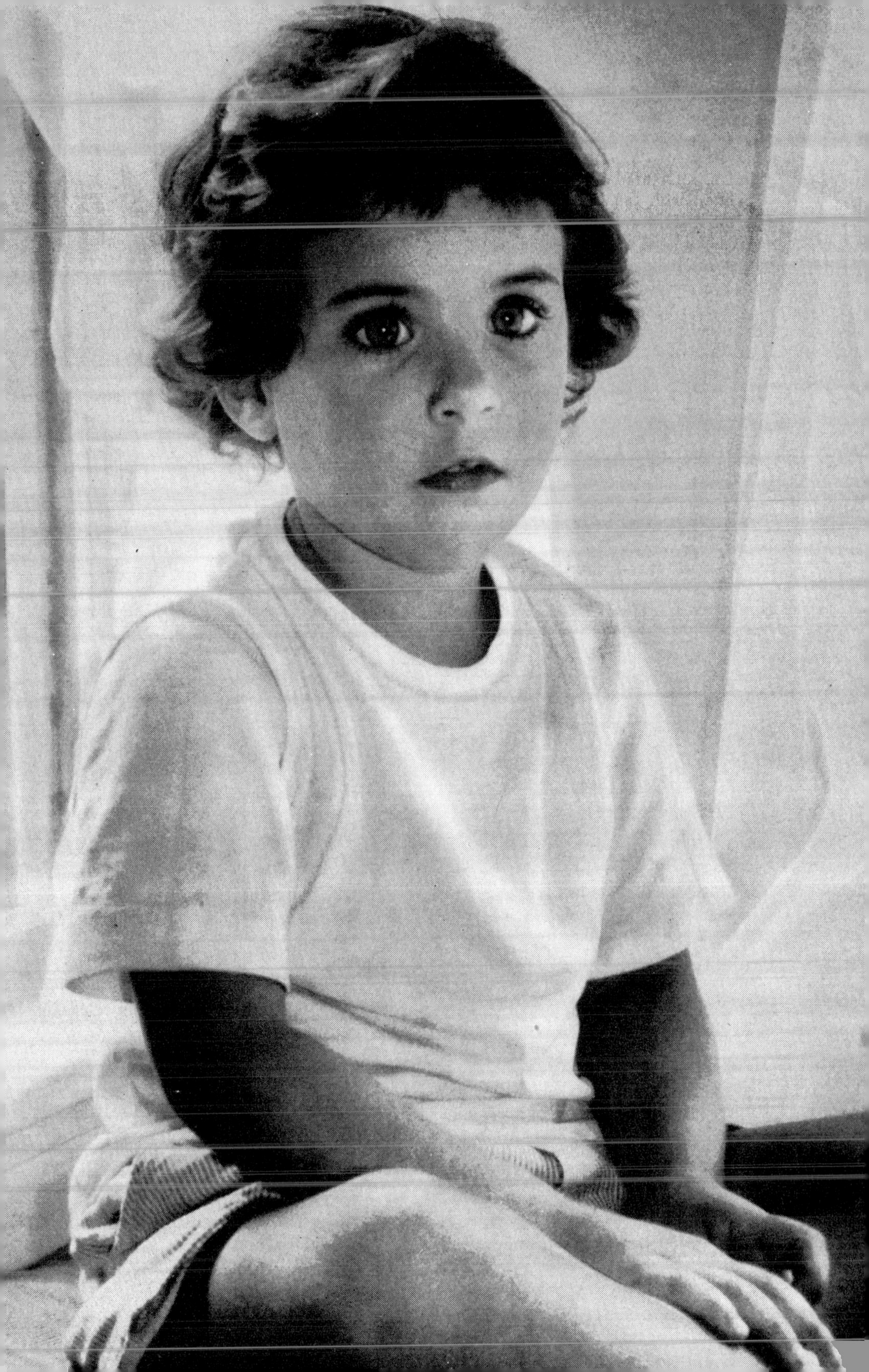

THE WINK-LIGHT

With 3000 speed film, this repeating flash lets you make snapshots indoors, without flashbulbs.

THE POLAROID WINK-LIGHT is a unique repeating flash light which, in combination with 3000 speed film, makes it possible to take a wide variety of indoor snapshots without the need for using flashbulbs.

The wink-light is not a substitute for flash in the sense that a speed light is. Ordinarily, when using flash or speed light, both those high powered light sources provide the only illumination—the room can be dark or lighted, but it usually doesn't affect the final result.

Not so with the wink-light. The low-powered flash from it is designed mainly for use in normally lighted rooms in which it would be almost possible to make a good picture with 3000 speed film. The brief flash is meant as a booster, to raise the general light level slightly, or as "fill light" to eliminate or reduce dark shadow areas in subjects up to about 8 ft. away. Most indoor snapshots are made within this distance.

In addition, in a darkened room, at distances up to about 6 ft., the wink-light supplies enough illumination for use as a main light source (like a flashbulb), but this is not its main purpose.

Any room in which people are reading, eating, playing cards, doing office work, or carrying on other normal social or business activities, usually has some areas bright enough to permit a snapshot to be made with 3000 speed film. However, the light frequently is highly directional—as from a lamp or window. One side of the subject is likely to be bright enough for a snapshot, but the other side is in deep shadow. Or, as is often the case, your subject is just outside the area of bright light—not in the dark, but in a darker area than that in which you could make a snapshot with 3000 speed film.

It's precisely for those situations that the wink-light is most useful. Its weak flash, plus the available light, plus the extreme sensitivity of 3000 speed film, make it possible for Polaroid Land camera users to take snapshots easily under conditions which would otherwise make photography difficult, if not impossible, without the use of flashbulbs. (However,

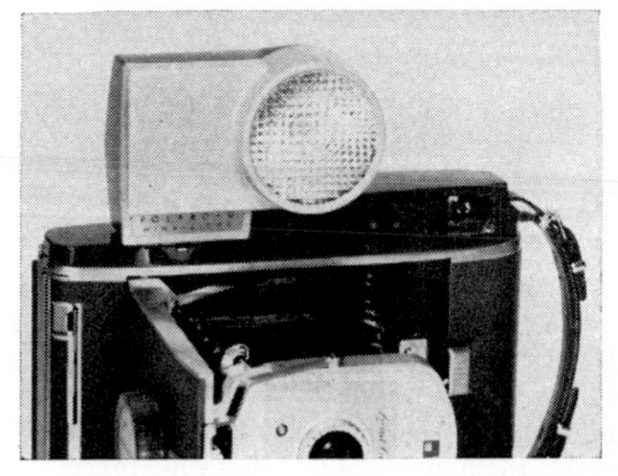

THE WINK-LIGHT: It attaches to the camera's accessory shoe. There are several models, which differ only in the type of connection used. The chart on page 188 tells which one fits your camera.

BALANCED LIGHT: This little girl was sitting with her back to a bright window; her face was in shadow. The wink-light filled in the shadows, softened the contrast between dark and light areas, preserved a natural look without overpowering the existing light, as might have happened with the brilliant light of a flashbulb.

◁ LAURIE SEAMANS

WITHOUT WINK-LIGHT: There was plenty of light on far side of bust, but it was coming from high left and behind sculptor John Terken, so his face was practically concealed by heavy shadows.

it does not work well with the Model 95.)

The wide lens openings and great range of shutter speeds of the Pathfinder models make them particularly suitable for pictures with 3000 speed film and the wink-light. The results possible are amazing.

For lighting conditions or subjects which are beyond the abilities of the wink-light, the Polaroid Wink-Light Flasher #256 is supplied with each wink-light. This is a tiny reflector and socket designed for the jelly bean size AG-1 flashbulbs. It plugs right into the wink-light (see photos page 62) and is powered by the same battery. It converts the wink-light into an extremely capable flashgun.

Incidentally, before attempting to use 3000 speed film with the wink-light please read *The 3000 Speed Film.*

How it works

The wink-light draws its power from a small 45-volt battery. When the wink-light is connected to the camera, the battery begins to charge a capacitor, a device for storing electricity. When the shutter flash contacts close, a powerful jolt of electricity goes to a small 12-volt tungsten lamp. The single shot of electricity is so brief that the lamp burns brightly for an instant, without being damaged.

After about 1000 flashes, the battery gets weak or quits, and the bulb starts to deteriorate. Replace them both together (see *Care of Equipment*).

The wink-light attaches to the accessory shoe atop the camera. On those cameras with electrical contacts in the accessory shoe, the circuit to the wink-light is formed as soon as the unit is slipped into the accessory shoe. Remove the wink-light from the accessory shoe after using it; if left connected it will drain the battery.

On some model cameras the electrical connection is by way of a wire from the shutter to the wink-light. Disconnect the wire after using the wink-light.

When the flasher is plugged into the wink-light, don't leave an unfired flashbulb in the socket for any length of time. This also drains the battery.

Never connect the wink-light to the camera when the photoelectric shutter #440 is on the camera—that will exhaust the battery rapidly.

When using the wink-light with a Model 110A or 110 Pathfinder, set the shutter speed to 1/30 (or 1/25) sec. and the sync lever to M. Adjust the exposure with the lever that controls the EV numbers

WITH WINK-LIGHT: Same exposure, but wink-light illuminates former shadowed areas. Note that light parts of statue are not overexposed. Light has been added, but it did not overpower existing light.

and f-number settings (see *Using the Pathfinders*). With all other Polaroid Land cameras, no special adjustments are necessary. Use the EV number control to adjust exposure in the usual way. And be sure the I-B switch is set to I.

The effect of distance

The effectiveness of the wink-light depends almost entirely on two factors: the brightness of the room lighting, and the distance from wink-light to subject.

The wink-light has a fixed light output. You can't increase it, and the only way to reduce it is to drape a handkerchief or a layer of tissue paper over the front. However, the brightness with which it lights the subject depends on how far away the subject is.

At 3 ft. the light thrown on the subject is 4X as bright as it would be from a wink-light 6 ft. away. And when it has to travel 12 ft. it's only ¼ as bright as it was 6 ft. *The nearer the wink-light to the subject, the more effect the flash will have, and the further away, the less the effect.* This is important, for the same EV number that gives a nicely exposed picture from 7 ft. may cause overexposure if you come in to 3½ ft.

The effect of room lighting

Since the wink-light output always remains the same, its effect depends greatly on how brightly the subject is lighted by the available light in the room. If the available light is such that you'd need EV 10 or 11 to make an exposure, the wink-light can have a great effect on the scene. However, if your subject is near a window and one side is light enough for a snapshot at EV 15, the wink-light has no effect.

The wink-light is most effective when the available light on the subject is dim, and least effective when the available light on the subject is bright.

Even though the light falling on the subject is relatively dim (exposure for the bright side EV 11, perhaps) it may still be very contrasty. That is, the shadowed side of the subject may be so dark that nothing registers in the print when the exposure is correct for the bright side. *The wink-light is more effective with contrasty lighting than with soft, even lighting on the subject.*

Correct exposure in lamp light

The majority of wink-light pictures will be made in rooms lighted by house lamps.

Auxiliary flasher for AG-1 bulbs converts wink-

DIRECT FLASH: AG-1 bulb in Wink-Light Flasher #256 gives highly directional light with sharp, unpleasing shadows and flattens out detail in subject. Compare this with photo below.

BOUNCE FLASH: With reflector swiveled toward ceiling, light spreads out over room, floods statue of Edison like daylight, gives it form. See page 75 for photo of reflector swiveled for vertical picture.

The procedure is simple. Turn on all the lights in the room to raise the general light level. In an average well lighted home, you could make an exposure with 3000 speed film at EV 11, but there would be dark shadow areas. So, try EV 11 with the wink-light, for subjects about 6 ft. from the camera.

If you come near (3-4 ft.) close down to EV 12 or 13. If you back off to 8 or 10 ft. the effect of the wink-light will be reduced greatly; you'll need at least EV 11, maybe EV 10. *These are slow shutter speeds—don't shake the camera.*

Often, your subject will be sitting next to a lamp with one side of the face brightly lighted and the other side dark. Here you can use your exposure meter to help get correct exposure with the wink-light. Take a meter reading from the bright side of the face (see *Correct Exposure*). Back off to 6 ft. and set the camera for the same EV number indicated by the meter. If you come in close (3-4 ft.) set the camera one EV number higher than recommended by the meter. Lighting conditions vary too much for any definite recommendations to be 100% accurate, but these are good beginning points for many picture situations.

Correct exposure by window light

If the light from the window is filling the whole room, or a large part of it, fairly evenly, take a meter reading, set the camera accordingly and start shooting with the wink-light from about 6 ft. If you come closer (3-4 ft.) turn the control to the next higher EV number.

If your subject is right by a window, with one side well lighted and the other in shadow, take a reading off the bright side. If the meter indicates an exposure of EV 14 or higher, the wink-light won't

light into capable direct or bounce flashgun.

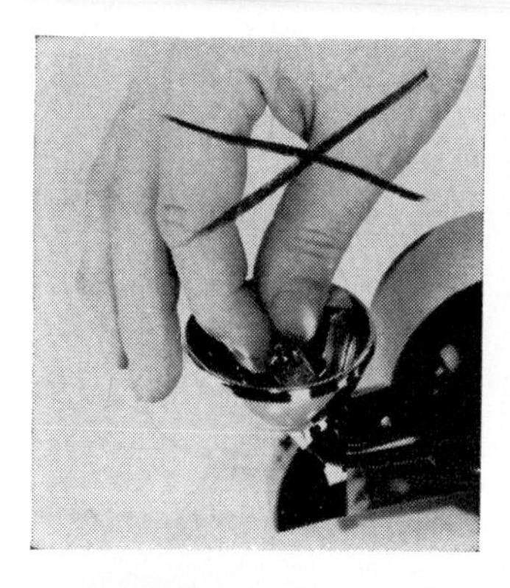

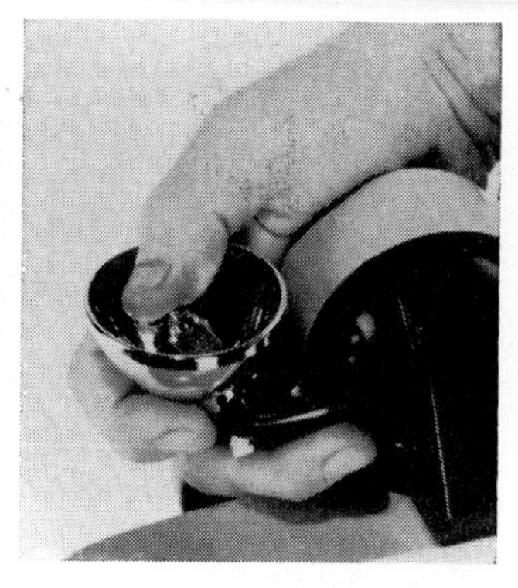

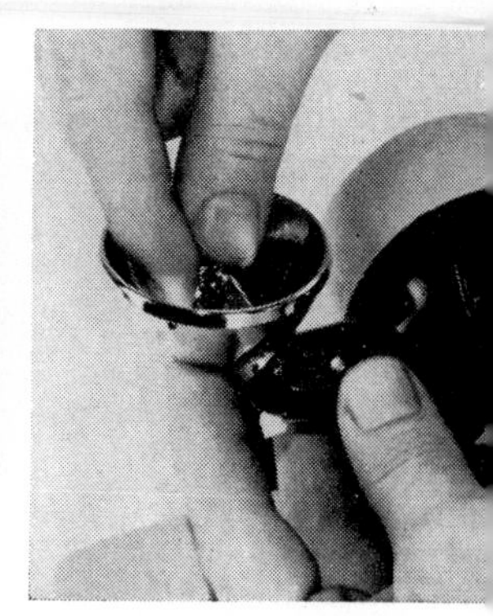

INSERTING BULB: Don't just push it into socket (left). Repeated pressure, even if light, may loosen connectors. Support reflector underneath, as shown. Wire contacts on some bulbs may be pressed in, may fail to make contact in socket. If so, pry them out slightly with fingernail. It's soft wire; do it gently.

help that shadow. Instead, take an "average" reading as shown on page 51, and make the exposure without the wink-light. This should lighten the shadows.

The Wink-Light Flasher #256

Obviously, there are many situations in which lighting conditions and/or the subject make it impossible to get a picture by available light or with the wink-light. Then you just plug the auxiliary flasher into the side of the wink-light. This little device takes the tiny AG-1 flashbulbs. The reflector swivels so you can use it for direct or bounce flash (photos, page 62) in either horizontal or vertical position. The soft, even light of bounce flash is preferable. Despite the small size of the AG-1, this bulb and 3000 speed film make a spectacular bounce flash combination.

The flasher and AG-1 bulbs can also be used with PolaPan 200 and 400, but the picture taking range is more limited than when using 3000 speed film.

Below is a bounce flash guide giving exposure recommendations when using the wink-light flasher, AG-1 bulbs, and various Polaroid Land films. For more details about flashbulbs, flashguns, synchronization, etc., see the chapter *Flash.*

BOUNCE FLASH GUIDE FOR USE WITH WINK-LIGHT FLASHER #256

Camera model ↓	Film type ↓	For close-ups 3-4 ft.	**For most pictures of people 5-8 ft.**	For distant subjects 9-12 ft.
		Set exposure control to number indicated below		
All except 95, 110A & 110	47-37	EV 17 or #8	**EV 16 or #7**	EV 15 or #6
	42 & 32-400	EV 13 or #4	**EV 12 or #3**	EV 10-11 or #1-2
110A & 110; use 1/125 or 1/100 sec. Set sync lever to "M"	47	f/32	**f/22**	f/16
	42	f/8	**f/5.6**	f/4.5 use 1/25 sec.

With Type 44 film, set exposure control one number (or one f-number) higher than recommended for Type 42.

BOUNCE FLASH GUIDE is for use with AG-1 flashbulbs in the wink-light flasher, with reflector pointed toward ceiling, under "average" conditions—that is, both photographer and subject are standing under white ceiling 8 to 10 ft. high, in moderate-sized room (perhaps 15 x 18 ft.) with medium dark walls. Estimate carefully distance in feet in straight line from flashgun to subject. Set exposure control to number recommended for that distance, focus camera and shoot. If picture is too dark, reset exposure control to next lower number (or f-number); if too light, reset to next higher number. Try again. Variations from "average" conditions (photographer and subject both seated, for example) may affect exposure; see *Flash* for details.

PHOTOELECTRIC SHUTTER #440

It sets correct exposure automatically, stops fast action, ensures extra sharp pictures.

THE PHOTOELECTRIC SHUTTER #440 is an accessory which fits onto the front of the camera, and is designed to improve bright daylight snapshots by automatically providing correct exposure and sharp focus.

It is a combined photoelectric exposure meter, variable speed shutter, and lens attachment, intended for use only with the 3000 speed film. It will not function with other Polaroid Land films. The shutter fits all Polaroid Land cameras except the Pathfinders, Highlanders, and the original Model 95. The shutter, and the 3000 speed film, should be used only with cameras which have either built-in or added light seals, as described in the chapter *The 3000 Speed Film.*

How it works

The brightness of the light reflected from the subject to the photocell of the exposure meter automatically sets the shutter speed at the moment the picture is snapped. The shutter speed ranges from 1/1000 sec. (in brightest light) to 1/10 sec., depending upon the brightness of the light. Under normal bright snapshot conditions, the shutter speeds are high enough to stop fast action and there is little likelihood of unsharpness due to camera shake. Thus, pictures are sharp.

The shutter blade passes across a tiny, fixed lens opening (equivalent to f/54).

OVERALL FOCUS: Tiny lens opening (f/54) in shutter brings near and far objects into focus at same time. With camera set for 6 ft., everything from about 3½ ft. to infinity will be in focus in the print, as shown here.

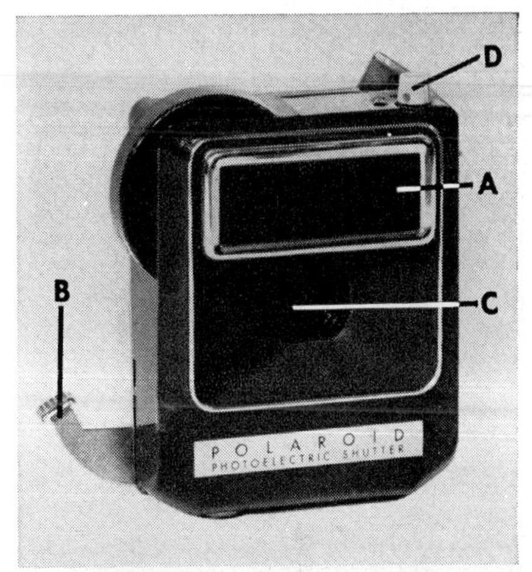

THE SHUTTER: Front view, above, shows: grid over photocell (A); release lever (B); glass plate over lens opening (C); exposure adjustment knob (D). In back view, below, are: lens opening (C); latching lever (E) that actuates parts holding shutter to camera; insufficient light indicator (F).

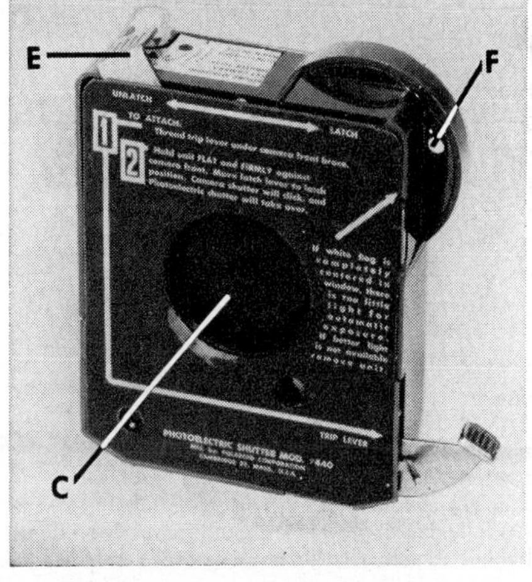

How to attach the #440 shutter to the camera.

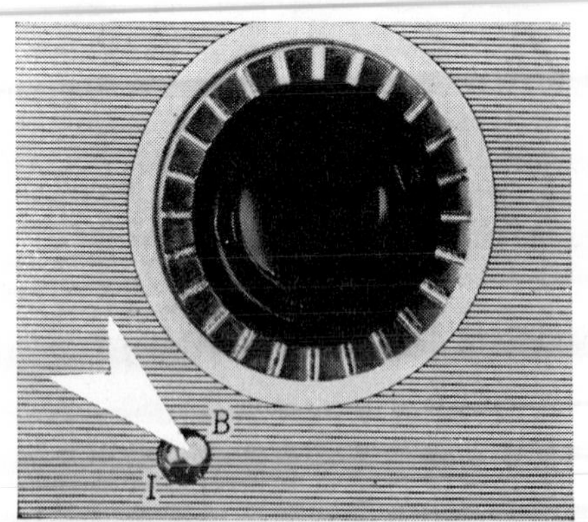

1. SET CAMERA: Always set exposure control to EV 14 (or #5) and move I-B switch to 8.

2. PLACE SHUTTER: Insert release lever (A) under camera shutter housing support (B) and slip #440 shutter over lens mount so it lies flat.

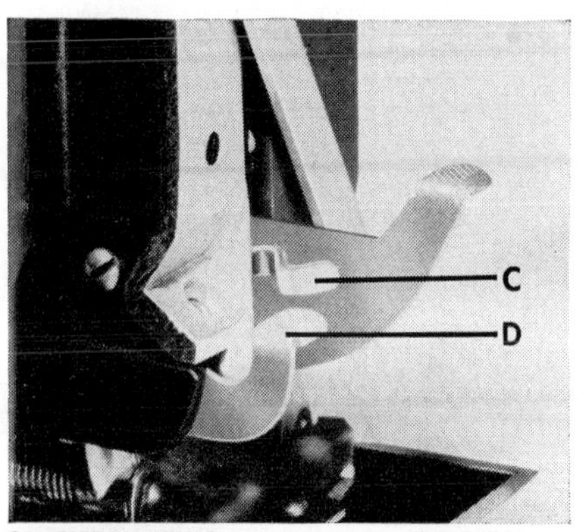

3. CHECK THIS: Arm (C) on #440 shutter should be directly over camera shutter release lever (D). If not, remove and replace #440 shutter.

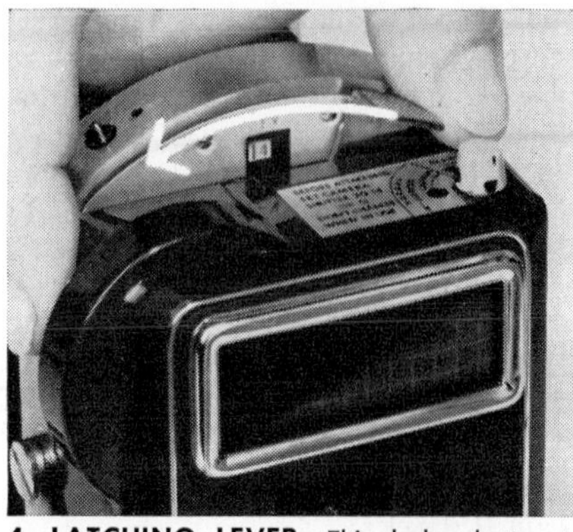

4. LATCHING LEVER: This locks shutter to camera; swing it to far side of housing. Camera shutter must click, as when snapping picture; if not, depress camera shutter release until it clicks.

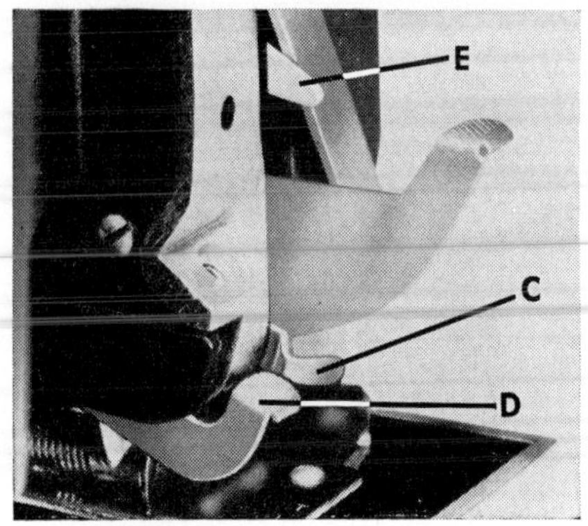

5. CHECK THIS: After latching lever is locked, arm (C) should depress camera's shutter release (D) fully. Locking arm (E) should be firmly wedged behind camera shutter housing support.

6. SHUTTER ON CAMERA: This is how it looks in place. Camera cannot be closed with shutter on.

MORRIS H. JAFFE ▷

The effect of this tiny aperture is to bring both near and distant objects into focus at the same time. In fact, with the camera set for 6 ft., everything from about 3½ ft. to infinity will be in focus in the print. This virtually eliminates the need to focus the camera.

When the #440 shutter is on the camera and you are snapping average subjects, always use the 6 ft. setting, even for pictures of distant objects. If you set the camera for a greater distance, such as 25 ft., 50 ft., or infinity, the corners of the print may be dark and part of the subject may be cut off.

When the light's dim

Because the lens aperture is fixed, the only control over exposure is the speed at which the shutter blade travels, and this in turn is controlled by the brightness of the light reaching the photocell of the exposure meter in the shutter. The shutter reaches its top speed (1/1000 sec.) only when the subject is in brightest sunlight. If the day is overcast or dark, or the subject is in the shade, the shutter speed slows down considerably. It cannot stop such fast action as in bright light, and you must be careful not to cause camera shake. Depress the release lever smoothly.

When the light gets too dim for the shutter to operate efficiently, a white dot appears in a window on the back of the shutter (photo, page 68). Then you should remove the shutter and operate the camera as usual.

Get used to the release

The release lever of the #440 shutter travels a long way—about an inch—before the shutter blade moves. Most of this movement causes the exposure meter mechanism inside the shutter to set the correct exposure. Only the last ¼ in. or so of travel is for releasing the shutter

ACTION STOPPING: In brightest sunlight, photoelectric shutter has top speed of 1/1000 sec., fast enough to stop most action. As light dims, shutter slows down; 1/10 sec. is slowest speed.

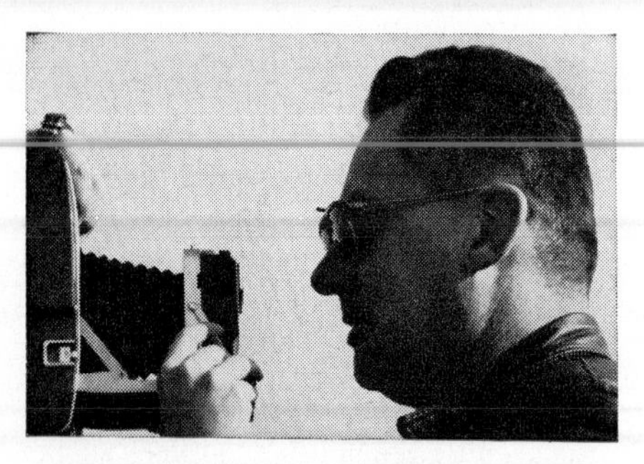

METER LOCKING TECHNIQUE: If light is behind subject, or subject and background are of widely different brightness, meter is "fooled" and gives incorrect exposure. Bring camera close enough to exclude stray light and background (don't cast shadow), depress shutter release lever to "meter locking point," move back to desired distance and shoot. Text explains this fully.

itself. So, the lever must go all the way to the bottom. Don't punch it—depress it smoothly to avoid camera shake.

Attaching the #440 shutter

The basic steps necessary to fit the shutter to your camera are shown on page 66. Here are some important pointers.

Always set the I-B switch to B before attaching the shutter. If the switch is left at I, the #440 shutter mechanism may shift it to B—and it may not. If the switch is not set to B, you'll get a completely black picture. In that case, remove the #440 shutter, move the I-B switch to B, and replace the shutter.

Be sure the exposure control is set to EV 14 or (#5) *before* swinging the latching lever (photo 4, page 66), and be careful not to accidentally move the exposure control wheel when moving the lever. If the exposure control wheel is moved *after* attaching the shutter, the camera's shutter may stay open when the #440 shutter is removed, thus fogging the next picture. If the camera shutter stays open, turn the exposure control to EV 10 (or #1) to clear the jam.

Adjusting the exposure

Under ordinary snapshot conditions the #440 shutter should give correctly exposed prints every time. However, if you are consistently getting slightly overexposed (a bit too light) or underexposed (too dark) prints, use the adjustment knob shown below. Ordinarily, the dot on the knob should match the dot on the plate. If the pictures are too dark, turn the dot towards "Lighten;" if too light, turn it towards "Darken." For brilliant, glaring scenes of snow, beach, or over water, turn the knob all the way to the right to line up the two arrows at the point marked "Glare Scene."

Special yellow filter

Regular Polaroid filters cannot be used with the #440 shutter. Instead there is a special square yellow sky filter (#450) which fits over the entire front of the shutter. It's described in *Filters.* With this filter in place the shutter can't produce its top speed, even in very bright light, so keep this in mind if you want to stop fast action.

Tricky exposure problems

The #440 shutter works best when the light on the subject comes from behind

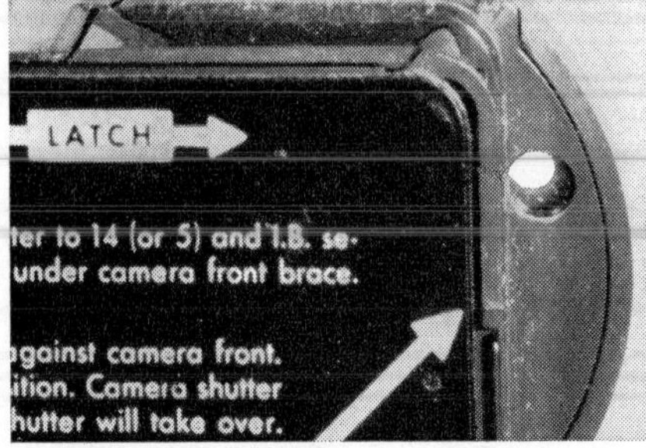

INSUFFICIENT LIGHT: This round opening is on back of shutter. When white dot fills opening, there's not enough light to use #440 shutter. Remove it and use camera shutter as usual.

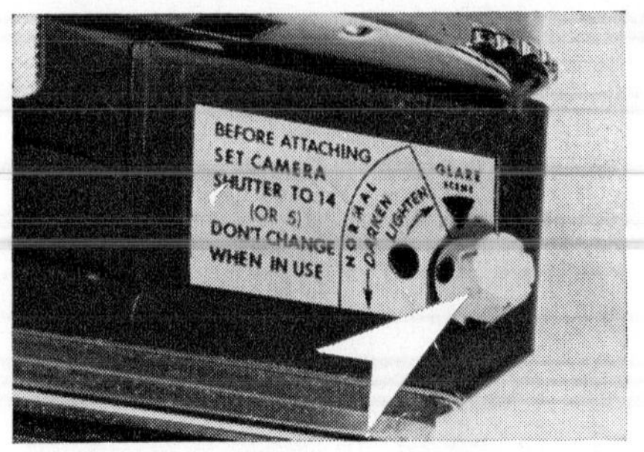

ADJUSTMENT KNOB: If pictures are consistently too light or too dark, this knob will adjust exposure. It's also for use with brilliant, glaring scenes. Text explains how to set it.

CLOSE FOCUS: Close-up lenses cannot be used with #440 shutter. However, with camera set to 3½ ft. everything from about 2 ft. to 10 ft. will be in focus. At that close range, viewfinder is inaccurate. Allow plenty of room between your subject and top and right side of viewfinder frame.

the front of the camera, and the background is about as brightly lighted as the subject. If the light comes from behind the subject, the direct rays may strike the photocell and cause a much underexposed picture. Underexposure may also occur if the subject is shaded or dark but the background is brightly lighted. The opposite effect (overexposure) occurs if the subject is brightly lighted, but the entire background is very dark.

For such situations there's a technique called "meter locking" which requires care, and practice with the shutter off the camera to avoid accidental exposures.

Depress the release lever about 4/5 of its travel—to the point where the top edge of the lever is next to a raised line at the corner of the shutter housing. At this point the lever will lock and won't return to its up position. By depressing the lever to this point you have set and locked the exposure mechanism to the correct exposure for the lighting at the time you depressed the lever. However, you have not released the shutter.

In effect, the shutter now "remembers" the correct exposure that would have been made if you had pressed the lever all the way, and will retain this setting until the lever is pushed the extra ¼ in. needed to release the shutter.

Therefore, you can bring the camera close enough to the subject so the photocell of the shutter "sees" only the light reflected from the subject and none of the background (photo, top of page 68), depress the lever to the "meter locking point" to get correct exposure, back off to the desired distance, and shoot. The bright light (or darkness) in the background will not affect the shutter.

FLASH

Where the wink-light isn't strong enough, or you haven't 3000 speed film, flash is the answer.

A FLASHBULB is the most compact, powerful, portable light source available for photography. Even with 3000 speed film there are many situations for which lots of extra light is needed, and for that the flashbulb fills the bill.

There are at present two Polaroid flash systems. The newer one makes use of the tiny AG-1 bulbs in the Wink-Light Flasher #256, in combination with the wink-light and 3000 speed film. This is described in *The Wink-Light.* The other system, an older type, employs the Polaroid flashgun, which was originally designed for use with films of medium high speed, such as PolaPan 200 and 400, and bulbs very much bigger than the AG-1. The principles by which good flash pictures are made apply equally to both systems. Only the equipment is different.

If you have only the wink-light and #256 flasher, the chapter *The Wink-Light* contains the basic information you need to get good flash pictures. This chapter is devoted to a detailed discussion of the principles of flash photography and how to use them with the Polaroid flashgun.

Recipe for wonderful pictures

With the simplest equipment and a little bit of care, Polaroid Land camera users can easily produce flash pictures which match in quality the finest one-flashbulb photographs made by professionals, and be worlds above anything the average snapshooter ever gets with a conventional direct flash camera.

The technique which makes top-quality flash pictures routine is called "bounce flash." It consists of pointing the flashgun upwards, and "bouncing" the light off the ceiling. This floods the room with what appears to be softly diffused daylight, and gives results such as you see on the opposite page. However, this is not a simple matter with conventional cameras and flashguns—few of them are adaptable to bounce flash. Even if the equipment is adaptable, you need considerable skill to do it right, and the results are often highly unpredictable.

Not so when you use the Polaroid Land camera. A special, simple bracket lets you bounce the flash off the ceiling, or shoot it directly at the subject with equal facility, as needed.

The high speed of the Polaroid Land films makes maximum use of the soft,

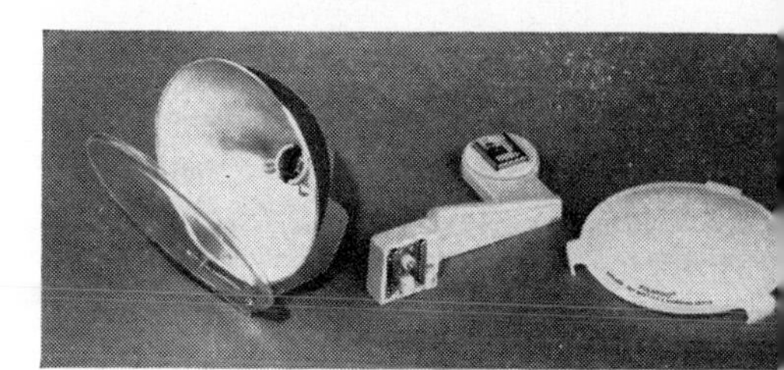

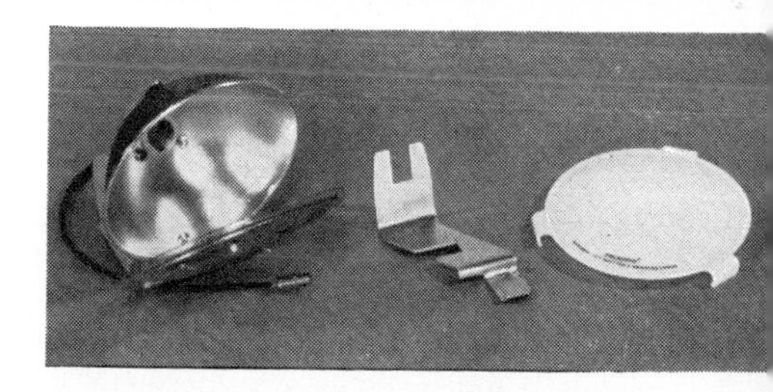

WHAT YOU NEED: Polaroid BC flashgun has hinged plastic shield, comes with white diffuser (right). Brackets (center) let you aim gun at ceiling for bounce flash. Outfit above fits Models 150, 800, 110A, and all Highlanders. Gun and bracket below are for Model 95B and various discontinued camera models. Text gives details.

CATCH THAT MOMENT! Flash is great for picture situations such as this. Polaroid bounce flash bracket gives you same soft, even light you see here. It's easy to use; text explains how. Picture was made on 200 speed film.

◁PETER GOWLAND

PETER GOWLAND

DIRECT FLASH: With flashgun on camera, pointing directly at subject, it is almost impossible to get even light distribution on both foreground and background. Results are like this. Unit above flashgun is wink-light with auxiliary flasher plugged in and aimed for direct flash.

even bounce light. The simplicity of the camera controls and the ease with which you can get correct exposure make bounce flash a method that anyone can use successfully—even a beginner. And if the picture is not quite right, you can do it over again on the spot. *You learn quickly how to make the next shot better!*

The device that makes bounce flash so simple and easy with the Polaroid Land camera is the bounce flash bracket, shown on page 71. There are two types of Polaroid bounce flash brackets and they are not interchangeable. The chart on page 188 tells which one fits which camera.

Why bounce flash?

Even when used most skillfully, direct-on-the-camera flash cannot produce the same pleasing effects as properly used bounce flash. The direct flash from a bulb is like a spotlight, and it "burns-up" skin tones. Subjects full face to the camera get virtually shadowless but harsh illumination which "flattens" features; there is no "modeling." Yet, if faces are turned at an angle, deep unpleasing shadows may appear.

Direct flash cannot give even illumination in both foreground and background, and even minor errors in figuring distance and exposure can affect the result drastically. Unless your subject is close to a wall or other object, the background light rapidly falls off into pitch darkness—people look "flat." The light is blinding and unpleasant.

None of this applies to correctly used bounce flash. The glare is directed upwards and does not bother your subject's eyes. The light bouncing off a white ceiling will fill an entire average living room with remarkable evenness (of course, background light falls off somewhat, but not to the sharply unpleasant degree characteristic of direct flash). Minor errors in exposure produce minor effects in the picture. Face shadows are soft and controllable. You get depth and "roundness" in your subjects.

Bounce flash is the ideal "in-the-home"

DIRECT FLASH gives harsh light; skin tones are poor. "One-way" lighting makes subjects look "flat." Shadows, if any, are unpleasing.

BOUNCE FLASH: With Polaroid bounce flash bracket in place, flashgun points towards ceiling which acts as giant reflector and diffuser, spreading light evenly over large area. Auxiliary flasher has swiveling reflector which may be turned up, as above, or to position shown on page 75 for vertical shots.

light source for formal or informal portraits of individuals and small groups, for action around the house, for office parties and any social gathering. *There is one absolute requirement: The ceiling must be white, or the palest tint of cream, pink, blue, etc.* Dark painted or natural wood finish ceilings will simply absorb the light aimed at them and make bounce flash difficult if not impossible to use.

Even a white ceiling must not be too high, or the flash will be dissipated on the trip up and back down to the subject. With the Model 150 and Type 44 film, it is possible to get good pictures under a white ceiling up to 20 ft. high. The faster lens of the Pathfinder lets you use a somewhat higher ceiling. In general, bounce flash with PolaPan 200 and 400 is ineffective in high ceilinged auditoriums, gymnasiums, and similar structures. However, the combination of 3000 speed film, a Polaroid flashgun, and a No. 5 or Press 25 bulb opens up almost unbelievable new opportunities for bounce flash in large indoor areas, particularly with the Pathfinder cameras. Conditions will vary so much that no exposure recommendations are possible. But with the results visible in a minute, a few practice shots should supply the information to make "impossible" pictures possible.

When to use direct flash

Although bounce flash is by far the best method for most of your flash pictures, we can't ignore direct flash—in some situations it must be used.

Here are some examples: the ceiling is too high, or is dark colored; you are outdoors at night without any overhead covering; for subjects more than 12 ft. from the flashgun.

The powerful little gun

The Polaroid BC flashgun is a remarkably compact and usable device. The body is of tough plastic, and the reflector is satin-finished aluminum alloy. In front of the reflector is a hinged

BOUNCE FLASH gives soft light, pleasing shadows; skin tones are excellent. Light hits subjects from all directions, gives them "depth."

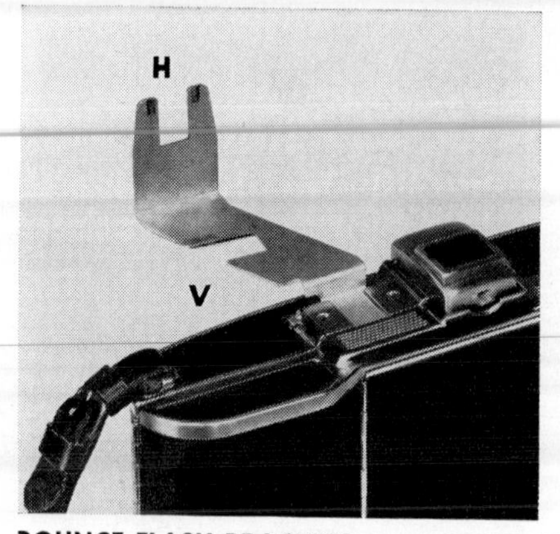

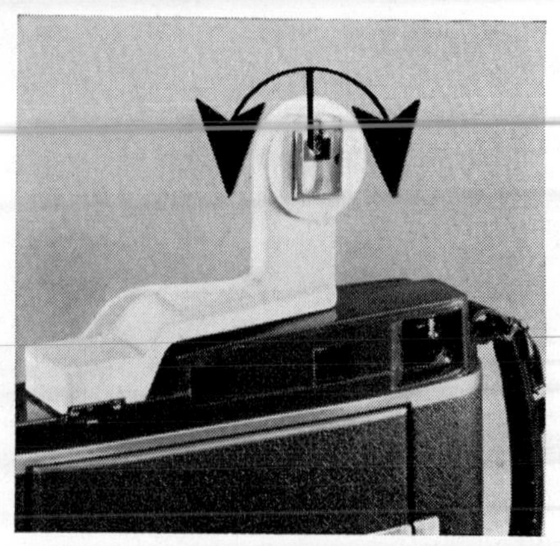

BOUNCE FLASH BRACKETS: No. 292, right, is for flashguns which make electrical contact through foot of gun that goes into camera's accessory shoe. Gun fits into connecting shoe on bracket which swivels (arrows) for horizontal or vertical pictures. No. 290, left, is for flashguns with connecting wires.

clear plastic shield, protection against the chance that a bulb might explode.

The gun is powered by a *battery-capacitor* or BC circuit. The battery is tiny but powerful. Current from it is fed in small amounts to a capacitor, a device for storing electricity. When the shutter contacts close, the capacitor sends a single but potent shot of high voltage current to the flashbulb. Be sure to read *Care of Equipment* for important information on how to keep your flashgun in top shape and get the maximum life from the battery.

With each gun comes a translucent plastic *Diffusing Filter* which clips on over the flash shield. This accessory is used for direct flash pictures to cut the light from the bulb and soften shadows. Don't use it for bounce flash.

WATCH THAT WIRE: It can get in front of lens unless it is led under bellows and around base of shutter housing to connector (arrow).

The flashguns and connectors

All Polaroid flashguns are similar in construction, but they are made with distinctly different types of electrical connections to match various camera models, and they are not interchangeable. Let's sort them out.

Camera models 150, 800, 80, 80A, 110A, all take the Model 281 flashgun, which has its electrical contact in the foot of the gun that slips into the accessory shoe on the camera. For bounce flash with this gun and those cameras use Polaroid Bounce Flash Bracket #292 (top, right). *Caution:* When using this bracket do not insert the bulb until both bracket and gun are in place on the camera. Otherwise, the bulb may go off.

Camera models 95B, 95A, 95, 100, 700, all take the Model 202 flashgun, equipped with connecting cord about 14 in. long which goes to an *ASA bayonet* type fitting recessed in the front of the shutter housing (photo at left). For bounce flash with these guns and cameras use Polaroid Bounce Flash Adapter No. 290. This is a simple piece of bent metal with slots to hold the gun.

The Pathfinder Model 110 will accept only the Model 222 flashgun, which has a short cord leading to an *ASA two-post* connector on the side of the shutter. For bounce flash, this combination also uses the No. 290 adapter.

Caution: When using direct flash, be sure the foot of the gun is all the way into the accessory shoe. On some models the

 To convert numbers on older model cameras to EV numbers add 9.

flashgun is secured by a small latch on the shoe. If not so secured, the flashgun may fall off the camera. To remove the gun it is first necessary to push aside the latch. Since it's hidden under the gun a small lever is provided on the bottom of the flashgun—move the lever and the latch opens. When using the No. 290 adapter for bounce flash it also must be securely latched in place.

Which bulb to use?

There's an incredible variety of flashbulbs on the market today, but you need concern yourself with only a few types—the very powerful No. 5 or Press 25 (which are essentially similar), and the very much smaller M5. The No. 5 and Press 25 have the right base to fit the Polaroid flashgun socket. The M5 has a different type of base—in order to use it in the Polaroid flashgun you need an inexpensive little adapter available at your photo dealer. Although the M5 is only a fraction of the size of the No. 5 and Press 25, the light output is almost as great. Wherever you can use the larger bulbs, the M5 will also serve if you set the camera's exposure control to the next lower EV number.

Standardize your flash methods

For in-the-home shots stick to bounce flash wherever possible, and for it use No. 5 or Press 25 bulbs with Polaroid 200 or 400 films. Type 44 is the best choice because its extra speed lets you take advantage of the deep zone of sharp focus at EV 14, 15, and 16 (or f/11, 16, and 22). With Type 42 or 32-400 films the exposure control would have to be set one number (or one f-number) lower to get equivalent exposure. For close range direct flash, M5 bulbs give enough light.

Where you need maximum light (pictures of large groups, long shots in factories or outdoors at night, etc.) use direct flash, with No. 5 or Press 25 bulbs.

Getting the exposure right

The amount of light from the flash which can enter the camera is regulated in the same way as for a daylight exposure—by varying lens opening and/or shutter speed. On all models except the Pathfinders, the single exposure control does the trick; on the Pathfinders, conventional separate lens opening and shutter speed controls are used. With either system (and both bounce and direct flash) the principle is the same: If the light reflected from the subject is very bright, cut it down with a small lens opening such as EV 16 or f/22. If the light is not very bright, let more of it in to the film through a larger lens opening—maybe EV 13 or f/8.

Exposure for bounce flash

For bounce flash pictures, here's a system of exposure which is so simple that many people won't believe it works—but it does, and amazingly well. It's designed to give you reasonably accurate expo-

FOR VERTICAL PICTURES: Flashgun is turned like this for bounce flash verticals. Don't forget to turn gun in bracket when changing from horizontal to vertical format, or vice versa. Auxiliary flasher for wink-light, below, swivels to this position for vertical bounce flash shots.

sure *on the first try* for pictures in the home, which is where the great majority of flash shots are made. It has been figured out for use under the following "average" conditions: the ceiling is white and 8 to 10 ft. high; the room is of moderate size (perhaps 15 x 18 ft.) with medium dark walls; both the photographer and the subject are standing. Here's how it works.

Practically all in-the-home flash shots are of subjects between 4 ft. and 12 ft. from the camera. You'll find that within those distances you can shoot most of your pictures with a single exposure setting, plus an occasional shift to a second setting. Let's assume you're using a Model 150, Type 44 film, and No. 5 bulbs in an "average" living room. Your basic setting will be EV 15 for people 5 to 8 ft. from you. For someone at the far end of the room (up to 12 ft.) just shift to EV 14. For a close-up portrait (3 or 4 ft.) shift the other way to EV 16. And that's all there is to it.

If the picture is too dark, use the next lower exposure number; if too light, use the next higher exposure number.

The bounce flash guide

The simplified exposure system described above has been made into a bounce flash exposure guide (below) which can be used with any Polaroid Land camera.

To use the bounce flash guide estimate carefully the flashgun-to-subject distance in a straight line (use the rangefinder if your camera has one) and set the exposure control to the number recommended for that distance. And don't forget to set the camera for that distance.

Conditions affecting exposure

The distance from flashgun to subject is not the only factor which affects exposure. Here are some others; in each case it's assumed that the room has an "average" ceiling.

If both photographer and subject are sitting, the light must travel further to the ceiling and down; this reduces its intensity. For any given subject distance, set the exposure control one number (or one f-number) lower than recommended in the bounce flash guide.

In small rooms with light walls, the flash is bounced back to the subject from every part of the room, and the general light level is higher than under "average" conditions. Set the exposure control one number (or one f-number) higher than recommended.

If walls are very dark or far distant (20-30 ft.), light in the room will be reduced noticeably. This has little effect in close-ups, except to sharpen facial shadows. If the subject is more than 8 ft. away, count on setting the exposure control at least one number (or one f-number) lower than for "average" conditions.

A light-colored wall directly behind the photographer acts as a reflector which throws more light onto close subjects and lessens facial shadows. The effect is most

BOUNCE FLASH GUIDE FOR USE WITH NO. 5 OR PRESS 25 BULBS

Your subject is this far from the flashgun ►	For close-ups 3-4 ft.	**For most pictures of people 5-8 ft.**	For distant subjects 9-12 ft.
All models, except 110A & 110, with Type 42 & 32-400 film.	Set exposure control to number indicated below		
	EV 15 or #6	**EV 14 or #5**	EV 13 or #4
Model 110A & 110, with Type 42 film; use 1/125 or 1/100 sec. Set sync lever to "M"	f/16	**f/11**	f/8

With Type 44 film, set exposure control one number (or one f-number) higher than recommended for Type 42. With M5 bulbs, in adapter, set exposure control one number (or one f-number) lower than recommended for No. 5 bulbs.

BOUNCE FLASH GUIDE is for use with Polaroid bounce flash bracket under "average" conditions—that is, both photographer and subject are standing under white ceiling 8 to 10 ft. high, in moderate-sized room (perhaps 15 x 18 ft.) with medium dark walls. Estimate carefully distance in feet in straight line from flashgun to subject. Set exposure control to number recommended for that distance, focus camera and shoot. If picture is too dark, reset exposure control to next lower number (or f-number); if too light, reset to next higher number. Try again. Variations from "average" conditions (photographer and subject both seated, for example) may affect exposure; some are listed above.

EV SHUTTER SETTINGS — TYPE 42 ROLLS For #5 or Press 25 flashbulbs only								
Dist. (Feet)	3½	4	5	6	8	10	15	20
DIRECT FLASH	18*	18*	17	17	16	16	15	14
BOUNCE FLASH	←—— 14 ——→					13		12
*Or #16 with diffuser over shield.								

SHUTTER SETTINGS FOR TYPE 42 ROLLS For #5 or Press 25 flashbulbs only								
Dist. (Feet)	3½	4	5	6	8	10	15	20
DIRECT FLASH	9*	9*	8	8	7	7	6	5
BOUNCE FLASH	←—— 5 ——→					4		3
*Or #7 with diffuser over shield.								

FLASH EXPOSURE GUIDES: Instruction sheet for medium fast films carries two kinds. EV settings, left, are for current cameras; Polaroid numbers, right, are for older models. Suppose you have Type 42 film, No. 5 bulb and are 10 ft. from subject. Look along distance line to 10 ft. Correct setting for direct flash is EV 16, for bounce flash, EV 13. With M5 bulbs, in adapter, set exposure control one number lower than recommended for No. 5 bulbs. Chart on page 76 gives more bounce flash information.

noticeable in a room with a high ceiling. Ordinarily, no change in exposure is necessary, and the effect is beneficial.

A light-colored wall behind the subject (but not behind the photographer) has no effect on exposure for the face. However, since the background is light, there appears to be more "separation" between it and the subject.

For very dark subjects, it may be necessary to set the exposure control one number lower than recommended; *for very light subjects,* you may have to set it one number higher than recommended.

Pointing the camera sharply up aims the flash back over the photographer's shoulder, wasting much light.

Pointing the camera down tilts the flashgun forward and throws slightly more light across the room.

The effect of ceiling height

In bounce flash the important thing is the height of the ceiling above the flashgun and the subject. Under the "average" conditions of our bounce flash guide, the ceiling is 3 to 4 ft. above the flashgun (and also over the head of the standing subject). If the ceiling is higher than "average," or if photographer and subject are both seated, the flash must travel further, which cuts down its intensity on the subject. However, the "higher ceiling" causes a much more even distribution of light over a wide area. This is particularly noticeable and beneficial at flashgun-to-subject distances of 10 to 12 ft. A contrary effect is seen if the ceiling is closer than "average" to the subject and flashgun. While the light on the subject is very bright, the flash cannot be evenly distributed over a wide area.

If you and your subject are standing under a 12-14 ft. ceiling, set the exposure control at least one number (or one f-number) lower than recommended; under a 16-18 ft. ceiling, set it at least two numbers (or f-numbers) lower than recommended in the bounce flash guide.

Controlling contrast, shadows

Bounce flash pictures of subjects 3 to 5 ft. from the camera may show pronounced shadows under eyes, nose, and chin. This is due to the straight-up-and-down path of the light. As the flashgun-to-subject distance increases, the light hits faces at more of an angle, shadows get smaller, and the high contrast of close-ups diminishes. At 7 or 8 ft., shadows and contrast seem normal; beyond 10 ft. shadows are virtually invisible, and lighting is "flat."

Unpleasing face shadows in close-ups can be reduced or eliminated by a slight uptilt of your subject's head (looking down exaggerates such shadows). Or, if possible, place your subject to take advantage of natural reflectors (such as a white tablecloth or an open magazine) which bounce light into the shadows.

Changes in development time can be important in controlling shadows and contrast. For the 3-5 ft. range, where lighting is inherently contrasty, use the "normal" developing times recommended on the film instruction sheet. At greater distances, if the lighting is definitely "flat", you can pep up contrast by developing 1½-2 minutes.

Ultra close-up bounce flash

Record shots of very small objects can easily be made with close-up lenses (see *Close-ups*) and bounce flash. Set up your subject and camera in the usual manner for an ultra close-up, and fit the flashgun for bounce flash. Make a "ceiling" to bounce the light by holding a piece of

SET PATHFINDER SYNC: Models 110A, 110 have adjustable synchronization. Set sync lever at "M" for No. 5, Press 25, M5, AG-1 and similar bulbs at all shutter speeds; 1/125 sec. (or 1/100) is best for general use. Set lever at "X" for electronic flash at any shutter speed. Also, at "X" setting, and at shutter speeds up to 1/30 or 1/25 sec. only, any type of flashbulb may be used.

ordinary brown or gray cardboard (about 11 x 14 or 16 x 20 in.) directly over camera, flashgun, and subject, about 12 in. or more above the flash shield. EV 16 and 17 give good results.

Exposure for direct flash

On the instruction sheets for PolaPan 200 and 400 you will find a flash exposure guide similar to those shown on page 77. This provides reasonably accurate direct flash exposure information for those films.

Let's assume that the camera is loaded with Type 42 film and you have No. 5 bulbs. *Estimate carefully the distance in feet from flashgun to subject* (use the rangefinder if your camera has one), and set the camera focus accordingly. Suppose that the distance is 15 ft. Look along the distance row of the flash guide to 15 ft. and then down to the direct flash line. The recommended exposure setting is EV 15, so turn the exposure control wheel to that setting and shoot. If the picture is too dark, try the next lower number; if too light, go one number higher and try again.

It's the bulb-to-subject distance that determines how brightly the subject will be lit by the flash, and errors in distance judging can cause serious over- or under-exposure, particularly at close ranges. Try to estimate distance as accurately as possible—at least within a foot or so.

Remember: Flash guides are just that —guides. They do not guarantee correct exposure, but they help you to get it.

Direct flash with Pathfinders

With the Pathfinders which have conventional shutter speed and lens opening controls, you're likely to get best results by using the *flash exposure guide number* system which is standard for conventional cameras. Below is an abbreviated guide number chart for use with Type 42 film and No. 5 bulbs.

up to 1/30 or 1/25 – 300
1/125 or 1/100 – 270
1/300 or 1/400 – 180

To use this system you divide the guide number by the flashbulb-to-subject distance in feet. The result is the lens opening (f-number) to use. Here's an example. Suppose you have Type 42 film, a No. 5 bulb, and are using 1/125 sec. (the best shutter speed for general use). The guide number is 270. The subject is 17 ft. from the flashgun. Divide 270 by 17. The result is approximately 16. Set the lens opening to f/16 for correct exposure. If the flashgun-to-subject distance happened to be 10 ft. the correct exposure would be 270 divided by 10, or 27. You would set the lens opening control to f/27, or about halfway between f/22 and f/32.

This is a useful, flexible system. You only need to know one or two guide numbers and you can get correct flash exposures any time. Write the guide numbers on a bit of paper and stick it on the back of the flashgun reflector.

Remote flash

Wonderful pictures can be had by using the gun off the camera, at a remote point, but connected to the shutter contacts by a long extension cord (can't do this with Models 150, 800, 80, 80A). For example, you can set up a flashgun for bounce flash *inside* a room (but out of the camera's view), run an extension cord *outside* to the camera, and take a picture through the window, which will be glare-free since all the light is on the inside. Figure exposure as though you were inside the room. Your camera shop can supply an extension for remote flash.

Getting maximum light

Here's how to squeeze the last bit of light out of a flashbulb for either bounce or direct flash if you need more light.

Most flash shots are made at EV 13, 14, 15, 16, 17; all of these have shutter speeds of 1/100 sec. and the fast blade action clips off a bit of the light. For maximum light with all cameras except the Highlanders and Pathfinders, try EV 12, at which the shutter speed is 1/50 sec.—this catches the "tail" of the flash, and puts noticeably more light on the film. If there is some light from other sources, try EV 10—the slow shutter speed of 1/13 sec. will catch all the flash and also permit some of the existing light to register. On the Highlander, use EV 11 for maximum light from a bulb. With the Pathfinder, set the sync lever (photo, opposite) to "X" and use 1/30 or 1/25.

Tips for better flash pictures

Keep the reflector clean so it will work at full efficiency; also keep the flash shield clean.

Don't carry unused bulbs loose in pocket or gadget bag—they can be damaged or broken. Keep them in the sleeve until ready to use.

Always examine bulbs for damage. Never fire a cracked bulb. If a bulb does not go off, don't fuss with it; try another one. If the room is dimly lit, there is no need to advance and waste a film when a bulb fails to fire; with PolaPan 200 & 400 not enough light will reach the film to register any images. Just shoot again.

Check the contact point on the base of each bulb. If it's tarnished or greasy, give it a quick rub on a piece of rough cloth, or on a leather shoe sole.

Insert the bulb firmly in the socket, so as to assure good contact.

Don't look right into the reflector when inserting a bulb in the socket. A short circuit, or an accidental push on the shutter release, may fire the flashbulb prematurely.

Wait a few seconds before ejecting and handling flashed bulbs—they're hot enough to burn your fingers.

Don't leave used bulbs lying around where children or animals can get at them, nor under foot where adults can step on and smash them.

FILTERS

You'll be amazed at how these bits of glass improve your pictures. They're easy to use, too.

MAGIC is the right word for the effect that a properly used filter can have on the average outdoor snapshot.

For with no effort on your part, this simplest of all accessories can make the difference between having a dull, lifeless picture, and one that is vibrant with beautiful white clouds, full toned skies, and striking contrast. Once you start to use a filter, and see for yourself just what it can do, you'll find that not only are your pictures better, but you're having a lot more fun taking them.

As a Polaroid Land camera user you enjoy a unique advantage when using filters. Since you have the picture in a minute, you can see immediately whether or not the filter has achieved the effect you wanted. If the sky and clouds are not quite as you think you'd like to have them, try a different filter, change the exposure, or experiment with a combination of both. If a photograph of a multi-colored subject looks disappointingly monotoned, you can try various filters, to lighten or darken single colors in the subject, and immediately see if the picture is improved.

Bothered by glare on a window or other surface? Knock it down with a polarizing filter, compare "with" and "without" prints to check your progress.

No user of a conventional camera can be absolutely certain as to how his print

◁ **CLOUD PROBLEM:** How do you make them stand out against blue skies? With a Polaroid Filter Kit, and the ability to see your pictures in a minute, it's a simple matter. Four photos on the next two pages show exactly how cloud effects similar to these can be achieved. This picture was made with 200 speed film.

WHAT YOU NEED: Polaroid #541 Filter Kit includes three filters—orange, polarizing, and half-step, and carrying pouch. Important companion accessory is #545 lens shade, below.

HOW IT WORKS: Merely slip filter over lens mount, then fit lens shade over filter. Friction holds them in place. Lens shade can be used alone; then you put it over lens mount.

◁ J. W.

Clouds add dramatic element to scenics, and

1. NO FILTER: On a bright day, with camera set at EV 17, Polaroid PolaPan film records only faint suggestion of clouds which fill sky. There's little contrast in water; far shore appears dull.

2. WITH ORANGE FILTER: Now there's strong contrast between sky and clouds (this is how they really were). Note how heavy filtering effect fades towards horizon. Setting is EV 15.

will come out until long after leaving the scene just photographed. But you can know every time, in a minute. Consequently, it takes hardly any time at all to learn to use filters expertly with the Polaroid Land camera. Try them, when next you go out with the camera—you'll be amazed.

How a filter works

Almost everyone has seen a photographic filter at some time or other. Usually it's a disc of colored glass which fits over the camera's lens. You may wonder why a colored glass should have any effect on a black-and-white picture. There's nothing mysterious about this; in fact, it's quite a simple principle which has to do with the nature of light.

Daylight, which we ordinarily think of as being white, is actually made up of a mixture of many colors which can be made visible by passing the light through a prism. (Remember the last rainbow you saw?) The predominant colors which go to make up daylight are blue, green, and red; if they are mixed in the proper proportions, we see the result as white light.

The purpose of a colored filter is to stop light rays of certain colors from reaching the film. The glass is so made that rays of some colors pass through freely, while other colors are held back partially or completely. The filter itself appears colored because it has this ability to pass some rays of light while holding back others. For example, a red filter appears to be red because it is passing red rays freely, but is holding back green and blue rays.

A green filter appears to be green because it is passing green rays freely, but

correct use of filters brings out the clouds.

3. WITH ORANGE PLUS POLARIZER: At setting EV 13, combination of filters gives extreme contrast. With these filters and under-exposure, you could simulate night scene.

4. WITH YELLOW SKY FILTER #450: Clouds are visible, but less distinctly than when orange filter is used. Sky filter is for use with Photoelectric Shutter #440.

is holding back red and blue rays.

A blue filter appears to be blue because it is passing blue rays freely, but is holding back green and red rays.

The rule for judging the effect of a particular filter is: *The filter passes freely light of its own color, and holds back light of any other color.* A "weak" filter (one that is rather pale in color) holds back light of other colors only partially. A "strong" filter (one with a deep, rich color) may hold back almost completely light of any color other than its own.

With those principles in mind, let's look at the two colored filters which will be used most by owners of Land cameras—the orange and the yellow. As the orange one is far more important than the yellow, we'll dispose of the yellow first.

The color yellow is a mixture of the colors green and red. Thus a yellow filter passes green and red light freely, but holds back some of the blue rays. It is a comparatively "weak" filter. The only yellow filter currently marketed by Polaroid Corp. is the Polaroid Sky Filter #450, which is a 2 x 2 square designed for use with the Photoelectric Shutter #440.

The orange filter also passes green and red rays (but in different proportions, which is why it appears to be orange) and holds back much more blue light than does the yellow filter. The orange filter is "stronger" than the yellow filter.

Question: Why are we so anxious to hold back blue light? Here we come to the first and most common practical application of filters for picture taking—to control the contrast of skies and clouds in outdoor pictures.

It so happens that photographic films are much more sensitive to blue-violet

Filters can help translate a colorful scene

J.W.

1. WITHOUT FILTER

2. WITH RED FILTER

light than to rays of any other color. So, when we take a picture, any blue registers in the print as if it were light gray or white. We've all had the disappointing experience of snapping a scene in which fleecy white clouds floated in a deep blue sky, only to find that in the final print the sky and clouds form one blank white mass, as in photo 1, page 82. And that's where our filters come in.

If you put a yellow filter over the lens, it will hold back some of the blue-violet rays from the sky and reduce the exposure for those areas of the film which are recording the blue sky. Since the exposure for those areas is reduced, the blue sky will register as a shade of gray, and the white clouds begin to be visible in the print, as in photo 4, page 83.

If you use a "stronger" filter, such as orange, a greater proportion of the blue light is held back from the film. Thus the sky recording areas of the film get a greatly reduced exposure; because they are underexposed they register as dark shades of gray, while the white clouds stand out in dramatic contrast (photos 2 & 3, pages 82 & 83, show this).

Putting a colored filter over the lens cuts down the total amount of light reaching the film; unless you compensate for this by increasing the exposure, the picture is likely to be underexposed (but not always, as you will soon see). The amount of extra exposure needed (called the "filter factor" in technical jargon) depends on the color and "strength" of the filter, and the type of film with which it is being used. (A complete chart of filter factors for a wide variety of filters, when used with Polaroid Land films, is included in the *Technical Facts* section). With conventional cameras, films, and filters, the filter factor is usually a bit of a problem, for you have to remember how much to change the exposure for each filter-film combination. Not so with the Polaroid Filter Kit.

On the rim of each Polaroid filter is a printed instruction telling you exactly how much extra exposure to give. On the orange filter, for example: "Average setting two numbers lower." There's a similar instruction on the polarizing filter.

into a meaningful black-and-white print.

3. WITH BLUE FILTER

1. WITHOUT FILTER, PolaPan 400 film "sees" yellow top and light blue lower half of bus as quite similar gray tones. This picture does not tell you that bus is painted in sharply contrasting color scheme. But a filter can change things.

2. WITH RED FILTER over lens, entire meaning of picture changes. Red filter holds back light reflected from blue surface, which is recorded as dark gray; it passes freely red component of yellow light (yellow is combination of red and green), which registers as almost white. Blue sky is also darkened, emphasizing lightness of bus top. This is the same bus as in photo 1.

3. WITH BLUE FILTER, apparent color scheme is completely reversed. Blue filter passes freely light from blue portion of bus, which film records as light tone; it holds back light reflected from yellow areas, which register in photograph as dark shades of gray. Still the same bus.

When two filters are used in combination, be sure to compensate for *both* filters by increasing the exposure sufficiently. With the orange and polarizing filters used together, you'd set the exposure control two numbers lower for the orange and two more for the polarizer, for a total of four EV numbers lower than for the same exposure without filters.

There are two Polaroid Filter Kits: the #541 kit for all models except the Pathfinder, and #551 kit for the Pathfinder. First, a glance at the #541 (see photo page 81). It's a slender leather pouch containing three filters, each in a metal rim designed to slip on the camera's lens mount, where it is held by pressure of the "fingers" on the filter rim. If the filter fits too loosely, it may fall off—just bend two or three of the fingers in a little bit. If it's too tight, loosen the fingers. They should grip firmly, but not so tightly that it's a struggle to get a filter on or off.

Caution: When slipping a filter on or off, hold the shutter housing with the other hand to avoid putting undue pressure on the supports which hold the front of the camera upright; don't strain them.

The filters currently supplied in #541 kits are: the orange #4, the half step #3, and the polarizing #2.

Of the three, the orange filter is by far the most useful and the one which will best improve your scenic pictures. *As a general rule, use the orange filter for all bright sun scenic type pictures.*

Here are a few of the things this filter will do for your outdoor pictures. Blue skies show up in prints as medium dark shades of gray, against which white clouds stand out strongly. Even if there are no clouds, it provides a darkened sky background for light colored objects on the ground, such as white buildings, blossoms, clothing, and so on.

For architectural pictures it increases the contrast between light and shadow areas on stone work. It's a must for marine scenes, pepping up the contrast by darkening the water, making white sails stand out strongly against dark skies. Used in combination with the polarizing filter, the orange filter can produce highly dramatic contrasts in skies and clouds.

Special filters for use with 3000 speed film.

SKY FILTER #450 & 4S LIGHT REDUCER: Yellow sky filter, left, is 2 x 2 in. hard plastic in aluminum frame for use with #440 shutter. It covers both lens opening and light cell, so there's no need to change exposure to compensate for filter factor—it's done automatically. With light reducer in place, center, exposure settings with 3000 speed film are same as for 200 speed film without light reducer. Rubber ring is important light seal; lip must cover I-B knob (arrow). For Pathfinders, remove filter from ring, reverse it and replace in ring. For Highlanders, right, remove ring.

And, if the two filters are used together and the picture is deliberately under-exposed, pseudo-moonlight effects can be achieved in bright sunshine.

The orange filter will put dramatic life into sunsets, particularly where there are heavy clouds and bright red streaks.

When you look across a valley to a distant scene, it often appears to be veiled in a blue haze, even on clear days. This is caused largely by small particles of dust and water vapor which scatter the light. The haze contains large amounts of ultra-violet rays (invisible to the human eye) to which film is extremely sensitive. So, the haze registers in the print, and in so doing casts a veil over all distant detail. The orange filter cuts this haze noticeably, so always use it for distant scenics where you want full detail in the subject. However, it won't clear up fog or mist.

The filter as a light reducer

As pointed out previously, the presence of a filter over the lens cuts down the amount of light entering the camera. The darker the filter, the more the light is reduced. This characteristic is useful.

The half step filter #3 is neutral in color (it's called a neutral density filter) and is so designed that when placed over the lens it reduces the light by one-half the amount that it would be reduced if the exposure control were moved to the next higher number (from EV 15 to EV 16, for example). This half step change provides a more precise control over exposure than is possible with the eight EV

WANT ADDITIONAL FILTERS? Wide variety of colors for special purposes is available. Filters are fastened to lens mount by adapter rings, which come in many sizes (Series V, 32mm is shown). To assure correct fit of filter and ring, take your camera to your photo dealer.

numbers on Polaroid Land cameras (this doesn't apply to the Pathfinders, which have a different type of exposure control).

If the print is just a bit too light with the camera set for EV 15, and a bit too dark at EV 16, try EV 15½—EV 15 plus the half step filter.

Another neutral density Polaroid filter, the 4S Light Reducer, is shown at left. One of these is packed with each wink-light and photoelectric shutter. It's intended for use with the 3000 speed film outdoors, when you don't have or are not using the photoelectric shutter on the camera. The 4S Light Reducer cuts the light the equivalent of four EV numbers (four "stops" in photo jargon—thus 4S Light Reducer) and makes it possible to use the 3000 speed film in bright sun without getting tremendous overexposure. It also has other important functions as a light seal. All this is explained in detail in the chapter *The 3000 Speed Film.*

The orange filter reduces the light an amount equal to about two EV numbers. Sometimes, on the beach or over snow or water, with PolaPan 200 or 400 in the camera, you may get overexposed (too light) prints even with the camera set to the highest EV number. Put on the orange filter, and leave the exposure control as is. If the next try is too dark, use the next lower EV number. If the orange filter alone isn't enough to prevent overexposure, add the polarizing filter on top of it.

If you're using 3000 speed film in a Pathfinder, the orange and polarizing filters used together are a suitable substitute for the 4S Light Reducer and will also improve scenics. This is not recommended for the other camera models, as the 4S Light Reducer also acts as a light seal for those models.

Five hints for sky control

Sometimes filters don't produce the sky and cloud control results which we think they ought to produce. The following paragraphs may explain why a filter appears to be failing to do its job.

1. A misty sky photographs lighter than a clear blue sky. Filters will have little effect on a gray, overcast sky.

2. Filters have least effect at the horizon (except for sunsets), do more for the high, blue sky.

FILTERS FOR PATHFINDERS

FILTER KIT #551: It includes orange and polarizing filters and plastic lens shade. These clip on around lens of Model 110A, below. For older Model 110 you need spacer ring and tiny wrench shown (to get them free of charge write Customer Service, Polaroid Corp.). Ring goes around lens mount, is secured with set screws, builds up lens mount to size so filter and lens shades fit. Kit comes in leather "pillbox" case, not shown.

HOW THEY ATTACH: Slip filter over lens mount. Light spring tension holds it in place firmly.

LENS SHADE: It clips onto filter, or on lens mount without filter. Lens shade also fits onto close-up lenses (see *Close-ups*).

Polarizer controls glare, improves contrast.

NO POLARIZER: Windshield and paint reflect blinding glare and man behind wheel is completely hidden. Type 44 film, setting EV 14.

WITH POLARIZER: Invisible subject appears because glare was "wiped off" by polarizer. It also picked up contrast in paint. Setting EV 12.

3. Filters have little effect on the bright light area near the sun.

4. Don't overexpose—that lightens the sky, reduces the filter's effect.

5. Underexposure will exaggerate the effect of the filter.

Besides the filters marketed by Polaroid Corp., there are standard filters of other colors with which special effects can be achieved. Some of these filters are shown on page 86.

Often a subject will contain two colors (perhaps shades of red and green) which will reproduce in the print as practically the same shade of gray. By adding a red or green filter, the tone relationships are completely altered, as shown on page 84. Such tone control is wonderfully handy for bringing out contrast in pictures of flowers, clothing, signs, automobiles, maps, or other multi-colored subjects.

The remarkable polarizer

The polarizing filter has a number of abilities which make it unique. It can darken skies and make clouds stand out, but to a lesser degree than does the orange filter. Combined with the orange filter, the polarizer can produce extreme sky darkening effects when they are desired.

It will knock down glare and reflections on water, glass, pavements, shiny foliage, or painted surfaces, permitting the film to record detail which would otherwise be obscured by the glare. But it all depends on how you use this remarkable device.

The polarizer has its maximum sky

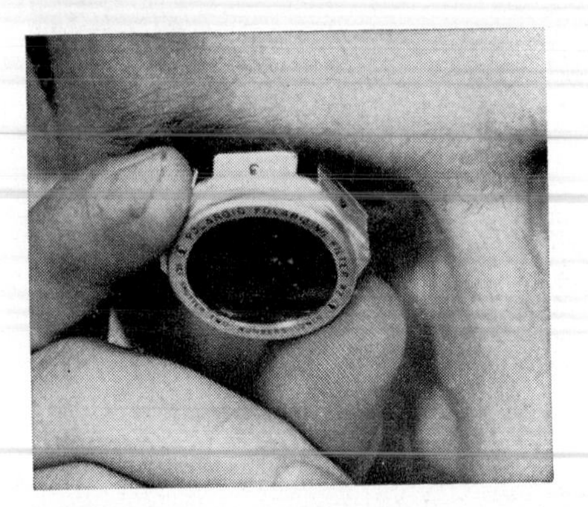

USING THE POLARIZER: Look at the scene through polarizer, slowly rotating filter until desired effect is reached. Lower filter from eye without rotating it, note which number is up (here, 3). Slip filter over lens in exactly same relative position.

darkening effect when the camera lens is pointing in a direction at right angles to the sun. That is, when the subject is strongly side lighted or the sun is directly overhead. It has little or no effect when the camera is pointing towards the sun or directly away from it. Whether you are using the polarizer to reduce glare or increase contrast, you must set the exposure control two numbers lower to compensate for the light it cuts out. Of course, you can also employ it with fast films merely to cut exposure, without compensating for its presence over the lens.

The wonderful thing about the polarizer is that you can look through it, aim it at your subject and see just what it will do. Around the rim are equally spaced numbers from 1 to 6. You hold the polarizer to your eye (as though you were the camera) and rotate the filter until the maximum effect is seen. Then, without turning the filter, lower it from your eye and note which number is uppermost (see photo. opposite). Put the filter on the camera in exactly that same relative position. Don't turn the camera from a horizontal to vertical position (or vice versa) without changing the filter position, or it will have no polarizing effect. And with the Highlanders, be sure to focus the lens *before* putting on the filter; if you rotate the lens *after* placing the filter, the polarizing effect will be lost.

To knock down glare, the camera should be at an angle from the reflecting surface—about 33 degrees for maximum effect at close range. Stand at that angle and look through the filter, rotating it until maximum effect is achieved. Note the uppermost number, and install the filter on the camera as described above.

The important lens shade

Some of the most effective outdoor pictures are taken with the camera aimed fairly close to the sun—dramatically back-lighted clouds, silhouettes, against-the-light portraits, are some examples. However, if you let the sun shine into the lens the picture will be fogged and streaked. A lens shade lets you aim closer to the sun without danger of light hitting the lens. It also controls stray reflections which might bounce off nearby walls, water, or other surfaces, and into the lens.

The #545 Polaroid lens shade fits all models except Pathfinders. Your photo dealer can get it for you. The lens shade for Pathfinders is in the #551 kit.

SHORT COURSE IN FILTERS

1. Keep filters clean and always store them in the case.
2. Darken skies, bring out clouds, cut distant haze for all scenics on bright, sunny days by using the orange filter with all films. When using the photoelectric shutter with 3000 speed film, attach the Sky Filter #450 designed for use with that shutter.
3. Remember to increase the exposure by setting the exposure control to a lower number as indicated on the rim of each filter.
4. Where light is too bright (beach, snow, etc.) and pictures are overexposed even at settings of EV 17 and 18, use a filter to cut the light. When the camera is loaded with 3000 speed film and you are not using the photoelectric shutter, cut the light with the 4S Light Reducer, or the orange and polarizing filters in combination.
5. Filters have little effect on skies on overcast days and will not cut fog, drizzle.
6. When glare or reflections interfere with the scene, the polarizer may help. Look through it, rotate it to get angle with maximum effect, slip it over the lens in that position.

CLOSE-UPS

You can make them with the Land camera, with the aid of a simple-to-use accessory.

IF YOU'VE NEVER shot a real close-up, you're missing out on a big picture-taking thrill, made even more exciting when you can see the results in a minute. Let's see how it's done.

Like any other fixed lens, short bellows camera, the Polaroid Land camera is limited in its focusing range—about 3½ ft. is as close as you can get. (With the Photoelectric Shutter #440 attached to your camera you can focus sharply as close as 2 ft., near enough for portraits or shots of large subjects.)

If you have a very small subject and want a big image of it on the print you must use a supplementary close-up lens, a simple device that slips over the camera lens (but can't be used with the #440 shutter). For the Land camera, such lenses come in kits to match the various models. These permit picture taking as close as 6 in. from the subject. At *that* distance the image on the print is about life size; details are startlingly clear.

Unusual portraits of people and pets; pictures of flowers, hobby subjects, small statuary and other art objects; record photos of pieces of machinery or small parts; quick copies of text or illustrations—all these are possible with close-up lenses. They also are a vital part of the Polaroid Copymaker, a special copying device (see *The Copymaker*).

Close-ups afford a certain number of chances for error. Fortunately, with the Land camera the picture—good or bad—is seen in a minute, and if a mistake has been made it's quickly corrected.

A Polaroid Close-up Lens Kit contains

◁ **SMALL SUBJECTS** can make big, exciting pictures, if you get close. Hand emphasizes kitten's tininess. Daylight, exposure control set to EV 16, with +2 close-up lens. 200 speed film.

HAROLD FEINSTEIN

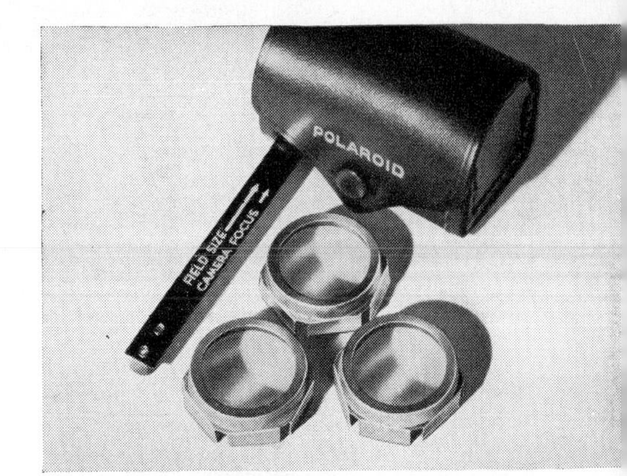

WHAT YOU NEED: Polaroid Close-up Lens Kit permits pictures as close as 6 in. from subject. Built in steel tape measures distance. Kit shown is #540 for all cameras except Pathfinders. Kit for Pathfinders is shown on page 92.

HOW IT WORKS: Close-up lens clips over camera's lens, is held in place by friction. For ultra close-ups two or three such lenses may be combined. Text explains how to do it.

Close-up lenses can produce excellent pictures

PORTRAITS: Closest focusing range of Land camera is about 3½ ft. *(left)*; face is small. A +1 lens lets you come closer *(center)*, produces bigger image. If you get too close, distortion may occur *(right)*. This was made with +2 lens. But, same lens produced beautiful results *(opposite)*.

three close-up lenses, and a flexible steel rule called the Data-Tape.

The lenses are numbered in the order of their "power." They start with the "weak" +1 and proceed to the stronger +2 and +3. These may be combined for even more strength—a +1 and +3 to make a +4, or +2 and +3 to make a +5, or all three to make a +6. (The kit for the Pathfinders includes a +4 instead of a +3, and these combine to make a +7.) When the lenses are combined, the strongest (highest numbered) lens goes closest to the camera, the weakest lens nearest the subject. (If a filter is needed for special effects or to reduce the light when using 3000 speed film, add it on top of the weakest lens, so the filter is nearest the subject.)

The stronger the lens, or combination of lenses, the closer you can get to the subject. And the closer you get, the smaller the area that gets into your picture. So, choice of lenses depends on the size of the area you want in the picture. Also, since the camera is too close to be focused as usual, distances must be measured. Now enter the Data-Tape.

First, you use the Data-Tape to measure the size of your subject, or the area to be included in the picture. This is called the "Field Size," which really means "how big your subject is." You must know this to pick the close-up lens that will include just about that same size area in the picture. Jot down the size.

Second, the Data-Tape carries information you need to pick the right lens, camera focus setting, and lens-to-subject distance for a subject of the size you

PATHFINDER KIT #550: Close-up lenses are large, to fit over camera's big lens. For Model 110A, kit contains only lenses and tape. For Model 110, you also need spacer ring and tiny wrench shown. Ring goes around camera's lens, is secured by set screws; close-up lenses then fit over spacer ring, same as on Model 110A.

CREATIVE CLOSE-UP: Camera was set to ▷ record hand and cigarette sharply. Zone of sharp focus at close range is small; face was placed to be partly but not totally out of focus. Photo was made with brief time exposure, at EV 17, with 200 speed film. For imaginative pictures like this, ability to see results in minute is great asset.

of people, if used with care to avoid distortion.

HAROLD FEINSTEIN

Close-up lens kit at work. Results on page 97.

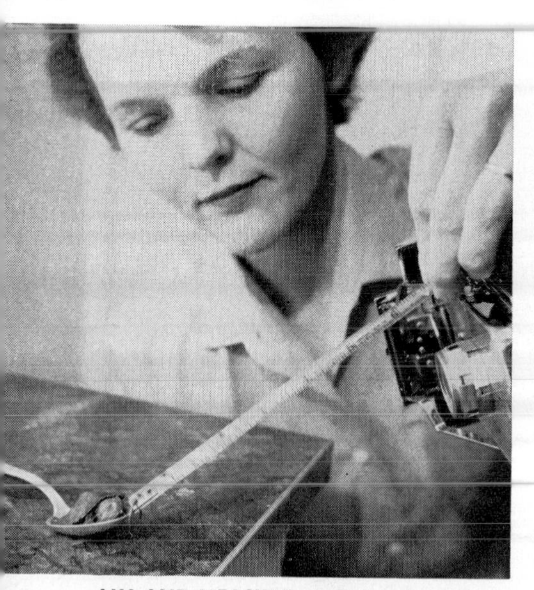

AIM AND MEASURE: Use Data-Tape for both. To aim, lay tape flat alongside camera, pointing straight ahead; turn camera so tape points in direction of subject. Measure from subject to edge of nearest close-up lens, as above. Measure last, *after* setting camera's distance scale.

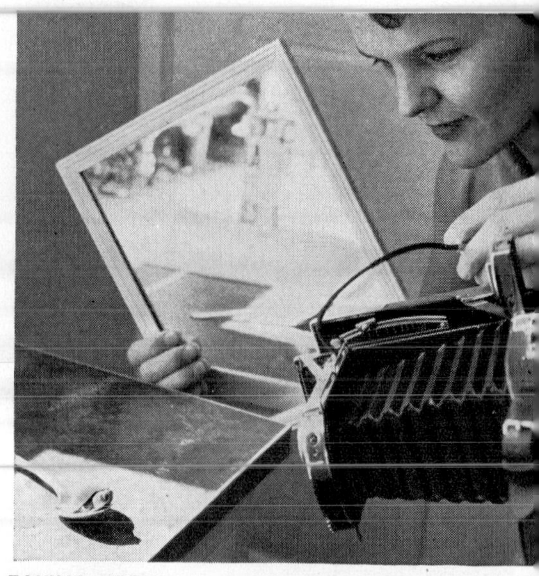

TAKING TIPS: Always use tripod; trip shutter with cable release if possible, to avoid shaking. Mirror or other reflector helps control daylight or floods. For tips on tripod use, cable releases, and what to do when light is too dim for snapshots, see *Time Exposures.*

have just measured. For this, the Data-Tape is sprinkled with strange looking numbers and symbols.

Third, the Data-Tape is the actual measuring device with which you place the camera the proper distance from the subject. And since the camera's viewfinder is useless so close to the subject, use the Data-Tape as an aiming device.

If you follow carefully the four steps in the Data-Tape chart opposite, close-ups will be as simple as A, B, C, D.

Getting "life size" pictures

How big a picture image you can get depends on the model camera in use.

With Models 150, 800, 95B, 95A, 700, and 100 the biggest possible image is 98 per cent of life size; +1, +2, and +3 lenses are combined, the camera focusing scale is set at 3½ ft., and the subject is 5⅞ in. from the front edge of the nearest close-up lens.

With the Pathfinders, a 1:1 (life size) picture is obtained with +1, +2, and +4 lenses stacked, the camera set for 6 ft., and the subject 5³⁄₁₆ in. distant.

With the Highlanders the limit is 72 per cent of life size, made with all three lenses, camera set for 3½ ft., and a subject distance of 5⅞ in.

With the Model 95, you get a 1:1 image with all three lenses, the camera set for 4 ft. and the subject 6 in. distant.

Portrait pointers

In close-up pictures, with any camera, the subject is likely to appear distorted. This is the main objection to using close-up lenses for portraits—noses and other parts of the body pointing to the camera are exaggerated (see page 92). For portraits, use a +1 lens at near maximum distance, arrange subjects so their features are in a single plane (half profile view instead of head-on, for example). Baby features don't protrude much—you can come closer. For maximum overall sharpness, with any close-up subject, keep all important parts in as flat a plane as is possible under the circumstances.

Here's a quick, handheld portrait technique for use with a +1 lens. Tie a string under the camera lens, with knots 24, 30, and 36 in. from the close-up lens. Subject holds the chosen distance knot next to an eye, tells when the camera is aimed straight, drops the cord; you shoot. Not much to that.

Lighting, exposure, setup

Almost any light source can be used for ultra-close-ups. Daylight and tungsten lamps are easier to control than flash and you can judge highlights and shadows *before* snapping the shutter. For portraits, the wink-light and 3000 speed film may be a useful combination.

Whatever the light, you need plenty of it, for close-ups should always be made with the camera set for small lens openings—EV 16, 17, or 18 (or f/16, 22, or 32 on the Pathfinders). This eliminates possible optical distortions by the simple close-up lenses, and also increases the zone of sharp focus (the near to far distances at which subjects are recorded sharply). Where the light's not very bright, the 3000 speed film makes it possible to avoid long time exposures.

Except for this requirement, close-up lenses have no effect on exposure. Follow the procedures in *Correct Exposure.*

The slightest camera shake will be magnified in a close-up. Always use a tripod (except possibly for a portrait). Best kind is one with a head that tilts sideways so it's easy to make a vertical picture, and a center pole raised and lowered by a crank. Examples are shown in the chapter *Time Exposures.*

Equally important, get the close-up lens-to-subject distance exactly as specified on the Data-Tape.

USE THE DATA-TAPE THIS WAY AND CLOSE-UPS ARE EASY.

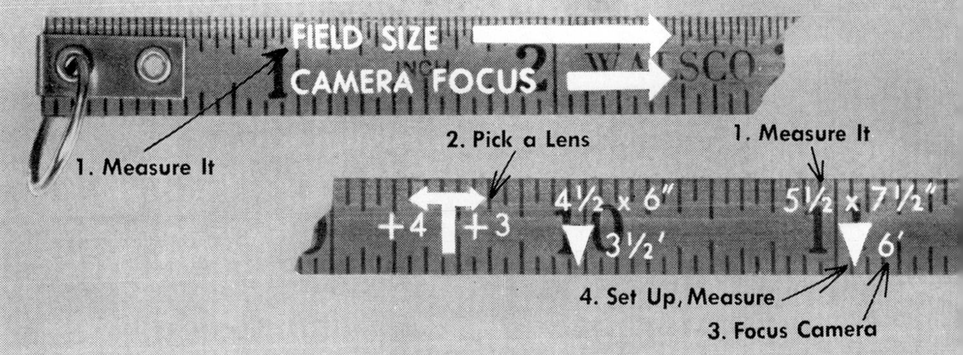

1. MEASURE IT:

As the camera gets closer to the subject, the area—or field—the lens can include in the picture gets smaller. So, first use the tape to measure your subject, or the area you want to get in the picture. This is the "Field Size." Now look along the top part of the tape to find a set of dimensions which come close to matching the size of your subject. Let's say the subject fills a space about 5 x 7 in. The Field Size markings closest to these are 5½ x 7½ in., so we start from that point on the Data-Tape *(above).*

2. PICK A LENS:

The Field Size, or area to be included in the picture, is directly related to the close-up lens used. At intervals on the tape are T-shaped, double-headed arrows. On each side of the arrow is a number, indicating the number close-up lens to use. You pick the lens number on the side of the arrow closest to your Field Size. Above, it's +3.

3. FOCUS CAMERA:

Along the bottom half of the tape, under each set of Field Size markings, is a number (a footage marking) telling you where to set the camera's focusing scale. *Above,* 6 ft.

4. SET UP CAMERA:

Put it on a tripod or other support. Stretch the Data-Tape so the free end is at the subject and the tip of the arrow under your Field Size is even with the front of the close-up lens nearest to the subject. Aim, shoot.

FROM MODERN PHOTOGRAPHY MAGAZINE

Close-ups with the Land camera can be topnotch.

ARTHUR KRAMER

HAROLD FEINSTEIN

△ **CROSS LIGHT** brings out shape of these small electrical connectors, emphasizes texture of skin. Close-ups of small parts are of great value in business and industry as aids in stock keeping, employee training, emergency reordering. Picture data: one photoflood placed close to hand, +3 lens, 200 speed film; EV 15.

◁ **BACK LIGHT** from window gives dramatic outline to chessmen, points up extremely shallow zone of sharp focus in ultra close-ups. This was done with Pathfinder using +4, +2, and +1 lenses in combination, f/32, brief time exposure. Nearest piece is virtually "life" size.

Here are four, same size as the original prints.

ARTHUR KRAMER

◁ **FLAT LIGHT** is best for copying; "north" light from a window is excellent. For students, researchers, who need to make quick copies for reference, combination of Polaroid Land camera and close-up lenses is useful. This photo was made with window-light, +2 lens, setting EV 15, and 200 speed film.

▽ **REFLECTED LIGHT** from mirror (shown on page 94) puts brilliant highlights on tiny subject. Reflectors let you turn daylight or flood to most useful angle, often take place of extra lamp. Photo below was made with +2 and +3 lenses, brief time exposure at EV 17, using 200 speed film.

LAURIE SEAMANS

To convert numbers on older model cameras to EV numbers add 9.

SPEED LIGHT

Want to "freeze" the fastest action? Looking for some portable daylight? Then try this.

ELECTRONIC FLASH is the wonder child of photographic light sources. Anyone who has done much picture taking with it finds it hard to be content with any other kind of artificial light. And hitched to a Polaroid Land camera (except the Highlander and the original Model 95), the combination is virtually unbeatable, for certain kinds of pictures.

Remember, we said: for certain kinds of pictures. Put it to work at jobs for which it's not suited and you'll be disappointed. Use it well for what it does best and you'll be thrilled at the results.

Let's see what the speed light offers.

1. It can stop the fastest action. Forget about telling your subject to "hold it." Most amateur-type units on the market today have a flash duration ranging from 1/750 to 1/2,000 second.

2. The flash is cool. You feel no heat from an electronic flash. In fact, it's over so fast there's little eye discomfort.

3. It gives daylight quality light. The composition and color of the speed light flash are almost identical with high noon daylight. Films give their maximum speed —usually about 1/3 more than they do with flash or flood lighting. And there's a certain quality to the prints which can be matched only in daylight.

4. No bulbs to carry and change. You take picture after picture, flash after flash —the unit needs no attention.

5. The flashtube never wears out. Well, hardly ever. It's good for many thousands of flashes. Of course, it can be smashed.

Against these unique advantages you must weigh some drawbacks: the smallest and most portable speed lights weigh a lot more and are bulkier than a Polaroid flashgun or wink-light; even "low-priced" speed lights of good quality cost almost as much as a Land camera; some of the portable types use expensive batteries; there's hardly an amateur-size speed light made today with a light output as great as that of a plain old No. 5 bulb in your flashgun.

Do you need a speed light?

That's an important question. You don't need a speed light: if you shoot a couple of flash pictures occasionally in the living room, and then put the gun away for weeks at a time; if you have no need to stop high speed action; if all the speed light pictures you take could have been done just as well with flashgun and bulbs, or a wink-light and 3000 speed film.

You can probably make good use of one: if flashbulbs are an important expense item because of the great number you use; if you find your picture taking handicapped by inability to stop fast indoor or night action with flashbulbs, or with 3000 speed film and the wink-light.

To help you pick a suitable speed light from the array on the market, here are some facts about how they work.

A speed light has three main parts: power unit, capacitors (devices to store electricity), and flashtube. The power unit provides a supply of high voltage direct current, which is fed to and stored in the capacitors. When the camera shutter's flash contacts close, all the electricity stored in the capacitors is "dumped" through the flashtube causing it to emit a

◁ **ACTION STOPPER:** Combination of speed light, Polaroid Land camera, and 200 speed film, caught this high flying youngster. Speed light is a specialized type of light source; unless you need its particular abilities, you may not find it worthwhile to buy such equipment.

PETER GOWLAND

brilliant, brief light. And the tube can flash thousands of times, provided that the capacitors are fully charged with electricity before each flash. The power unit and capacitors are usually combined in one assembly called the power pack.

One reason it's tricky to pick a speed light is that they vary widely in the type of power supply used to generate the high voltage DC, and the size of the capacitors (the bigger they are, the more power stored, the brighter the flash). There are three types of speed light power supplies which Land camera users should choose from, according to their needs: household alternating current; high voltage dry battery; low voltage dry battery.

The AC power pack draws its current from household lines, transforms it to high voltage direct current. Speed lights with AC power packs are good for work in a fixed location, where many flashes in succession are needed. AC units may be "portable" in the sense that they are small and light in weight, but they must be connected to a household AC outlet when in use, so your movements are limited. They consume very little current.

For a true portable you need a battery power supply. Some of the best units are powered by a high voltage dry battery, a compact but mighty source of electricity, which feeds directly to the capacitors to charge them. These are simple, rugged, powerful, rather heavy units. One battery is good for about 1,500 flashes, if used within a year (after that the battery starts to die of old age). These batteries cost about $16. Unless you know for certain that you'll shoot at least 1,000 flashes per year, and that you must have battery portability, this is an expensive and wasteful type of unit to operate.

Another type of battery power supply, now becoming popular, draws its current from several ordinary photoflash "D" cells. The "D" cells deliver a low voltage current which is raised to high voltage DC by a rather intricate electrical system. A set of batteries is good for only about 100 flashes, but a set costs about a dollar. Thus, this is a good type for the man who occasionally has real need for a portable speed light but also leaves it idle for long periods. If the batteries die meanwhile, it's no big loss. Most of these units can also be operated on 110-volt AC house circuits.

△ **REMOTE FLASH CONNECTION:** Here a small Ascor AC powered unit is connected to the camera's shutter by a long extension. Such a rig, good with bounce flash, lets you move around with the camera while the light stays constant. With 3000 speed film in the camera and the speed light aimed at the ceiling, you have a great and exciting picture taking combination.

◁ **TYPICAL PORTABLE:** Power pack is slung from the shoulder; the flashtube assembly is fitted to the camera. This is a Graflex Strobomite, powered by four "D" cells or 110 volts AC.

HOW TO CONNECT: Speed light outlet (except on Pathfinders) is atop the shutter housing. A tiny adapter cord (Polaroid #490) plugs in there and in turn connects to the cord on the speed light. Pathfinders must have the sync lever (arrow) set to "X" or the flash won't reach the film. On the Model 110A, disconnect the camera's flash fitting (at right) by lifting it straight off; fit the speed light plug to that outlet, as shown. On the Model 110, connect the speed light to the two-post flash fitting.

How to use speed light

Practically all modern speed lights must be used with camera shutters having "X" (zero delay) type synchronization—that is, the sync contacts close at the instant the shutter blades are wide open. You can't use such units with the Highlander and the Model 95, so better forget about speed light with those cameras. All Pathfinders, and all other models (at settings EV 13 to 17—#4 to #8 on older cameras) are synchronized for speed light. The connections are shown above.

The reflector assembly (sometimes called the light head) can be used on the camera for direct flash, in very much the same manner that a flashgun is used. You may have to buy a special bracket in order to attach it to the camera.

With 3000 speed film, even a small unit gives enough light for bounce flash, but it may be awkward to fit the speed light to the camera in bounce position. A more likely choice is remote flash; the light head is mounted on a light stand or other support instead of on the camera, as shown in the photo at left.

How to get correct exposure

There is little published information on using speed lights with the Land camera. You'll have to compile your own flash guide. Here's how to do it.

Ask someone to act as your model and to sit on a straight chair a few feet from the wall in an average room. Leave just enough light so you can see what you're doing—too much may affect the exposure somewhat. Mount the speed light on the camera, 10 ft. from the subject. Now make a series of exposures, using settings from EV 13 through 17 (#4 through #8 on older model cameras). From these pick the one with the best skin tones and general illumination. Let's say it's EV 15.

Using that as a basis, the following settings should give correct exposure also: At 14 ft., one number lower; at 20 ft., two numbers lower than at 10 ft.; at 7 ft., one number higher than at 10 ft., and at 5 ft., two numbers higher. The advantage of the Land camera is that you can see the results immediately, and thus work out the flash guide in short order.

Exposure with the Pathfinder

With the Pathfinder, follow the same procedure, (with 1/100 or 1/125 sec. shutter speed) starting at f/5.6 and closing the lens down one f-number with each exposure. Pick the best print and note the f-number of that exposure (let's suppose it is f/11). Multiply that f-number by 10—the result, 110, is your guide number. For other distances, simply divide the guide number by your speed light-to-subject distance in feet and that's the correct lens opening to use. Of course, as when using flashbulbs, guide numbers are just a guide—they help you to the correct exposure, but they are by no means a guarantee of same.

FLOODS

Tungsten lamps are inexpensive, dependable, and for some jobs you just can't beat them.

FOR STEADY, precisely controllable lighting, there is nothing to match photoflood lamps. Not even daylight is as sure and predictable in results.

You set up the lamps; you measure the illumination with an exposure meter; you balance it evenly (if that's what is wanted), or set the lights to throw shadows where desired. At every step you are in complete control of conditions, and can adjust them to get a particular result. Add to this the wonder of the Land process—in a minute you can see the actual picture, know whether or not it is satisfactory, immediately make adjustments to improve it, if necessary to do so.

Obviously, such precise and careful picture taking is not for snapshots. But this kind of control is just perfect for formal portraits, copying, still lifes, interiors, or any other type of picture in which the subject is not in motion. Try to use floods to record two youngsters and a puppy romping in the living room, and you're wasting time. However, if you need a record shot of some small parts, cross-lighted to bring out their shape, a flood is the right light for the job (example, the close-up on page 96).

The kinds of flood lamps

Until very recently, any discussion of flood lamps for photography was confined to the so-called photofloods. These are special lamps which burn very much more brightly than conventional lamps of the same physical size. However, they are not inexpensive, they have a burning life of only 5 to 10 hours, they draw large amounts of current (special wiring and fuses may be necessary when using them), they get frighteningly hot, and they are generally awkward to handle.

With the advent of the 3000 speed films, such lamps are no longer necessary for Polaroid Land camera users. If you already have photofloods and know how to use them, they'll perform better than ever with 3000 speed film. But, if you're starting from scratch, without lamps, don't bother with photofloods.

Instead, with 3000 speed film you can make pictures in a minute with any of a whole series of commercial or household lamps which are inexpensive, long lived,

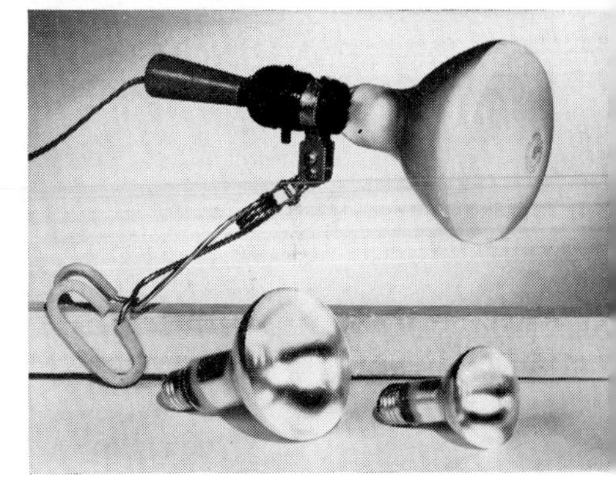

WHAT YOU NEED: The 3000 speed film lets you use the simplest, least expensive flood lighting equipment. Basic item is the clamp-on socket. In it is a 150-watt reflector flood (they come in various wattages). The smaller lamps are a 75-watt spot and a tiny 30-watt spot. Clamp-ons can also be used successfully with plain household lamps in a variety of aluminum reflectors.

◁ **SIMPLE LIGHTING:** One flood lamp to the left of the camera was aimed at the man; another at the far right illuminated the background. For portraits, floods provide easy-to-handle light. The 3000 speed film is ideally suited to this kind of photography.

PETER GOWLAND

◁ PETER BASCH

ONE LAMP AT CAMERA: Placed close to camera, one flood gives even, virtually shadowless light. Here, effect was heightened by dark drape across throat and shoulders, and by distant, unilluminated background. Setup can be duplicated in almost any room.

PETER GOWLAND

ONE LAMP, HARSH LIGHTING: By placing lamp low and front, mild-looking individual can be turned into horror story subject.

draw moderate amounts of current, and are easy to use. So, in this chapter, everything is based on the use of 3000 speed film with those flood lamps.

Any ordinary 100-watt household bulb can be put into a reflector and there you have a usable flood. But much more convenient than this are the lamps with built-in reflectors shown on page 103.

These reflector lamps are used for window displays, store lighting, etc. and are available at most electrical supply and hardware stores. You're unlikely to find them for sale in camera stores.

Some are designed to throw a wide beam of light—these are reflector floods. Others project a narrow beam of light—these are reflector spots. Both types come in a variety of sizes; the 75-watt and 150-watt are most useful for photography. There's also a tiny 30-watt spot, which is very handy to have around.

Which lamps to use?

Should you use plain floods with separate reflectors, or reflector photofloods? That depends on your needs. For the casual picture taker who wants to set up a couple of lamps once in awhile, reflector floods are far more convenient to handle and to store. A good assortment to begin with would be two floods—150-watt and 75-watt—and a 75-watt spot. Of course, your particular needs will dictate what kind of lamps and how many you must get.

The man who intends to do quite a bit of serious work with floods will probably do better with plain lamps and separate reflectors. And here's an important point: Stay away from paper reflectors, or any lightweight metal foil type of thing which rests right on the neck of the lamp. These lamps are quite safe to use, but they get hot enough to give your fingers a singe you'll long remember.

The best reflectors to use are made of spun aluminum and weigh a few ounces. They should have screw inserts at the narrow end which permit them to fasten securely to the lamp socket. The interiors are satin finished. They come in a wide variety of sizes and shapes. An 8 in. or 10 in. bowl is suitable for general work. Long, narrow shells act as a sort of modified spot, concentrating the light (rather inefficiently) on a small area.

Reflector helps to soften harsh shadows.

ONE LAMP, AT RIGHT: Single flood, moved away from camera, throws heavy shadows on face; undesirable, except for special effects.

ONE LAMP, PLUS REFLECTOR: White wall, cardboard, or other reflecting surface on shadowed side, reflects light into face.

How do you hold them?

The handiest device is a *clamp-on socket*, such as is shown on page 103. When you go to buy a clamp-on, get a good one— it costs only a few cents more than a junky one. The best place to get them is in a well stocked camera store, but a large electrical house will also have clamp-ons of good quality.

Look for: a powerful spring grip, with rubber covered jaws to protect furniture and trim; free movement of the socket on a ball joint, which should be adjustable for greater or less tension; a socket which will accept aluminum reflectors (ask the salesman about this); a knob or other handle on the rear of the socket, so the angle can be adjusted without touching the hot lamp and socket; a heavy-duty connecting cord at least 10 ft. long. Such a clamp-on can also handle a plain flood in a reflector.

You'll also need a long, heavy-duty extension cord, ending in a triple outlet capable of handling up to 500 watts.

The more serious picture taker may want to use light stands instead of clamp-ons. The tubular aluminum type are light and sturdy. Everything we've said about electrical equipment applies equally to lamps mounted on stands.

J. W.

ONE LAMP, IMPORTANT SHADOW: Single reflector flood, to left of camera and on level with pianist's head, gave general light and caused wall shadow. By moving lamp, shadow can be located wherever desired, or even made to disappear behind subject's body.

TWO LAMPS, DRAMATIC LIGHT: Floods were placed at right and left, somewhat behind subject and pointing slightly at camera. Compare this with the friendly portrait on page 102, also made with two lamps.

PETER BASCH

THREE LIGHTS, SOFT MODELING: Two lights right and left of camera (but close to it) were arranged to give almost shadowless illumination. Third light, high and behind girl, highlights her hair, adds sparkle to picture.

A common use of floods is for portraits. Even with 3000 speed film, you can't use the fastest snapshot shutter speeds, unless you concentrate enough light to almost fry the subject. So you'll probably have to use camera settings in the range of EV 10 to EV 13, with relatively slow shutter speeds. (Exception: the wide lens openings possible with the Pathfinders will permit shutter speeds up to 1/125 sec. without excessive amounts of light.)

A tripod is desirable to reduce the chance of camera shake, and having the camera fixed on the tripod makes it easier to compose the picture and arrange the lighting exactly as wanted. Follow the tips on tripod selection and use which are given in the chapter *Time Exposures*.

Keep the background simple. A light toned wall is always good, or a plain window drape. If the background is to be fairly light in the picture, place your subject just far enough away from it so that the lamps don't throw objectionable shadows on the wall, or arrange the lights to accomplish the same thing. For a dark background just move subject and lamps far from the wall so little light falls on the background. An independent light source, hidden behind your model, can be directed at the background to control the light on it, and that's a very flexible method. By adjusting the light on the subject, and the light on the background, you can achieve such divergent effects as a brightly lighted subject against a dark background, or a subject silhouetted against a light background.

How many lights?

It's possible to take an acceptable picture with a single flood placed at or near the camera position (see example, page 104). However, in order to get any real modeling and form into the picture the light should come at an angle, so it will throw some shadows. Control of the shadows and highlights is the essence of portraiture. It's difficult to do much with only one lamp. Two lamps give a great deal of flexibility. A third lamp can be very useful for controlling the background, as described previously, or to throw a direct light on the top and rear of the subject's head to bring out the detail in hair, or add some highlights.

On these pages are illustrations of what happens to highlights and shadows when floods are used in various positions.

To control the brightness of the light

on the subject, you move the lamps closer or further away. Just as with flash, *it's the lamp-to-subject distance* that counts. Starting at any point, if you halve the lamp-to-subject distance, the light on the subject will be four times as bright; if you double the lamp-to-subject distance, the light on the subject will be one-quarter as bright as at the original distance.

For pictures by floods an accurate, sensitive exposure meter is a must. The Polaroid #625 meter is excellent for this type of work. Use it, following the procedures shown in the chapter *Correct Exposure.* There's an important point to remember when using the meter.

Polaroid Land films, and most conventional films, are slower (less sensitive) in tungsten light than in daylight. For use with floods, the 3000 speed film has an exposure index of about 2000.

If you are using a meter other than the Polaroid #625 set it for an exposure index of 2000 (or the closest figure on the meter's scale) and use the meter in the normal manner. Set the film speed dial of the #625 meter to 3000, but take your exposure reading from the small line next to the arrow, as shown at right.

If there's so little light reflected from the subject that your exposure meter doesn't register it, you need more light. Move the lamps in closer. If that's impracticable, take a time exposure, using the methods shown in *Time Exposures.*

READING THE #625 METER: When using 3000 speed film, the film speed dial is set to 3000. With tungsten lamps, read the EV number next to the small red mark alongside the arrow. Here the mark is pointing to EV 12. In daylight, read the EV number next to the arrow.

Other uses for floods

Floods provide a simple, inexpensive light source for identification pictures. One or two lamps are arranged near the camera to light the subject evenly.

For indoor pictures by window light, a flood can be very helpful by adding a bit of fill-in light for the shadows, or to illuminate the background. Or one or two floods can be bounced off ceiling or wall to raise the light level in a room a moderate amount.

Floods are a good light source where much copying has to be done. Use two lamps, one on each side of the camera, and at a moderate angle (45°) to the material to be copied. Make sure the light is even overall.

Floods are useful for all sorts of commercial and record shots of equipment, furniture, and so on. Don't be appalled if you have a large dark machine to photograph and only one or two floods at hand with which to do it. You can *paint with light*, as the old-timers do when they want shadowless illumination. Mount the camera on a tripod, turn the exposure control to a high number, such as EV 16 or EV 17. Set the shutter for a time exposure. Either ask someone to hold the shutter open or use a cable release which has a plunger lock for that purpose. Then start waving the flood in arcs so that the light covers whole sections of the machine to be photographed.

Don't aim the light into the open lens, and don't stand between camera and subject (you can walk through if you don't linger). Walk all around your big machine, keeping the light in continuous motion. It may take 3 to 5 minutes to cover every bit of it with light. Then close the shutter and develop the print. If it's not right, try again.

TIME EXPOSURES

What do you do when the light's too dim for snapshots? Here's a way to save the day.

THERE ARE THREE things to be concerned with when making a time exposure.

First, the camera must be rock steady. Use a sturdy tripod or stand the camera on some firm support. For verticals, a folding foot is provided (photos, far right, show this).

Second, the camera must be set for a time exposure—that means to "B." The shutter must be held open an appreciable time, perhaps for several seconds. Use either the regular shutter release lever or attach a cable release (photos, right). Incidentally, the setting "B" stands for "Bulb," obsolete jargon from the days when studio photographers squeezed a rubber bulb to open the shutter. *The Bulb setting has absolutely nothing to do with flashbulbs or flash pictures. Use it only for time exposures.*

Third, you have to figure the exposure. In dim light, exposure guides are useless; an exposure meter is a must. Polaroid exposure meters are intended mainly for snapshots. Nevertheless, they can be used for time exposures, as explained below. Be sure to set the film speed scale for daylight or tungsten lamps (see *Correct Exposure*) as directed in the film instruction sheet.

If the light reflected from your subject is too dim to move the meter needle off the lowest number on the scale, then do this. Hold the meter beside the subject with the meter window pointing directly at the main light source. (This is the exact reverse of what's done ordinarily to take a meter reading.)

With the meter aimed at the main light source, note the number to which the needle points. Then set the camera according to the chart below, and hold down the shutter release for the specified time. If the picture is too dark, repeat with an exposure at least twice as long; if too light, cut the exposure at least in half.

If the light's so dim that the needle doesn't move even with the meter aimed at the light source, try to get the subject and the light source closer together. If that's impossible, just guess and hope.

Important point to remember: The longer the time for correct exposure the less chance of error. On an exposure of 1 sec., an error of 1 sec. in timing means 100 per cent overexposure. But on a 10 sec. exposure, a 1 sec. mistake is only a 10 per cent error, with no noticeable effect on exposure. So, if you're making a time exposure with immovable subject and shake free camera, don't be afraid to use a high EV number and a relatively long exposure time.

TIME EXPOSURE GUIDE

When the meter reads	Set the exposure control to number	Hold down the shutter release about
EV 10 or #1	EV 13 or #4	4 sec.
EV 11 or #2	EV 13 or #4	2 sec.
EV 12 or #3	EV 13 or #4	1 sec.
EV 13 or #4	EV 14 or #5	1 sec.
EV 14 or #5	EV 15 or #6	1 sec.

Settings above are for use when shutter control is set to "B," and exposure meter is at subject with meter window pointing at main light source. Full details are given in text.

 To convert numbers on older model cameras to EV numbers add 9.

TIPS ON TRIPOD USE

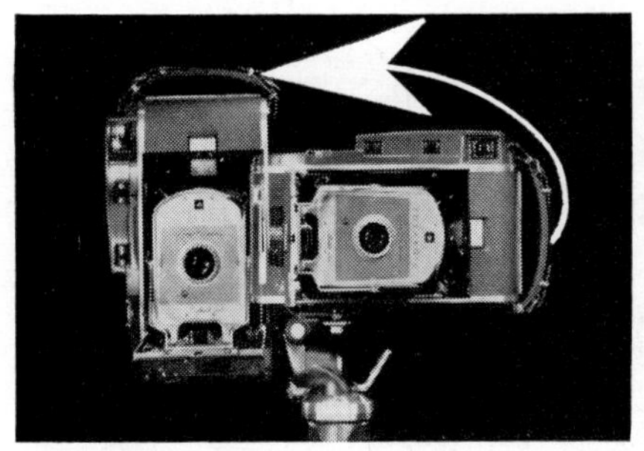

VITAL FEATURE: When buying tripod be sure its head is designed so camera can be tilted from horizontal to vertical, and vice versa, without having to loosen and shift tripod screw. If it won't do this, it's poor choice for Land camera.

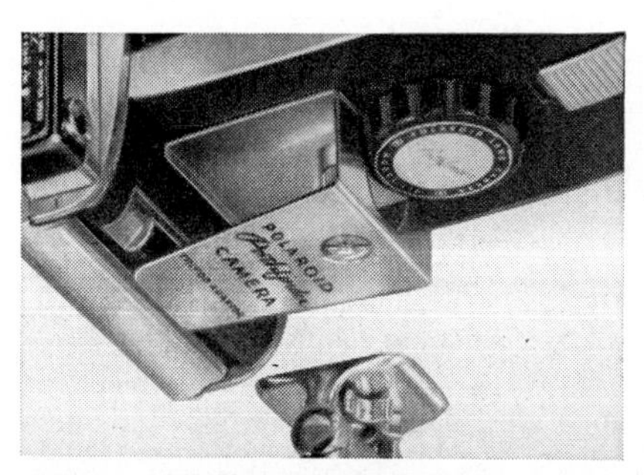

TRIPOD ADAPTER: Rangefinder knob interferes with tripod head when camera is in vertical position. Tripod adapter ($1.95) raises camera so knob and tripod head do not collide.

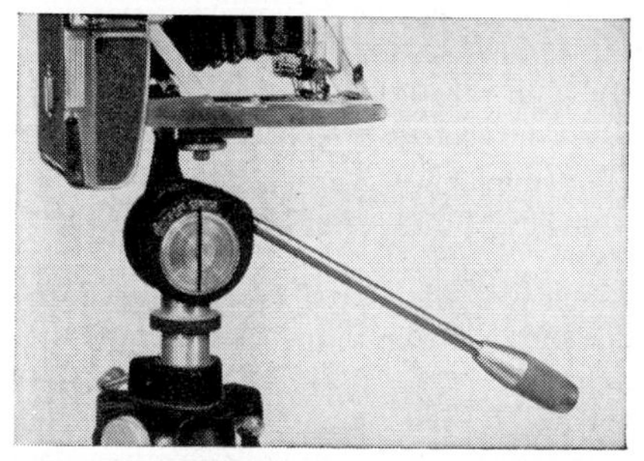

TRIPOD HANDLE: When using tripod socket under folding front of camera, tripod handle must face forward. If handle points to rear, it's impossible to pull tab in proper manner, or to load film without removing camera from tripod.

HOW TO SET THE CAMERA

ON ALL MODELS EXCEPT Highlanders and Pathfinders, flip switch (arrow) from "I" to "B". Use shutter release lever or cable release to hold shutter open; it will close when you remove finger from release. Locking screw on cable release helps for long exposures. Switch automatically returns to "I" after each time exposure.

ON HIGHLANDERS turn knob to "B" (arrow). This must be reset to "I" (snapshot) manually after time exposures; if not your next snapshot may be ruined. Note how cable release is attached; it is shown with shutter held open by lock screw on release.

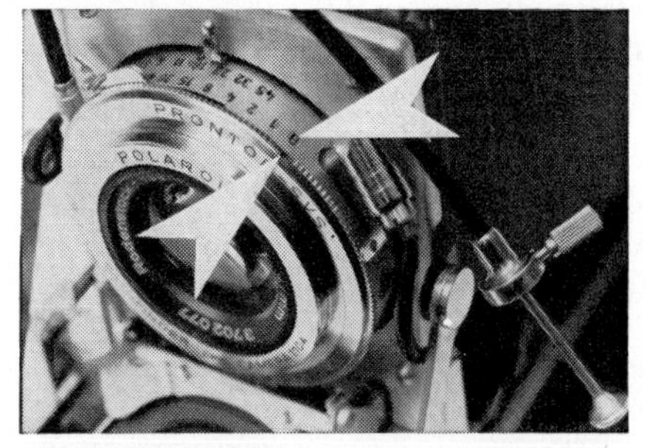

ON PATHFINDERS turn shutter speed control ring until indicator is at "B" (arrows). Shutter must first be cocked; then press release to open shutter, let go to close it. Model 110 also has "T" setting. Cock shutter, press release; shutter remains open as long as desired without pressure on release. To close, press release once again.

CARE OF EQUIPMENT

How to keep your camera and accessories in top condition for a long, useful life.

JUST A LITTLE CARE will keep your Polaroid Land camera in good health for years and years of service. The mechanism is simple and ruggedly built. But it also contains parts as precisely made as a good clock, and if they are allowed to deteriorate, the camera ceases to be a precision instrument and cannot perform properly. Here are some preventive maintenance hints which, if followed, will keep your camera and accessories serviceable for a long time.

Care in operation: With all models except the Highlander, *be sure* to set the focusing scale to infinity before trying to close the camera; if it's set for 50 ft. or closer distances, the moving focusing track will get jammed against the camera body, may cause damage.

If your camera is one of the models which have a wire frame as the front part of the viewing system, take care that it does not get bent. Also when closing, check that *both ends* of the wire frame viewfinder clear the camera body and the struts which support the folding front bed of the camera.

When small children are around, keep the camera out of hand's reach. Youngsters usually don't mean to smash things, but it happens.

When opening the back of the camera for loading or inspection, let the outer and inner doors down carefully—don't let them flop open with their full weight hitting the hinge stops.

There's a small foot on the bottom of the folding front—it's used to support the camera in a vertical position. Be careful not to hook this on the edge of the carrying case when putting the camera in the case. And don't put too much pressure on it in the open position—it's meant to support a camera, no more.

Keep it clean: Protect the camera from sand and dirt. Close the camera when it's not in use–dirt particles can work their way into the shutter, stop-pin and release mechanisms, cause wear and friction in the bearings of the steel pressure rollers, damage the bellows material. If dust gathers on any part of the camera, wipe it off carefully before closing—*never put away a dirty camera (of any kind).*

In ordinary use, foreign matter collects in the back of the camera. Some of this is excess reagent from the film pods—occasionally a bit leaks out from between film and positive paper during the developing process. A lightly water-dampened, clean, lint-free cloth will get rid of the reagent if you get it before the material hardens. If it cakes hard, scratch it loose with a fingernail, never a piece of metal, then use a slightly damp cloth.

The photo opposite is an actual example of how dirty a camera back can get if cleaning is neglected.

Before loading each roll, check the steel rollers to be sure they are free of any dirt—if they collect foreign matter you'll see evenly spaced white spots on your pictures. See *Picture Troubles* for an example of what this looks like. And, clean out the film roll chambers occasionally.

Bits of black enamel are likely to wear off, due to normal use. They'll do no harm, but clean them out of the camera back.

Easy on the oil: The only parts of the camera which should ever be oiled are the ends of the steel rollers. They may need *one small drop each* after about 100 rolls of film. Also, oil them if the rollers make noise when turned, or are stiff, or if it becomes consistently difficult to advance the film. Models 100, 700, 800, and 110A (except for a few early samples) have permanently lubricated, sealed bearings.

If the roller bearings become damaged or badly worn, they can't exert even pressure and the films won't develop properly.

Beware of moisture, heat: Cameras should be protected from dampness, salt air, and excessively high temperatures. Such conditions may damage the external metal parts and the bellows; if exposure is severe, moving parts will be affected.

If the camera gets wet or damp, wipe everything dry with a soft cloth, and don't close it until the bellows is thoroughly dry. Avoid storing the camera in very hot or very sunny areas, even if not loaded. Heat may also damage exposure meters.

KEEP THE CAMERA CLEAN: The crusty material (arrows) on the inner back is dried excess developer reagent—a bit of it may leak out between the edges of the print and the negative. Sometimes it gets onto the steel rollers. The text explains why such dirt causes trouble and how to clean it off.

Give it some exercise: A camera that lies idle for long periods can deteriorate more than if used occasionally. At least once a month it ought to be opened, bellows extended, and all controls operated. This is particularly true of the Pathfinder's shutter, a complex mechanism. It should be cocked and released once or twice at *all* speed settings, including B. (The older Model 110 also has a T setting.) On the Model 110A there's a self-timer—run it a few times, too. Unless the shutter gets this kind of exercise, stickiness develops and it may quit operating on some speeds, or altogether. Also on the Pathfinder, operate the f-number control and "X" and "M" sync selector lever. And if your camera (any model) hasn't been used for a while, click the shutter several times *before* loading a new roll of film.

Does your camera have a rangefinder? Check it occasionally, as follows: When it's set to infinity, the two images of a far distant object should coincide. If they are a bit off, don't bother with it; if they are 'way out of coincidence, the rangefinder needs adjustment by a competent repairman. The two images should also be on the same level. If one is higher than the other, a repairman is needed. Rangefinder images should be clear and bright. If they are dim and it's hard to see, clean off the outer windows as described in *Care of the lens,* below. If this doesn't help, a competent repairman should look at it. Same applies to the viewfinder.

Care of the lens: This is a piece of fine optical glass, and it's easy to scratch or otherwise damage it. No fingerprints!

Don't scrub at it with a damp handkerchief. Don't use those silicone coated eyeglass cleaning tissues on it. You ought to have a small lens cleaning brush, preferably one of the kind that has a rubber bulb attached, with which a stream of air can be blown at the lens. Any camera store will have a good lens brush.

If dust gets on the lens, first blow it off or brush it off lightly. Breathe *gently* on the lens—just enough to dampen the surface—and lightly wipe it clean with a soft wad of good quality camera lens tissue, or Kleenex tissue. And don't forget, a lens

CHANGING A WINK-LIGHT BATTERY & LAMP: Loosen the case lock screw five full turns. This releases two latches in the case. Carefully remove the front half of the case. The latches may stick slightly; if so, loosen the screw another turn. Remove the old battery and exchange bulbs. Install the new battery in the position shown. The end with the contacts must go in first and the contacts should be to the rear of the case. Replace the insulating block so it conceals the battery connections. Then replace the front of the case and tighten the screw five full turns.

has two sides—occasionally get at the back of the camera and clean the rear element of the lens.

Filters, close-up lenses: Treat these with as much care as the camera lens gets, and clean them the same way. Incidentally, the Data-Tape in the Close-up Kit should be run in and out carefully—don't yank it out to its full length. The coil spring has just so much tension. If the tape shows signs of collecting dirt or rust spots, clean it off with a cloth lightly dampened with a thin machine oil.

Care of the exposure meter: This is a rugged little meter, but it's still a delicate instrument and hard knocks should be avoided. If you carry it on the camera, be certain that the accessory shoe grips it tightly, so it won't fall off. Keep the glass window clean.

Your exposure meter is sick if it displays any of the following symptoms: needle stays at zero or elsewhere; needle moves only one or two numbers, even in bright sunshine; needle moves erratically, or shows signs of stickiness. Don't try to operate on the meter. Instead, trot down to your camera dealer with it and ask to have it repaired. Or, if more convenient, pack it in a stiff cardboard box with plenty of padding and mail it to: Product Repair Dept., Polaroid Corp., Cambridge 39, Mass. Your name and address *must* be clearly marked on a tag or sticker attached to the meter.

Care of the Photoelectric Shutter: This device is a combination photoelectric exposure meter, camera shutter, and optical instrument. While it should have a long life, with reasonable care, it is subject to damage from shock, moisture, dirt, or extreme heat.

The following parts should be inspected frequently and cleaned, if necessary, in the same way as you would clean a lens or filter: the face of the gridded light cell; the glass over the front and the back of the lens opening.

To check whether or not the shutter is functioning, remove it from the camera and hold it so the light cell faces a bright sky, or other brightly lighted daylight scene. Look at the back of the shutter and press the release all the way. You should see a brief light spot at the lens opening as the shutter opens and closes. Repeat this, aiming the light cell at a houselamp, or some other moderately bright light source. The shutter should open and close more slowly.

In case of malfunction, do not attempt to open and repair this unit. Take it to your camera dealer, or pack it carefully (see *Care of the Exposure Meter,* above) and return it to Product Repair Department, Polaroid Corp., Cambridge 39, Mass.

Care of the wink-light: Treat this like any good piece of electrical equipment. Protect the connectors and the little pin sockets for the auxiliary flasher from dirt and moisture. Avoid heavy strains on the connectors or wire (if you have a model with a wire connection).

The wink-light is powered by a small but mighty 45-volt battery (Eveready #460 or Burgess #K30P). When the wink-light is placed on the camera, the battery begins to charge a capacitor, a device for storing electricity. When you snap the picture, the capacitor dumps a powerful but brief shot of current into a small tungsten lamp (G.E. #428) causing it to flash brightly for an instant.

The battery will last longer if the wink-light is flashed occasionally (once a week) than if it lies idle for several months. To avoid exhausting the battery accidentally, observe the following precautions: *Don't* leave the wink-light connected to the camera when not in use. *Don't* connect the wink-light to the camera when the Photoelectric Shutter #440 is on the camera (this will really drain the battery rapidly). *Don't* leave an unused flashbulb in the auxiliary flasher when the flasher is plugged into the wink-light.

The battery is good for about 1,000 flashes; so is the bulb. Replacement battery kits are available – these include a fresh bulb, which should be installed at the same time as the new battery. If your camera dealer has no replacement kits, write to Customer Service, Polaroid Corp., Cambridge 39, Mass.

Care of the flashgun: Like the wink-light, this unit is also a piece of good electrical equipment and it should be given proper handling and care.

Polaroid BC flashguns are powered by a tiny photoflash battery which is good for a year or two. In use, the battery charges a capacitor which, in turn, delivers a powerful jolt of current to the flashbulb to flash it. The capacitor draws current from the battery more economically if the flashgun gets moderate use than if it is left idle for months.

The circuit in the Polaroid BC flashgun is such that the battery will charge the capacitor *only* when a bulb is in the socket—a tiny current passes right through the bulb without firing it. So, when you take the camera out for its monthly exercise and inspection, put a flashbulb in the flashgun socket for a minute or two, and then remove it. *Never store a Polaroid BC flashgun with a bulb in the socket*—the steady current flow to the capacitor will exhaust the battery.

Other equipment: New types of Polaroid equipment and accessories are constantly being marketed. In case any of these malfunction in any manner, or if you have any questions, write to Customer Service, Polaroid Corp.

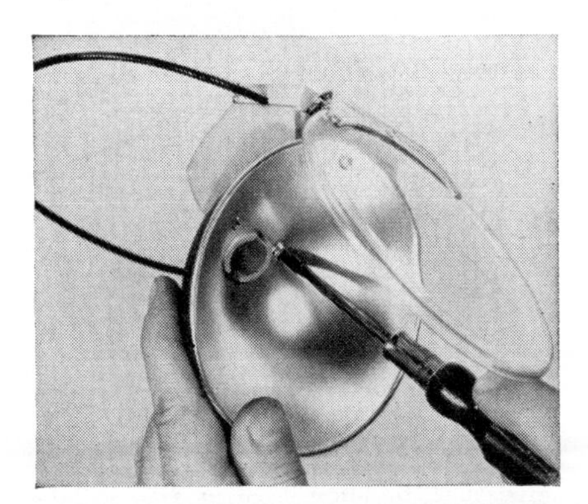

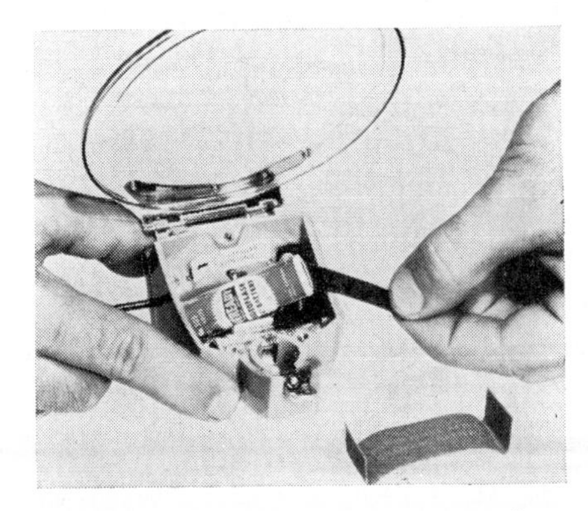

CHANGING A BC FLASHGUN BATTERY: First remove the screws securing the reflector. If you have no screwdriver, a coin will fit the wide screw slots. Lift out the fibre insulator strip (in foreground of picture). Pull up the end of the rubber band—this lifts the tiny battery out of its seat. Insert a new battery, looping the rubber band underneath—don't jam the band between the battery and flashgun electrical contacts. Replace the insulator strips, then the reflector. Try one test flash.

USING THE PATHFINDERS

These cameras have special lenses and shutters; here are the complete operating instructions.

THE PATHFINDER models make a picture in a minute, inside the camera, in the same way as any of the other Polaroid Land cameras. So, all the basic operations described in the front of this book apply to the Pathfinders.

They differ from all other Polaroid Land cameras in the methods used to get correct exposure. The Pathfinders do not have the single wheel exposure control found on the other models. Instead, they have separate, conventional photographic controls which regulate the size of the lens opening (f-numbers) and the shutter speed (fractions of a second) in order to get correct exposure.

The Model 110A also carries an EV (exposure value) scale numbered from EV 5 to EV 19. The numbers from EV 10 to EV 18 correspond in exposure value to similar numbers on other Polaroid Land camera models. The additional numbers (down to EV 5 and up to EV 19) simply indicate that the Model 110A can handle a greater range of exposure conditions than can the other models. Load a Pathfinder with 3000 speed film, and its picture taking ability in dim light is almost incredible.

These cameras have topnotch lenses and shutters. The Model 110A has a self-timer, the only Polaroid Land camera so equipped. It also has a folding lens cap with a shutter lock to prevent picture taking when the cap is closed. Now let's look at the controls (opposite).

MODEL 110A: It has integral coupled rangefinder, enclosed parallax-correcting viewfinder. Rodenstock Ysarex 127mm, f/4.7 lens is in Prontor SVS shutter, with speeds from 1 to 1/300 sec., plus self-timer. Camera is calibrated in EV numbers in addition to f-numbers and shutter speeds.

MODEL 110: Discontinued in 1957, this had coupled Kalart rangefinder, folding optical and wire viewfinder. Wollensak Raptar 127mm, f/4.5 lens was in Wollensak shutter with speeds from 1 to 1/400 sec., but without self-timer. Camera had only conventional f-numbers and shutter speeds.

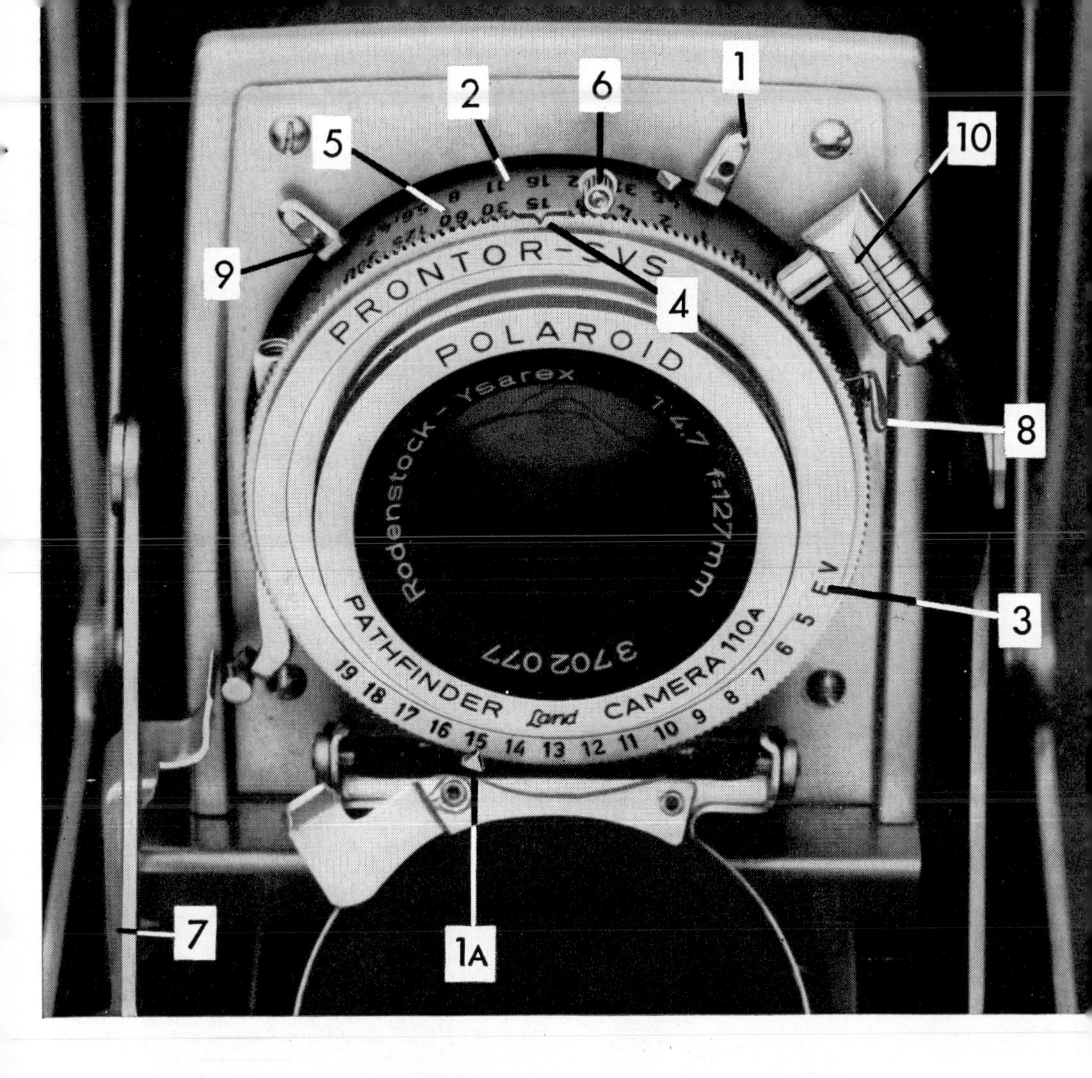

THE MODEL 110A SHUTTER: THE CONTROLS AND WHAT THEY DO.

The size of the lens opening is controlled by lever (1); as you move this, a pointer attached to it moves across the f-number scale (2), and at the same time the EV pointer (1A) on the other end of lever (1), moves the opposite way across the EV scale (3).

Shutter speed is controlled by turning the outer knurled rim (shutter speed ring) until the notch (4) comes opposite the desired setting (in fractions of a second) on the speed scale (5).

The settings now on the shutter can be described in two ways: In conventional photographic terms it is set for 1/15 sec. at f/45. Using the EV system (explained in the text) it is set to one of the shutter speed/f-number combinations which are equivalent to EV 15.

The cocking lever (6) sets the shutter; pressure on plate (7) snaps it.

Lever (8) operates an interlock between the shutter speed ring and lever (1). This is described in the text p. 115.

Lever (9) controls the choice of synchronization (for wink-light, conventional flashbulbs, or speed light), and also sets the self-timer mechanism.

A push-on plug (10) on a wire connects the flash outlet on the shutter with the camera's accessory shoe, into which either the wink-light or the flashgun fits. For use with speed lights, the plug (10) is lifted off the flash outlet and the speed light plug is connected directly to the outlet on the shutter.

How to use the interlocking EV system on the

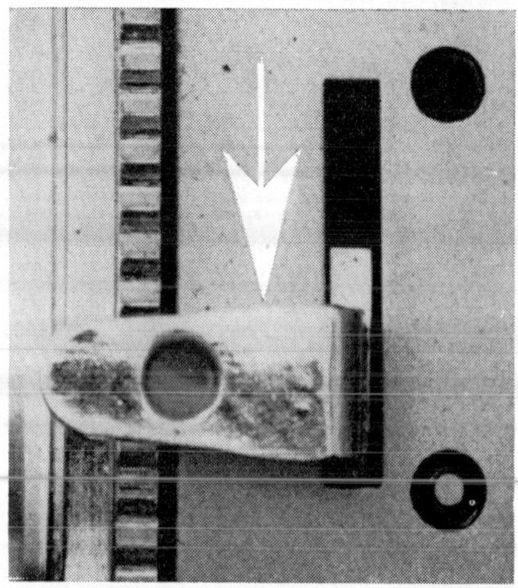

1. DISENGAGE THE INTERLOCK: This lever is on the shutter rim. Push in and move it to the dot with the hole. This disengages the mechanism which interlocks the shutter speed and f-number controls, so you can set the camera to the EV number for correct exposure (let's say it's EV 15).

2. SET THE EV NUMBER: Move the lever (1) so the EV pointer (1A) moves across the EV scale (3) to EV 15. If the lever stops before the pointer gets to EV 15, turn the knurled shutter speed ring (outer rim) to bring EV 15 to the pointer.

4. CHECK THE SHUTTER SPEED: The camera is set for EV 15, but a glance at photo 2 shows the shutter speed ring (4) at 1/15 sec., too slow for a snapshot (the f-number pointer (1) is at f/45, a very small lens opening). Turn the speed ring to a faster speed (such as 1/125, arrow, above); as you do so the interlock also moves the f-number pointer to f/16, a larger lens opening, to compensate for the faster shutter speed. And the camera is still set at EV 15 (1A) despite the change.

5. COCK THE SHUTTER: In contrast to the self-setting shutters on other Polaroid Land cameras, the Pathfinder shutters must first be cocked to tighten the springs inside. To do this, move the lever in an arc as far as it will go. Now you are ready to snap the picture, as in photo 6. Although it does no harm to leave the shutter cocked for a while, it's a good idea to release it before putting the camera away after use. This also applies to the Model 110.

Model 110A shutter.

3. ENGAGE THE INTERLOCK: Push the lever in and move it to the solid dot. This interlocks the knurled shutter speed ring and the lever which moves both the EV pointer and the f-number pointer. When interlocked, if the ring is moved, the lever also moves along with it the same amount.

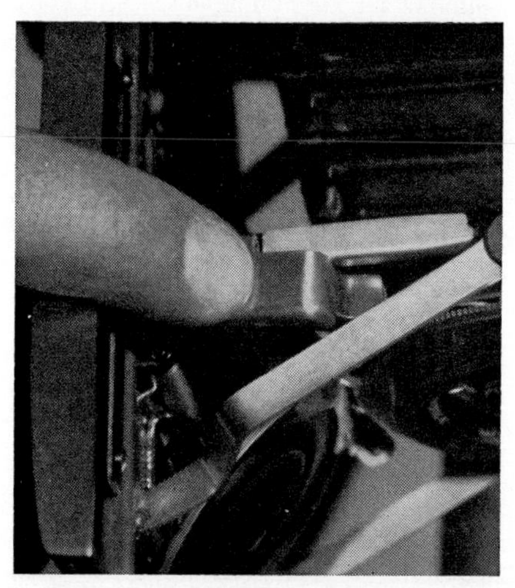

6. PRESS THE SHUTTER RELEASE: Squeeze the metal plate in gently; it travels about ¼ in. before the shutter snaps. Don't jab at the shutter release; you'll shake the camera. Even though the Model 110A has a shutter capable of very high speeds, you'll probably be using 1/125 sec. for most of your shooting. So, camera shake can still be an important cause of unsharp pictures. Hold the Model 110A (and Model 110) as shown in the chapter *Hold it Steady.*

CORRECT EXPOSURE WITH THE MODEL 110A

There are three quite different methods of using the exposure controls on the Model 110A camera.

Method 1. It can be operated like any conventional camera with f-numbers and a multi-speed shutter. When so used, the EV interlock must be disengaged, as in photo 1, at left. You should use an exposure meter calibrated in f-numbers and fractional seconds—the Polaroid meters won't do. Unless you have such a meter and are already skilled in the use of it and the exposure controls of a complex conventional camera, this is the least desirable way to use the Model 110A.

Method 2. This makes use of the EV scale, and is recommended as the simplest way to use this camera for outdoor snapshooting where the light conditions are fairly constant. The EV interlock must be disengaged, as in photo 1, at left. You can follow the exposure guide on the film instruction sheet, or use a Polaroid meter to find the EV number which gives correct exposure.

Let's assume that you're outdoors. Set the shutter to a suitable snapshot speed —1/125 is good as it will stop moderate action and reduces the chance of camera shake. It's a moderately bright day and the meter recommends EV 15. So, you just move the EV pointer to EV 15, as shown in photo 2, at left. This automatically adjusts the lens to the proper opening for correct exposure at 1/125 sec. under those light conditions. That's it.

Perhaps it was a very dark day, or you were in deep shade, and the meter recommended EV 10. With the shutter set for 1/125 sec. the EV pointer won't go to EV 10—it stops at EV 11½. That's immediate warning that the shutter speed is unsuitable for the light conditions. So you rotate the shutter speed ring until EV 10 gets under the EV pointer (don't move the pointer accidentally) thereby setting the shutter to a slower speed, more suited to the dim light.

Method 3. This also makes use of the EV scale, but with the interlock engaged. All the steps are shown at left.

SELF-TIMER: To use it, first set shutter to desired speed, cock shutter, then move lever (lower left) to "V" position. When shutter release is pressed, timer in shutter runs for several seconds before shutter snaps. When set for self-timer, shutter automatically goes to "X" type sync, suitable for speed light at any shutter speed, or for any type of flashbulb at 1/30 sec.

It's recommended where the camera is used in a variety of lighting conditions.

Reviewing the interlock

Here is a brief summary of the EV interlock system with reference to the photos on pages 116-117. With the interlock disengaged (photo 1) you set the EV number recommended by your meter (photo 2), and then engage the interlock (photo 3). Check the shutter speed setting. If it's suitable for the type of picture, you're all set to cock the shutter (photo 5) and shoot (photo 6). But if the shutter speed is unsuitable, just turn the speed ring to the desired speed. This automatically sets the lens to the proper opening for correct exposure. The interlock also prevents you from using too fast a shutter speed for a given light condition, because it will stop the shutter speed ring if you try to turn it beyond the correct exposure setting.

Correct exposure with Model 110

This discontinued model has conventional f-number and shutter speed controls (similar in operation to those on the Model 110A), and for best results it should be used with a similarly calibrated exposure meter. However, a conversion scale on the rangefinder housing (below) makes it possible to use a Polaroid exposure meter or printed exposure guide with the Model 110.

Flash and speed light settings

The Model 110A and Model 110 have shutter synchronization adjustable for wink-light, conventional flashbulbs, and speed light. Details are given in *The Wink-Light, Flash,* and *Speed Light.* For all three types of lighting, the Model 110A should be used with the EV interlock disengaged, as in photo 1, page 116.

With the wink-light, set the sync lever to M and use 1/30 or 1/25 sec. With No. 5 or Press 25 flashbulbs (M sync) and speed light (X sync) 1/125 or 1/100 sec. is suitable for most situations.

The direct flash exposure guides on the film instruction sheets are made up with EV numbers. You can use these with the Model 110A (but not the Model 110) as in Method 2, page 117.

The bounce flash exposure guide (see *Flash*) is made up with both EV numbers and f-numbers. With the Model 110A use either set of numbers; with the Model 110 use the f-numbers.

With both cameras, flash and speed light exposures can be computed by the guide number system described in the chapters *Flash* and *Speed Light.*

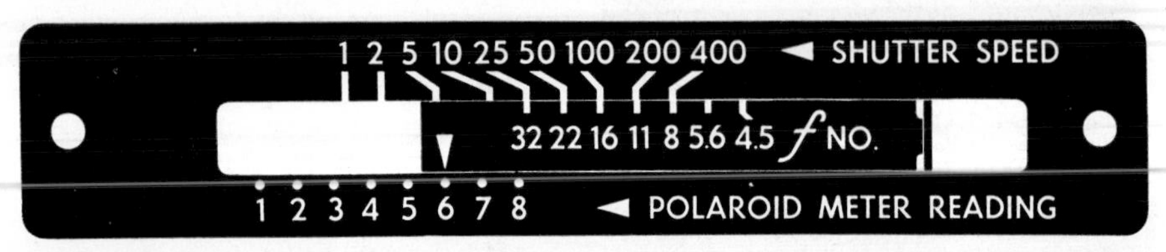

FOR MODEL 110 USERS: Scale on rangefinder housing converts Polaroid Exposure Meter reading to equivalent conventional f-number and shutter speed combinations. Simply set center arrow opposite Polaroid meter reading number, then take your choice of lens and shutter settings.

POSTCARDERS

On the road or in your own home, it's fun to make personal picture postcards in a minute.

SOME OLD KILLJOYS say that there's no point in taking a camera on a trip because you can buy better pictures on postcards.

Maybe so, but how would you like to be able to get the exact scene, the particular time, place, and people (even including yourself) onto picture postcards which you make right on the spot?

With Polaroid Postcarders you can do just that. These are of stiff paper stock, coated with a pressure sensitive adhesive. Remove the protective cover, press on your Polaroid Land print, and there's a strictly personal postcard ready to mail. And, you don't *have* to be on a trip. Pictures around home can make fine postcards, too.

Postcarders come in packages of 25, for 95 cents. One size takes prints from any Polaroid Land camera. Simple directions are on each Postcarder.

Caution: Do all writing on the Postcarder *before* sticking the print to it. *Important:* Coat every print thoroughly before mailing your Postcarders.

WHAT YOU NEED: Package of Polaroid Postcarders and suitable pictures. Postcarder with protective cover is at top left. When used with prints from Highlander cameras, border of protective material remains (lower left). Prints from big cameras cover entire Postcarder (right).

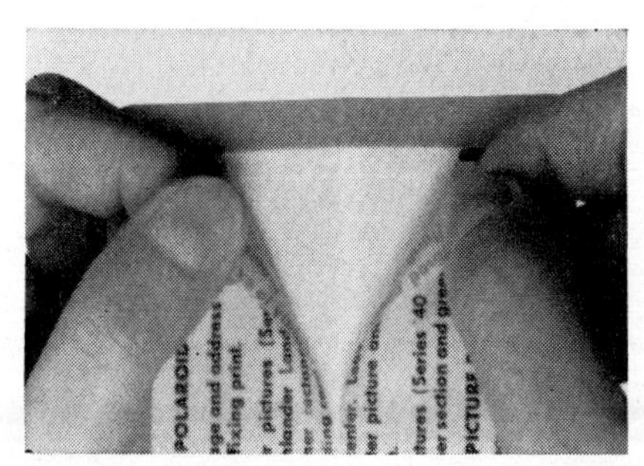

REMOVE THE COVER: It's in two pieces. Only inner rectangle is removed for prints from Highlander. For larger prints strip off green border, too. Full instructions are on each Postcarder.

WRITE FIRST: Do all writing on Postcarders before joining them to prints; if not, pressure from pencil or ball point pen can cause writing marks on face of picture, may break coating.

TRAVEL

Your Polaroid Land camera offers unique advantages on a vacation or business trip.

MOST PEOPLE carry cameras when they travel, but not everybody comes back with pictures. You probably know someone who came home from a trip with a batch of films, sent them off for developing, and only when they were returned discovered that the camera had a light leak, or the shutter was out of order, or they should have extended the lens, or some other horrible mistake had ruined half the lot.

There is only one camera with which this cannot happen. When you see the picture in a minute you *know* you took it right (or wrong). And if it's wrong, it's a simple matter to correct it on the spot and get it right.

If this were its *only* advantage, the Polaroid Land camera would still be a powerful contender for the title: "The traveler's companion." But beyond the security of *knowing you have the picture*, the camera offers other unique advantages that make it an ideal choice for many people who are going on trips.

Want to meet people?

Let's suppose that you are alone on a cruise, or at a resort, and it's the usual too short vacation. There is no faster, surer way of meeting people than to unlimber a Polaroid Land camera and start shooting. Does she (or he) look well on a horse? Snap it, and show her (or him) the picture in a minute. The wonder of it never fails to start a conversation. "Would she (or he) like to try one?" Why, of course.

Start flashing away at a party or dance and you'll be overwhelmed by people who were strangers just a few moments ago.

Travelers in distant communities often are afraid to take pictures of the people there—they sense a feeling of resentment. But all people like to see pictures of themselves, and no one has discovered a place in which the "locals" fail to be fascinated by the wonder of the picture in a minute. There is no question about it—when you want to "break the ice," nothing can match the Polaroid Land camera. Few people who travel, even in their own state, or in other parts of the U.S.A., ever get to know many residents of the communities they visit. Invest a few rolls of Land film in a "make friends" project and you'll be amazed at the results.

How to open doors

Your pictures are potent for other purposes, too. A snapshot of a flight hostess, deck steward, purser, ticket agent or a member of the local constabulary, can make the difference between stand-off accommodation and friendly help. At least two young men have traveled halfway

◁ **KEEP A RECORD** of every place you go, all the wonderful things you see. Having your picture in a minute lets you know that it "came out" right. All the pictures in this chapter were made with Polaroid Land films. Here, Type 42 would be a good choice; to silhouette the dark shapes, expose for the bright areas (EV 16 or 17).

FRITZ HENLE

SEND HOME PICTURES: Tucked in with a letter or attached to a Postcarder, such a snapshot will give the home folks much more pleasure than an ordinary postcard. You can usually find someone willing to snap the shutter for you, or maybe your camera has a self-timer which lets you get into the picture too.

around the world, trading pictures made in a minute for lodging, transportation, and food. We don't recommend it, but it *has* been done.

Of course, a lot depends upon how you go about it—no one wants to feel that he's being traded a snapshot for some extra service. But no matter where you are, a fine picture, presented in a friendly, straightforward manner, will help to establish friendly contact.

Traveling businessmen know the importance of such contacts, and many of them carry a Polaroid Land camera for exactly that purpose. There is no surer, better way to leave a friendly memory with a person than to take his (or her) picture and leave it with him (or her). Next time you pass that way, that person will remember you.

Send them in letters

What a difference between getting a hastily written letter or run-of-the-mill postcard, and an actual photo of someone you know in a distant setting! Look at the picture of the two girls (*left*) with the Eiffel Tower in the distance. This spells "Paris" and travel, and having fun, more than any ready-made card ever could. It saves you time and writing, and it reassures the family at home by giving evidence that you're well and having a good time. A particularly convenient and novel way to do this is to use the Polaroid Postcarders.

How to travel with a camera

By all odds, the best way to transport your camera and accessories is in a regular carrying case. Polaroid Corp. has a variety of sturdily made compartment cases designed to hold the various camera models and their particular accessories.

Which accessories to take? Certainly the exposure meter, filter kit, close-up kit, and wink-light, so you'll be ready for any kind of outdoor or indoor picture opportunity. Also, you ought to have your lens brush and a locking cable release.

Of course, you don't have to carry all this with you all the time. You can leave the case in your hotel room with items you're sure not to need for a day's outing. Or, you can just leave the "not now" items in the room, fill the case with film and take it along.

The film supply

There's no denying that packages of Polaroid Land film are bulky, and you may wonder about carrying a big supply. This is not as much of a problem as it might appear at first.

Let's consider the usual two-week domestic vacation. If your destination is near some large community with camera stores, you're sure to find Polaroid Land film there, so you need carry only enough for the trip.

If you're off to a resort by train, bus, or air, and are doubtful as to the opportunity of getting into a town with a camera store, it's still no problem. Have your photo dealer mail a supply of film on ahead, but be sure to do this sufficiently in advance so it's there when you arrive.

Of course, if it's a trip by car there's no difficulty. Just pile everything in, with at least 50 per cent more film than you think you can possibly use. But, don't leave film and camera in the car trunk, or in a tight locked car, broiling in the sun for hours. The heat can damage the film, and it doesn't help the camera.

Many people go off for the entire summer to remote beach or mountain spots, or to work in camps. Same thing as for a two-week vacation—if you're near a large town with a camera store, film's available. Otherwise, arrange with your local photo dealer (or one closer to the vacation spot) to supply you with film by mail.

With 3000 speed film and a wink-light for indoor shots there's no need to worry about supplies of flashbulbs. And the tiny AG-1 bulbs for the wink-light flasher #256 are so small that it's easy to carry a good supply. If you're toting a flashgun, No. 5 bulbs are widely available.

Problems of foreign travel

Once you leave the U.S.A., the film supply situation is entirely different. There should be film available in photo stores in the major cities and resorts in the Western Hemisphere. Elsewhere, however, you cannot count on getting film.

For information as to whether or not Polaroid Land films can be had in Europe, Asia, The Far East, and other places, write to Customer Service, Polaroid Corp., Cambridge 39, Mass. List the countries you intend to visit, and approximately when; also give some idea of the amount of film you are likely to require. You'll get the latest information and will then know whether you should take all or just part of your film supply with you.

You should also communicate with the consulate or tourist office of the countries on your itinerary. Ask how much film can be brought in by travelers; also whether or not it is possible to have film mailed to that country from the U.S.A. There are all sorts of regulations which vary from country to country and are subject to change. You will probably find liberal rules in the countries which most American tourists visit. However, it pays to be sure, so inquire.

JOHN ROSS

MAKE FRIENDS: So you photograph a couple of strangers. Then you develop the picture, right then, and show it to them. They like to see themselves; you explain the way it's done. This leads to more pictures. Soon they are no longer strangers. 200 speed film used for these photos.

SHIPBOARD FUN: Cruises and ocean crossings end quickly. Make a record of the good times you were having and the nice people you met.

J. W.

What kind of pictures?

What makes travel exciting? You see new places, new people, have novel experiences. The pictures of your trip should carry the story of why your trip was a wonderful success. The people you met, the places you enjoyed most, the things you did—record them all. *And be sure that a good percentage of the pictures include you and your companions in the act of enjoying yourselves.*

You'll find loads of picture taking ideas, as suitable for travel as for home, in the chapters following.

OUTDOOR PICTURE

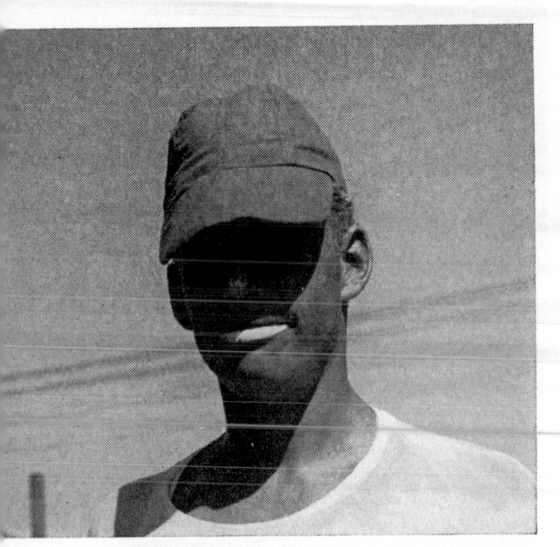

NOT THIS: Perfect bad example of high noon, bright sun snapshot. Avoid this by using natural or artificial reflector to throw light into shadows, or turn subject so face is in bright shade, or do both, as demonstrated in photo below.

Bright sun portraits.

Bright sun is a poor light for portraits, unless you know ways to control it.

Manufacture bright shade, simply by turning your subjects around so their faces are out of the direct rays. Let the harsh light hit their hair, glance off a cheekbone or ear. But keep the eyes and main features in the soft light of bright shade. EV 14 and 15 will be good settings with PolaPan 200 and 400. Use a lens shade. If using the photoelectric shutter, keep direct sun out of the light cell, or you'll get underexposed pictures.

White sand, concrete pavements, light walls, are all excellent natural reflectors, will project light into heavy shadows, if you place your subject nearby. Or, use a white sheet, cardboard, crumpled metal foil. Even a newspaper can help a lot.

PETER BASCH

BRIGHT SHADE, NATURAL REFLECTOR: Sun is just as bright and high here as in picture above, but girl was turned so brilliant rays merely add sparkle to her hair. She's resting on hood of light-colored car which reflects soft light into her face.

To convert numbers on older model cameras to EV numbers add 9.

TAKING IDEAS

PETER GOWLAND ▷

◁ FRITZ HENLE

FACES UP OR TURNED AWAY: At right, face is up-tilted just enough to get shadows out of eyes which, of course, must be closed. With low sun, turn your model's eyes into shade (left). Bring exposure meter close, to avoid getting direct sun in light cell. Expose for shaded side, or give "average" exposure —halfway between readings for bright and dark sides.

HARSH PORTRAIT: Same shadows which would be disadvantage in full-face portrait are put to use as dramatic accents in unusual profile. To get this near, you must use close-up lens. With photoelectric shutter on camera, you can come almost as close as this, but not quite, without close-up lens, which cannot be used in conjunction with photoelectric shutter.

HAROLD FEINSTEIN

BRIGHT HAZY DAY: Best kind of light for outdoor portraits. It's bright (you can use EV 15, 16, 17) but soft; gives plenty of modeling, without harsh, unpleasing shadows.

△ HAROLD FEINSTEIN ▽

REFLECTORS are important in dim light, too. Newspaper bounced fading twilight into elderly reader's face. Even at dusk this would be an easy-to-take snapshot with 3000 speed film.

PETER BASCH

IN THE CAR there's plenty of light, plus an exposure problem. Don't let bright sun outside lead meter astray; take reading close to face, expose for shaded areas. You could take this easily with any Polaroid Land film.

Portraits in any light.

The high speed of the new Polaroid Land films adds tremendous scope to your picture taking—almost any kind of daylight is good enough. Here are six examples of what can be done; none of them presents a difficult picture taking problem.

Of course, you can't shoot at twilight with the same settings as in bright shade, but that's what exposure meters are for. And you'll find that when shooting under widely varying kinds of illumination, the ability to see the picture in a minute is an enormous asset—if you don't get exactly the desired result the first time, take it again, right then.

You'll discover new excitement in picture taking when you try portraits under lighting conditions similar to those shown.

PETER BASCH

WINDOW MAKES FRAME for rainy day portrait; drops on glass tell story. Face is raised to catch maximum of dim light, cause soft shadows; without these, picture would be "flat."

GRAY, FOGGY DAY: Light is so even that fully lit face is likely to be shadowless, uninteresting. Have subject turn or tilt head until soft shadows appear. Incidentally, filters will do nothing for sky in such weather. ▽

J.W.

GROUPS: Snap them in bright shade; in direct sun, strong shadows are all over faces, any head turning complicates matters. In bright shade, people can look anywhere, still be well lit. In dappled light, as here, expose for brightly lit face to get detail in features; wide range of new Land films (200 speed here) will easily record bright shade detail.

HAROLD FEINSTEIN

HAROLD FEINSTEIN

MAKE A CHOICE: Correct exposure for both shaded foreground and brilliant background was impossible. Choice was for shadows; highlights are overexposed. But it could be reversed—highlights correct, shadows underexposed.

J. W.

PSEUDO NIGHT: "Moon" is actually late afternoon sun. Exposure was for highlights only—sun and glinting wavelets. Other areas are heavily underexposed. Try EV 17 with orange filter, plus polarizing filter, over lens (see *Filters*).

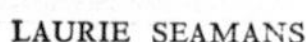

LAURIE SEAMANS

BACKLIGHT: High light source and lens shade keep direct rays out of lens. Unless you want silhouette, expose correctly for shaded side.

Light, exposure, mood.

These three factors are completely intertwined in a fine photograph. Alter either lighting or exposure and the mood of the picture will change. In turn, you can change the mood by altering one or both of the other factors. This is easy to do; the results can be startling.

You have to make a choice sometimes, and this is where pictures in a minute offer unique advantages. You can shoot the scene one way, study the print in a minute, decide whether or not you like it that way. If not, you are still at the spot and can reshoot. That is the beginning of creative photography. After you have done this a number of times, under widely varying conditions, you'll begin to know instinctively how to light and expose to create a certain mood and you can use your exposure meter to best advantage.

FRED PLAUT

DAY AND NIGHT scenes of same subject provide interesting contrasts. For day scene, try EV 16 o
Night shot would require time exposure, steady support such as tripod or car hood with PolaPan
or 400, but with 3000 speed film it's a snapshot. If buildings have lighted windows (but no floodlight
best results are had at late dusk, when there is still light in sky to outline structures.

J.V

SKYWRITING is usually done against clear blue sky to make letters stand out. Treat it like clouds—always use an orange filter for maximum effect. But picture needs more than just sky and writing. Here silhouettes of man and railing pattern were used to add dramatic punch to scene.

J.W. ◁

JOHN COLLIER, STANDARD OIL CO. (N. J.) ▽

HOLIDAY SEASON: You'll see this in thousands of communities; be sure to make your shot after snowfall. Snow is excellent reflector, bounces light into areas that would otherwise be dark. Time exposure, or 3000 speed film.

COOK-OUT: There's lots of light in that fire, but subjects must be pretty close, as above. Use 3000 speed film, try EV 10, 11, 12, with and without the wink-light. Even if someone moves slightly, it won't matter.

JACQUES LOWE

FLASH INTO NIGHT is special problem. For close subjects (6 to 10 ft.) exposure is just about same as if indoors in large room, so follow flash exposure guide (see *Flash*). At greater ranges, as here, set camera one number lower than recommended by flash guide.

Light and the night.

Years ago, anyone who could turn up with a good outdoor night picture was thought to be pretty skillful with his camera. Now, with 3000 speed film, a whole new world of photography is open to you.

Unfortunately, there are no hard and fast rules or techniques for outdoor night pictures—the conditions are too varied. Under some conditions even the ultra-sensitive #625 exposure meter may be of little value. However, that's no great problem with *your* camera. With the result before your eyes in a minute, it's a simple matter to change exposure, focus, or composition to get a certain effect.

With PolaPan 200 or 400 film snapshots may not be possible, so try the techniques described in *Time Exposures*.

AFTER RAIN is one of best times for night pictures. Pavements reflect lights; if they are really wet, beautiful patterns occur. Picture was made at dusk, when there was still enough light to separate objects from sky. Without this, scene would lose much of its interest. ▷

JOHN R. WHITING

COMBINATION: Direct flash at camera lighted men, horse, and building exterior; brief time exposure afterward recorded lights in building and under shed. You can use same technique to photograph your home at night.

HAROLD FEINSTEIN

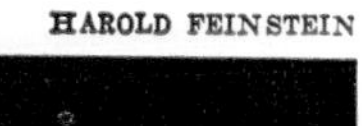

DICK WOLTERS

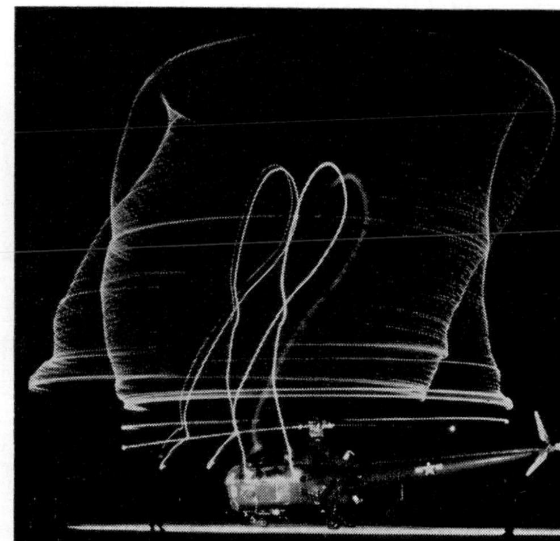

MOVING LIGHTS: Looks difficult, but really isn't. To record patterns such as these, you need dark background, moving light or lights, camera on tripod or other support, set at EV 10 or 11, with shutter open for time exposure. These lights were on rotor tips of helicopter which took off, hovered, landed. Principle is same for moving car headlights, or track of flashlight waved in air. See *Time Exposures*.

CARL K. SHIRAISHI ▷

J. W.

CLOUDS OVER WATER: For brightly lit marine scenes always use orange filter to darken sky and water, emphasize sails and clouds.

ARCHITECTURAL subjects look best with side-lighting to cause shadows, bring out form of structure. Use orange filter to darken shadows, add contrast. Try setting EV 15 or 16.

J. W.

SUN BEHIND CLOUDS produces dramatic sky effects; catch them with orange filter and expose for brightest area (setting EV 16 or 17). All objects in shade of cloud will be underexposed and silhouetted against bright sky.

Ways to better scenics.

Everybody who has ever had a camera has tried to take scenic pictures with it. For most people this has been a singularly disappointing experience. Somehow, the scene in the print never looks quite as grand as it did to the eye. This need not be so, as the pictures on these four pages show; even though they are reproduced in modest size, each is a strong, simple statement about a certain combination of place and time.

That is an important point about scenics —keep them simple. Don't try to photograph a whole forest or city—concentrate on a few trees or buildings, or a silhouette that says "city" or "forest," as in the New York skyline on page 134.

Filters are indispensable for scenics, particularly the orange #4. Film? Polaroid PolaPan 200 and 400 are the best choices for outdoor pictures.

FOREGROUND INTEREST is important in scenes which have main objects of interest in distance. At left, scene is static, foreground adds nothing to picture. Then photographer noticed youngsters at right, moved his camera, produced charming result. Generally, foreground objects add most interest if at bottom or sides of print rather than at top, but there are no hard and fast "rules" about this.

SNOW AND ICE provide exciting picture material, particularly if bright sun provides strong cross- or backlighting. Remember: It's cold, and development time must be adjusted accordingly. For information about this, see instruction in film package, and also *The Films*.

PHOTOS BY CARL K. SHIRAISHI

MORE ON SCENICS

TED RUSSELL

LOW HORIZON: If scene includes spectacular sky, tilt camera up slightly to take advantage. Ground objects will tilt in a bit, but who cares? Orange filter, of course.

J. W.

CONVERGING LINES which draw eye from foreground to distant, tiny object always make for strong picture. Here, foreground is most important, camera is aimed low, horizon is high.

EDWARD BURKS

FRAMING distant scene with foreground silhouette gives sense of depth to view which would be meaningless without it. Girl's outline at side adds element of interest. Concentrate on getting foreground sharp; hills are so distant and hazy that detail there is unimportant.

CARL K. SHIRAISHI

TWO VIEWS OF SAME SUBJECT may vary widely, according to location of camera, lighting, angle. Why limit yourself to only one approach? Start with long shot, then come in close; shoot against light, pick out details and record them. You'll find that single simple subject can provide material for whole afternoon of interesting shooting if you try out various camera viewpoints.

BAD WEATHER is no reason to put away camera. On dull gray day, snow is textureless, flat (compare with page 133) and by itself would make poor subject. To get "tone" into snow and provide maximum contrast with dark objects (trees, footpath), base exposure on reading from snow itself. As with picture opposite, concentrate on sharp focus and correct exposure for foreground, where detail should be visible.

CARL K. SHIRAISHI

A new look at action.

To many people, photographing action means only one thing—stopping it dead. And you can do that now by adding to your camera the Photoelectric Shutter #440. In brightest sunlight it can produce shutter speeds as high as 1/1000 sec.

But what if you don't have that accessory? How much action can you stop with 1/100 sec.? That's the top shutter speed on all current Polaroid Land cameras except the Model 110A, which has shutter speeds to 1/300 sec.

For all ordinary picture taking, 1/100 sec. will stop a lot of action, particularly if you carefully choose instant and angle as shown in the two photos on this page.

But why freeze *all* action? Its very essence is movement, and the most exciting action pictures are those which give this impression of movement. Look at the pictures on the opposite page. Would any one of them have been improved if the photographer had decided to use a higher shutter speed?

PEAK ACTION: What goes up must come down, but before it comes down it will be motionless for brief moment. Shoot then to stop action.

△ HAROLD FEINSTEIN ▽

TAKE AN ANGLE: Fast moving objects are most difficult to stop when they pass at right angles to camera (top of opposite page), easiest to stop when coming head-on. For firsthand information on this, snap series of moving traffic stream from various angles of approach. You'll be amazed at variety of results possible.

ERNEST G. SCARFONE

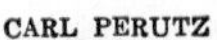

CARL PERUTZ

IMPRESSION OF SPEED is most pronounced when some part of picture is blurred by movement; photos in which all action has been "frozen" rarely give you feeling of rapid motion. Here are two ways of saying "speed." At left, camera was held steady while race car hurtled out of view far too rapidly for shutter to stop it. At right, camera was "panned" (turned) to follow course of fast rolling cycle, dissolving background in process. Techniques could have been reversed—girl might have been blurred against sharp background, car could have been sharp on blurred crowd.

EDWARD BURKS

IMPRESSION of people in rush is easy to produce. All you need is brief time exposure (one second or less) to register their movements. Do it when light is such that EV 11 or 12 would give correct snapshot exposure. Instead, turn control to EV 17 or 18, or set shutter to "B," make time exposure. If necessary, add orange and/or polarizing filter to reduce amount of light entering lens. Camera must be on tripod or some other steady support.

PETER GOWLAND

EMPHASIZE SMALLNESS by pointing camera down at tiny subject. Ordinarily, children and pets are best pictured at "eye level," but this is example of picture which might have been ruined by conventional approach.

Look up, look down.

Plenty of paper has been covered with instructions to *always* hold the camera straight and level. That's a good recipe for dull pictures. True, accidental tipping of the camera can make a botch of a "straight and level" scene. But many subjects just have to be photographed with the camera pointing up or down. And those are good directions in which to look for interesting picture possibilities.

Here's an important point to remember when snapping buildings or monuments. If you aim the camera up, perspective will be distorted, and buildings will tilt inwards. If buildings tilt slightly, it usually looks like an accident. However, if you point the camera up so sharply that they tilt an alarming amount, and if the effect appears to have been caused deliberately, you are being "creative."

H. W. HANNAU

PETER GOWLAND

RECLINING FIGURE is most easily photographed from elevation. Four simple tricks add much to this picture: diagonal placement, "S" curve of figure, separation of feet, straight line from shin to pointed toes.

PICTURES OF SIGNS can form wonderful record of time and place. Here, shape and pattern are most important and silhouette against bright sky is best technique. Where main interest is in words or illustration, take reading of that with exposure meter, set camera accordingly.

DELIBERATE DISTORTION can play important part in adding drama or humor to picture. Here, by coming close, nose is emphasized and appears much larger in relation to rest of head. By placing hand and carrot in same plane as end of nose, photographer was able to focus sharply on all three.

BEAUTY UNDERFOOT is often ignored by hurrying snapshooters. Wild flowers, small plants, sea shells, interesting rocks, all make good subjects. For these, close-up lens is needed.

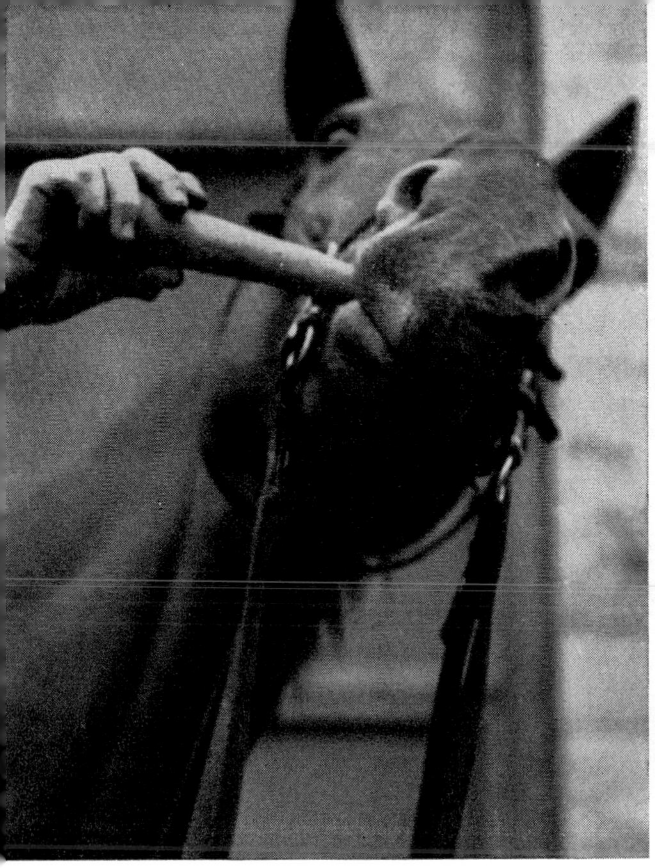

BURT OWEN

CARL K. SHIRAISHI

HIGH PEOPLE are special problem. For better view of face, head must be bent; this puts features in shade, requires accurate use of exposure meter. Be careful to avoid distortion of feet and legs, which will be much closer to camera than face. Here, girl is leaning over rail at sharp angle; lower part of her body was placed back from railing to keep it out of picture.

ANITA EKBERG, BY PETER BASCH

J.W.

PATTERN: This picture draws almost its entire interest from pattern of light and shade. If arches were flatly lit, as they would be at different hour, this would be merely another dull record of masonry (to emphasize architectural shadows, use orange or red filter). You can find fascinating patterns in nature, in groups of people, in buildings, in piles of materials and equipment—they are everywhere, if you but look for them.

Making an eye-stopper.

If you dissect these pictures and examine the separate parts, you may be surprised at the commonplace subject matter. Only one (the cat and dog) depended on the element of chance. None of them involved anything more technical than getting correct exposure and using a filter. Why are these eye-stoppers?

One reason is that they are simple; despite their small size, each tells its story well. For the rest, it just amounts to careful picture taking with due regard to principles so obvious that most of us usually ignore them. But you won't be able to ignore them very long when you start making pictures in a minute. You'll see immediately how the picture can be improved, and you'll have both the desire and the opportunity to do so, right then.

SCALE: Big and little are only relative terms, without meaning unless you supply some basis for measurement. This simple-to-take picture has impact because its terms of measurement are stated clearly and in an uncomplicated manner.

BURT OWEN ▷

◁ WM. R. HEICK

▽ JOHN VACHON, STANDARD OIL CO. (N. J.)

CONTRAST: You may never find subjects as perfectly placed as in photo at left, but this picture illustrates one important principle: Separate subjects from background by contrast. What would happen if cat and dog exchanged places? Take advantage of surroundings, areas of light and shade, choice of angle, to make separation certain. Often, you can manufacture contrast by use of filters, as at right, where sky was darkened to make white subject stand out (see *Filters*).

CONCENTRATION OF INTEREST: Lines which lead (or drag) eye to single point of interest are powerful compositional element. Here, everything is subordinated to that purpose; even steps have been reduced to mere zigzag stripe by carefully chosen edge-on viewpoint. Composition of this type is most effective when point of interest is off-center. Even without dog, this would be eye-stopping photo.

PETER BASCH

MASS: Junked truck becomes dramatic subject. How? Mainly by low, close viewpoint which exaggerates height and width, adds to feeling of weight and power. Strong lighting, heavy shadows help, too. All this applies to pictures of any massive subject.

BURT OWEN

ISOLATION results from unconventional subject placement, plus careful exposure meter use. Exposure was based on reading of child's dark, sun-tanned skin, to assure full shadow detail. Thus, white sand is somewhat overexposed, little detail is visible; child's figure stands out.

J. W.

REFLECTIONS: They'll come out best when subject (building reflected in glass) is lit brightly. Reflecting surface (showroom window, here) should be out of direct sun. For sharp reflected image, set lens focus for total distance from camera to reflecting surface to subject (infinity, here). Picture data: Type 42 film, EV 12.

"Different" pictures.

The only thing "different" about these pictures is in the ideas that created them. Place the little girl plumb center in the print and you have the duplicate of many you've seen before. Snap the truck from eye level and 20 ft. distant, and it's just another pile of junk. Come down on the sand and ask the man to "hold it" and what have you?

This is the field of creative photography —taking everyday, garden variety subject matter and turning it into something special, without a single technical trick.

This is the kind of work which you can do best with pictures in a minute. You can *see* the result while you are still on the spot; you *know* whether or not you have the picture; you can do it over again, *right now*, if it's not exactly as you think it ought to be.

PETER BASCH

STORMY SKIES make fine pictures. Trick is to expose for bright areas (set to EV 15, 16, or 17 depending upon light). Then all other sky areas will be dark and threatening in contrast. Here, feeling is enhanced by wet concrete apron on which planes are standing.

HAROLD FEINSTEIN

IMPORTANT SHADOW: Look for subjects like this in early morning or late afternoon when sun is low. Be sure to set camera for correct exposure in highlight areas (EV 15, 16, 17) so shadows will be dark and strong; for even more contrast, use orange filter.

OUTFITS: Kids wear strange rigs—coonskin hats, cowboy suits, space helmets, baseball uniforms. They carry giant pistols and other weapons ranging from medieval to supersonic. All this is great picture material. Don't miss it!

A time to remember.

Have you looked at many pictures of children in family albums? Pretty bad, most of them. True, you can frequently identify the subject, but that's about all. There's no breath of life; there's little that tells you what kind of boy or girl that was. And in later years, even parents can forget much of that period. Don't let that happen with *your* youngsters.

Start now to keep a record of everything they do. Snap them at play, with friends, around the house, on all "occasions" such as birthdays, or starting on the first Scout hike.

You'll get more out of this project than just wonderful pictures. In the process, you'll be learning more about your children by sharing activities and experiences with them. And no one has yet found children who aren't fascinated at the prospect of seeing themselves in pictures in a minute. First thing you know, they'll be snapping you, too. And why not? It's easy enough with this camera.

IMPRESSION: No need to spell everything out in detail. This says "winter sports" just as clearly as if she zoomed by on ice. And it has lost none of its charm because her face is invisible.

PHOTOS BY BURT OWEN
EXCEPT AS INDICATED

LOW ANGLE: You don't have to get on your knees for this; let that active youngster leap onto bench or boulder. This problem is common to all makes of eye-level cameras.

KIDS AND ANIMALS: Greatest combination for heart-warming snapshots of children. Don't pose them—just bring them together and let nature take its course. And, snap that look of wariness, or wonder, that's bound to come when child meets horse, or is introduced to first deer or elephant at zoo.

JOHN COLLIER, STANDARD OIL CO. (N.J.)

HOBBIES: Couple of amateur geologists at work. Whatever your youngster's hobby is, be sure you have pictures of him (or her) at it. And he (or she) will find pictures in a minute helpful in keeping track of collections.

CARL K. SHIRAISHI

ACTION: Snapping kids in full flight is no mean feat. One way is to pre-focus camera for certain distance, wait until action flows your way, then shoot. For more helpful hints on shooting action, see pages 136 and 137.

PICTURE FUN IN YOUR SOCIAL LIFE

Pictures in a minute can add fun to your social life in so many ways that we couldn't possibly list them all. Here are just a few ideas.

Next time you have a party, be sure to invite your Polaroid Land camera. No matter what the activity, pictures in a minute will help to stir things up, keep them moving, "break ice" between strangers, start plenty of talk.

Snap your guests laughing, dancing, singing, dining—doing almost anything or nothing. Pass the prints around, or stick them up in some central spot.

Games, anyone? The most serious charade is likely to break up in a laugh riot when you present a print of someone "acting out" before the charade is finished.

Want to make a hit with the sponsors of your next local charity or church bazaar? Offer your services and camera for a "gag" shot setup like that shown opposite. It's really amazing how people will flock to such a booth, and pay willingly. Before you start, make some tests to be sure that the focus is sharp, exposure correct, and that the light(s) will give the effect you desire. Have a table or counter at which an assistant can coat prints, open rolls of film, collect money. If you don't own a speed light, you can probably rent or borrow one from your local photo dealer for the occasion.

Many people like to make up personalized greeting cards built around a family portrait. Pictures in a minute are perfect for this, for you can keep at it until just the right print turns up. In case you happen to be shy about putting a picture of yourself on the card, why not build it around some fine seasonal snapshot which you took? Send the print to Polaroid Corp. for a copy negative, from which your local photo dealer will make up quantities of any of a variety of cards.

GUEST BOOKS AND AUTOGRAPH ALBUMS take on new meaning and value when they also include the signer's picture. Years from now such photos will revive many memories. Keep prints in Polaroid Land Picture Albums. *Signature should be on album paper, never on prints.*

JACQUES LOWE

CHARITY BAZAARS: Want to raise money, fast? Set up humorous prop with cutout for one or two heads. This is most easily done outdoors with daylight exposure; indoors, speed light is best light source, with floods next. Prints will be popular at 50 cents or $1 each.

PERSONAL GREETING CARDS: What could be better for holiday season, party invitations, social announcements of all kinds? Shoot them with a self timer, or have an assistant click the shutter. Try 3000 speed film, with existing light plus wink-light, or bounce flash.

PICTURE LETTERS: Say "Hello" to far-away relatives or friends; include in "thank you" letter after receiving gift or visiting; wonderful tonic for convalescents and "shut-ins" you can't visit. Postcarders are fun, too. Try some, soon.

PLACE CARDS: Snap pictures of arriving guests, surprise them later with prints set out as place cards. Guaranteed to start dinner conversation, and welcome as souvenirs. Or, after dinner put them in guest book (opposite page).

INDOOR PICTURE

J. W.

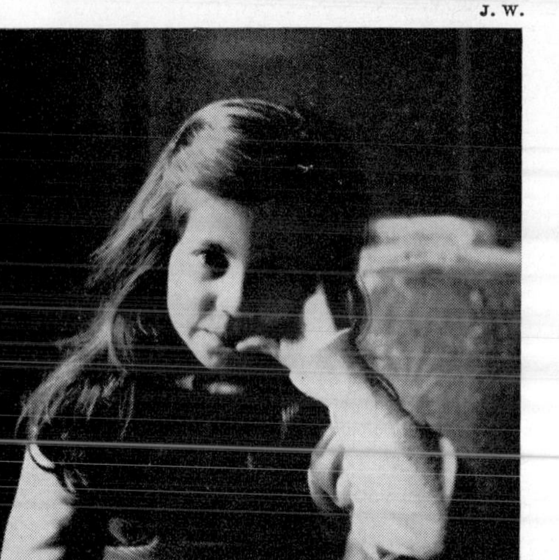

WINDOW LIGHT, WITH SHADOWS: This is common situation. If shadows are too deep, use wink-light, or big reflector, such as white sheet over cardboard, or mirror.

People and windows.

Some of the greatest portraits ever made were done by diffused "north" light streaming in a window. You'll find it an exciting and challenging light source to work with. Bright sun, on the other hand, is just as troublesome inside the house as it is outdoors. However, you can tame it somewhat with white curtains or other diffusing material.

The main problem in window portraiture is usually the background, which is likely to be cluttered. If you have a clear wall, that's fine. If not, try to arrange a simple drape, or a large sheet of white or gray (or brown) paper. To get variety into your window portraits, you should also be able to control the background illumination. This is most easily done with a single flood lamp. By moving it closer to or further from the background, you can get almost any degree of brightness. The other big problem is face shadows. Some of the pictures show different ways to use, control, or eliminate them.

JACQUES LOWE

AGAINST LIGHT: Two good ways to do this. Take meter reading of shaded side; set exposure control one number higher than recommended by meter. This gives semi-silhouette effect shown. Or, add wink-light, and with same camera setting described above shadows will be somewhat lighter.

TAKING IDEAS

JEAN SIMMONS, BY PETER BASCH

WINDOW LIGHT, MINIMUM SHADOWS: Place camera between subject and window, as here. For stronger shadows (left, and below, right) move camera to side, have subject turn head. Light is usually bright enough for snapshots; use meter. Here, low angle has eliminated background.

JOHN R. WHITING

WINDOW SILHOUETTE is simple, but dramatic effects can be achieved. Exterior light must not touch near side of face. Set camera so bright background is correctly exposed.

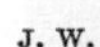

J. W.

WINDOW SPOTLIGHT: Here, camera is aimed at about right angle to direction of light. Subject should face light, but turn just enough to cause shadows, as desired.

CARL K. SHIRAISHI

FORMAL PORTRAIT: two flood lamps provided simple-to-use lighting for this excellent picture. Text at right explains setup.

Lighting for portraits.

Most of your pictures of people indoors will have to be taken with illumination other than daylight. With 3000 speed film, using the existing room light plus the wink-light and auxiliary flasher, you'll be able to get the picture under almost any conditions. However, there are definite limits to the variety of lightings possible with the wink-light and flash. That's where floods offer great possibilities for interesting portraits. With 3000 speed film, elaborate or hard to handle floodlighting equipment is no longer necessary. How to choose and use the lamps is explained in *Floods.*

For the portrait at left, one lamp high and to right provided the main light. Another, behind and above the subject, outlined the top of her head. Below are two other imaginative uses of floods, and in the chapter on *Floods,* you'll see several additional, simple but interesting, flood lightings. Try them all. You'll see the results in a minute, and both you and your subject will have a lot of fun.

J.W.

SIMULATE ROOM LIGHT: Main light could have come from floor lamp; actually, one flood was held high and to right. Stronger bulb was installed in table lamp for light to separate background from outline of head.

LAURIE WIENER ▽ J.W. ▷

SILHOUETTE: All you need is single flood aimed at plain wall, and willing subject to pose between camera and lighted wall. Pictures in a minute make this old-time party stunt more fun than it ever was before.

JACQUES LOWE

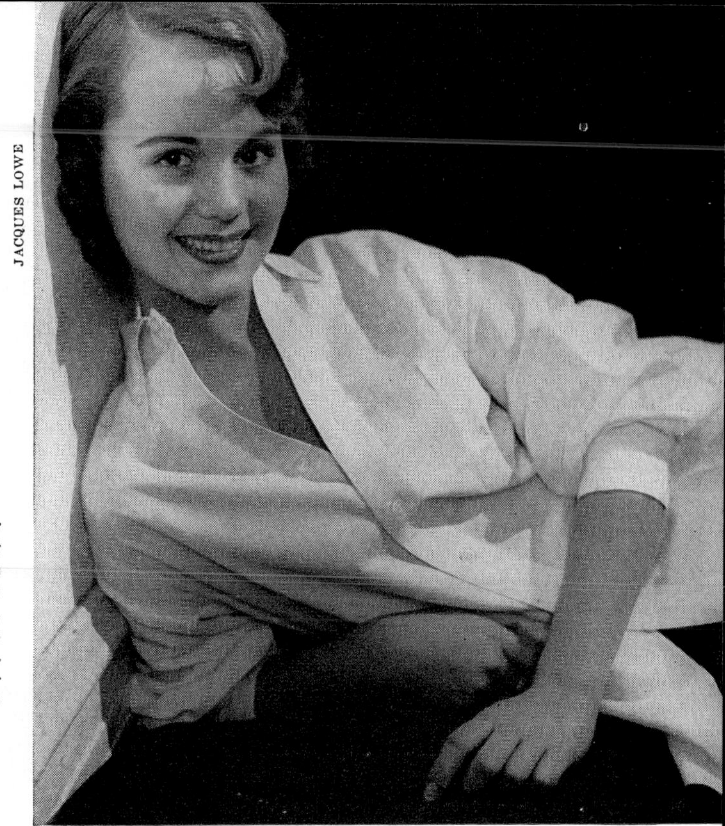

BOUNCE FLASH is fine for informal portraits. Use it when there's not enough room illumination for shooting with the existing light. The soft, even light of bounce flash is superior to that of direct flash, or illumination by the wink-light used alone. *See Flash* and *The Wink-light.*

AVAILABLE LIGHT: If you want to try this pipe-lighting pose, be sure to have additional light sources; if not, only small area of face will be illuminated. Here, most light came from bright gas lantern high and to left. With 3000 speed film, this would be a fairly easy snapshot.

MORRIS GORDON

REMOTE SPEED LIGHT: This is one way of getting distant view of group and surroundings while keeping flash close enough to group for proper lighting. Long extension cord connects speed light inside room with camera outside window. (See *Speed Light* for details.)

Tips on group shots.

Flash (conventional or speed light) is virtually a must for all indoor group pictures. The only exception might be in a room which was flooded with daylight. Even if you were able to line up enough floods to light your subjects fully, such a setup would be awkward to handle and uncomfortable for the group. Certainly, bounce flash is the method to use around the house. Use 3000 speed film with AG-1 bulbs in the auxiliary flasher of the wink-light or, with other films, No. 5 or Press 25 bulbs in the Polaroid flashgun with bounce flash bracket (see *Flash*).

What kind of pictures? Every kind—anytime you have a social or family group of any sort, that's a good subject. Snap them when there's plenty going on—people laughing, singing, eating, talking. And what excitement there will be when all those people see themselves in a print a minute after you snap the shutter! It's really a great party attraction.

NOT THIS: People slumped on couches or in easy chairs won't look their best in head-on pictures. Trouble is that feet are much closer to camera than heads, and are exaggerated.

LEONARD BALISH

THIS IS BETTER: Ask subjects to sit upright, and close to front of couch. Or, shoot from side, so that even if sprawled, entire body is about equidistant from camera.

J. W.

DIRECT FLASH is best in public places where rooms are very large, or if ceilings are high and dark. Shoot from high angle, if possible. Calculate exposure for flash aimed at center of group so as to get fairly even light distribution at all points.

BOUNCE FLASH: Use it wherever ceilings are light and of ordinary height, rooms are of moderate size. There is no better light source for snapshots of groups in average home settings.

PETER GOWLAND

PETER BASCH

INTERIORS: In public buildings, time exposure is best method to use (see text). Here, walls lean because camera was titlted up. In home, try time exposure or bounce flash.

Interiors, action, stage.

You'll be pleasantly surprised at how easily your Land camera can produce beautiful pictures of interiors of public buildings or private homes. You need: 3000 speed film; a tripod or other support; a time exposure.

The main problem will be to get everything in sharp focus from foreground to background. This is less troublesome in a large building, such as a church, than in a room of average size. For maximum near and far sharpness, you need the small lens openings provided by settings EV 15, 16, 17. Where it's 100 ft. or more to the most distant important object, set the focus to 25 ft.; where the far point is about 50 ft. away, focus at 15 ft. Sometimes, overall sharpness will be impossible, and you'll have to favor one area, leaving the rest unsharp. This is called selective focus. The most striking results are had at settings like EV 10 and 11, which give a minimum amount of near to far sharpness. Try it.

JACQUES LOWE

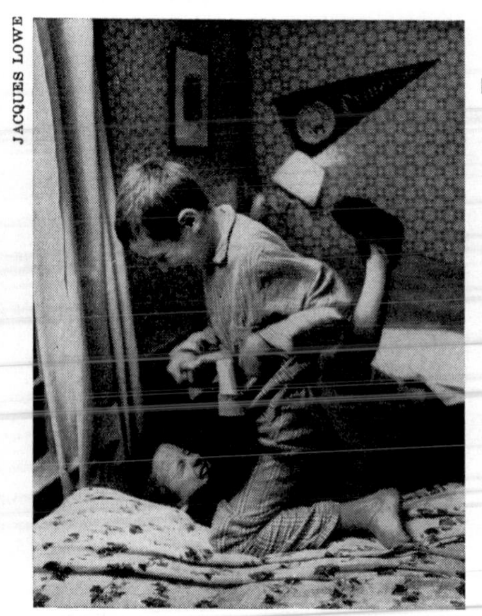

ACTION of this kind is best caught with bounce flash, which fills average rooms with soft, even illumination and is very easy to use.

J.W. ▷

AT CIRCUS: Take 3000 speed film. For overall lighting try EV 10, 11; beware of camera shake. Spotlights are bright enough for EV 13 or 14.

ESTHER BUBLEY, STANDARD OIL CO. (N. J.)

ACTION in gym or similar large area requires combination of direct flash, fast film. With no walls or ceiling near to reflect light, it's best to set camera one number lower than flash guide recommends. Speed light is good, too, and will usually be able to "freeze" fast action.

AMATEUR THEATRICALS: Conditions vary widely, but with all lights on, you can usually take snapshots with fast films. Try EV 10, 11, or 12. For records of sets, or of "mood" lighting, time exposures are best bet.

CARL K. SHIRAISHI, PRATT INSTITUTE PLAY SHOP

FOR THIS you need: bright, diffused window light; +1 or +2 close-up lens; EV 15, 16, or 17 and brief time exposure. Sheet of plain paper covers table, and is taped to wall for seamless background. By choice of filter, you can control contrast between fruits of different colors (see *Filters*).

HAROLD FEINSTEIN

NOVELTY: Start with sheet of stiff white paper and let your imagination go. Lay "subject" on floor, shoot straight down. Same taking data as for photograph of bowl of fruit above.

Still lifes, hobbies.

At one time or another practically all the great painters and photographers have turned their attention to still lifes. And you too should find this a fascinating aspect of picture taking.

Window light is the best illumination, but flood lamps also can be used. In most cases, close-up lenses are necessary to get a big image in the print. Here's a chance to do some real experimenting, and since the finished print is there in a minute, you will soon find out whether or not you like the results.

There are two main combinations of hobbies and pictures: snapshots of people enjoying their hobbies, and photographs by hobbyists of the results of their activities—crafts, collections, and so on. Taking these pictures generally presents no special problems, and having pictures in a minute adds a special "kick" to this kind of work.

◁ ANTHONY GUYTHER

J.W. ▽

ESTHER BUBLEY, STANDARD OIL CO. (N. J.)

AMATEUR CRAFTSMEN: Growth of "do-it-yourself" hobbies provides wide opportunities for relaxed, informal portraits. Use existing light, wink-light, or bounce flash.

AMATEUR MUSICIAN: Fast moving hand could have been "frozen" with speed light, but slight blur adds to picture. Direct flash, low angle, were used to cast wall shadow.

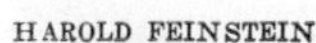

HAROLD FEINSTEIN

COLLECTORS of all kinds find pictures in a minute excellent way to catalog and record collection. In addition, some items make charming pictures. This resulted from combination of Pathfinder (with lens set to f/32), 200 speed film, +4 close-up lens, bright light from window and time exposure.

J.W.

BRIGHT SUN is good light for pictures of fur and feathers—it puts sparkle and highlights into dark colors and (with cross-lighting) brings out texture of coat. Since pets frequently get up on windowsills for sunning and gazing, you have many opportunities for fine snapshots.

HAROLD FEINSTEIN

ANGLE: Pets usually look best when snapped at "eye level"—but not always. Kitten's small size is emphasized by high angle and corner placement. 200 speed film, EV 10 used here.

Pets around the house.

For head portraits of dogs and cats, close-up lenses are a must. Be prepared for some slight difficulty in getting full cooperation from the subject while you measure and aim. Full length views are much easier—no close-up lens required, particularly if you include some of the pet's favorite surroundings.

If you use a close-up lens, pre-focus on a fixed perch, and make tests for correct exposure and focus *without* the pet. Even a turtle can get pretty active if he objects to being photographed, so fast shutter speeds are desirable. It's easiest to work outdoors in bright daylight. Indoors, speed light will stop all action and, with an extension cord (see *Speed Light*) you can place the light wherever necessary. If you're indoors and are not using a close-up lens, load with 3000 speed film and shoot as usual, allowing extra exposure for the color of dark fur, etc.

HAROLD FEINSTEIN

IMPRESSION: This is how Hunter looks going up stairs. Direct or bounce flash at camera could record event, but not this impression. With 3000 speed film, powerful flood lamp aimed down steps might be enough at EV 10 or 11. To ensure stopped action, use a speed light on a long extension (see *Speed Light* for details).

LAURIE SEAMANS

BURT OWEN

FISH are easily photographed by bright light from back, side, or top (not from front). Use +2 or +3 close-up lens, pre-focus on point in tank. When he swims by, shoot.

KIDS AND PETS are just as good subjects indoors as outdoors. Bright diffused window light and bounce flash give best illumination for such pictures. Model 95A camera and 200 speed film were used here.

BABIES

Bright ideas, simple techniques for better pictures of tiny but important people.

BABIES get more lenses aimed at them than almost anyone else (except maybe pretty girls), but they would get awfully discouraged if they could see what they look like in most of the resulting snapshots. For it's a sad fact that, by and large, most baby snapshots are not very good—to put it gently.

This sad state of affairs provides a fine source of living for professional baby photographers (some of whom don't do much better than the proud parents), but there is no good reason why this should be so. Very small children are usually charming; they laugh and wave arms and legs; they blow bubbles while they look at you with big eyes; until they get old enough to scuttle about like torpedo boats, they stay put in a crib, carriage, or someone's arms. All in all, very likely subjects for pictures. Why then are the results so often dull, or even worse?

Baby picture troubles

If you should study a great number of baby snapshots several reasons would become apparent. There are purely mechanical troubles—exposure, focus, double exposure. Then there are troubles of "seeing"—bad angles, wrong kind of lighting, poor relation of baby to surroundings, bad backgrounds. But the saddest trouble of all is lack of ideas. So let's attack that problem first thing.

◁ **SOFT LIGHT** of a bright hazy day was ideal for this close-up. EV 15, with 200 speed film.

HAROLD FEINSTEIN

Who sees baby most, watches the growth of expression and movement, has the greatest number of opportunities to take interesting snapshots? Mother, of course. But she may not have the time or desire to master the technicalities of conventional photography. And, if she's like so many busy people, the thought of having to finish off 12, 20, or 36 shots before seeing *any*, may kill the picture taking urge completely.

For her particular needs, the Polaroid Land camera offers definite advantages—ease of operation; shoot one picture and see it. So, the first half of the chapter is devoted to ideas for snapshots of baby alone in various situations.

Father has a slightly different problem—he wants pictures of mother and child. For *him*, the second half of the chapter is devoted to ideas for snapshots of both of them. What about pictures of father and baby? Well, at least half of the ideas for mother and child snapshots are applicable to father too.

Throughout, the chapter takes into account the baby's routine, shows where picture opportunities can be had, gives specific solutions for specific problems that are bound to arise when you aim your Land camera at a tot.

One thing we won't do is present a set of rigid rules—always do this, or that, under certain conditions. But if you simply follow the suggestions given here, you can hardly fail to get fascinating baby snapshots for your album.

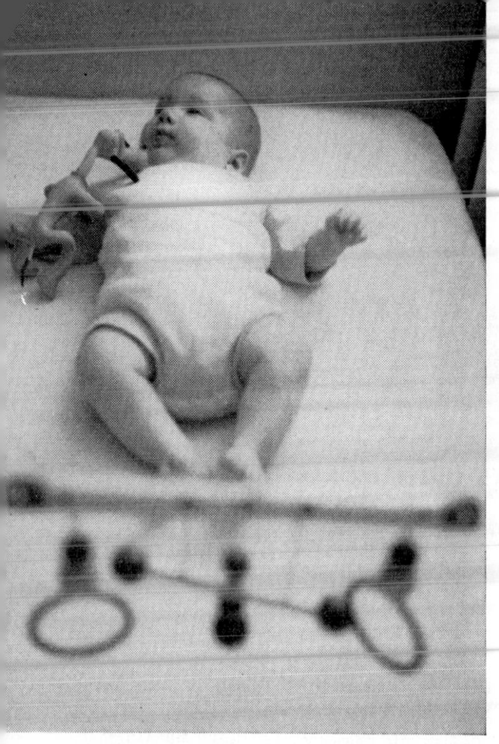

USUAL RESULT is something like this. Too much foreground, too high, too far away.

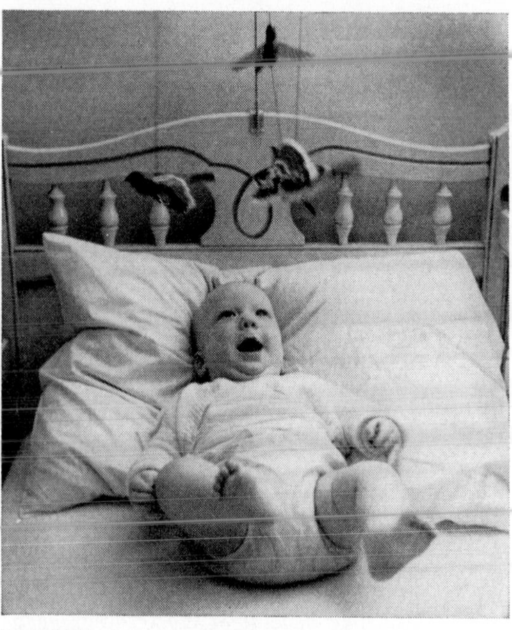

PILLOWS prop up baby too young to sit, permit full face view, better body perspective.

In the crib: 4 ideas for charming pictures.

The child's first world is a cradle or crib. Thus, a very large percentage of baby snapshots center around that article of furniture. Babies lie flat in a crib; cribs have high sides. This combination leads almost inevitably to the stereotyped result in the photo at top left. The other photos show how to improve on this.

Unless you are specifically trying for a downward look, keep the camera as low as possible—nothing to stop you from shooting between the crib slats, if they are separated widely enough.

Babies are tiny, and are likely to be almost insignificant in your prints unless you come quite close. You'll find the close-up lens to be a great help in producing a large image in the print (see *Close-ups*). Then *that* can be enlarged easily.

Lighting? It should be soft and diffused, in keeping with the surroundings. 3000 speed film is the perfect choice for such situations. Walls, bedding, clothing, are usually light colored and reflect light into the shadow areas.

Bright "north" window light is ideal. If it's not quite bright enough, put strong bulbs in the light fixtures, or aim a couple of floodlamps at light walls or the ceiling. (see *Floods*). If none of these methods is possible use the wink-light flasher #256 (or other flashgun) for bounce flash, which spares the child's eyes from the brilliant light of the bulb.

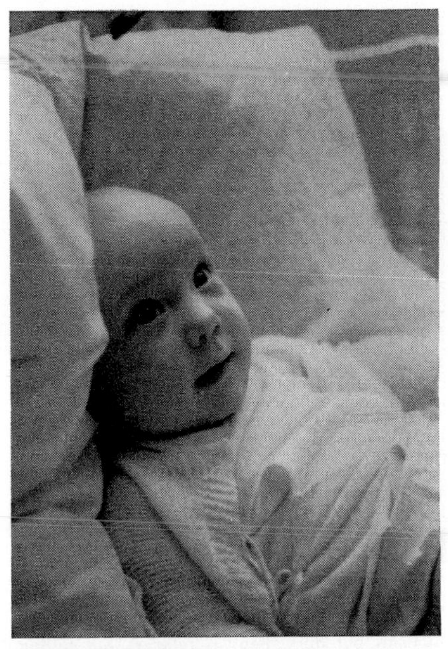

COME NEARER with a close-up lens. You can remove crib side, or shoot between slats.

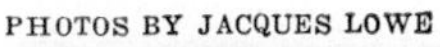

PHOTOS BY JACQUES LOWE

BABY ON TUMMY on pillows is raised to "eye level." Stuffed toy adds scale to picture.

IMAGINATION: Baby hasn't moved; camera was lowered and brought closer. If you try this, be sure to focus on baby, let the edge of the crib be un-sharp if necessary. This is a simple, straightforward picture with a big image, and would be ideal for enlargement.

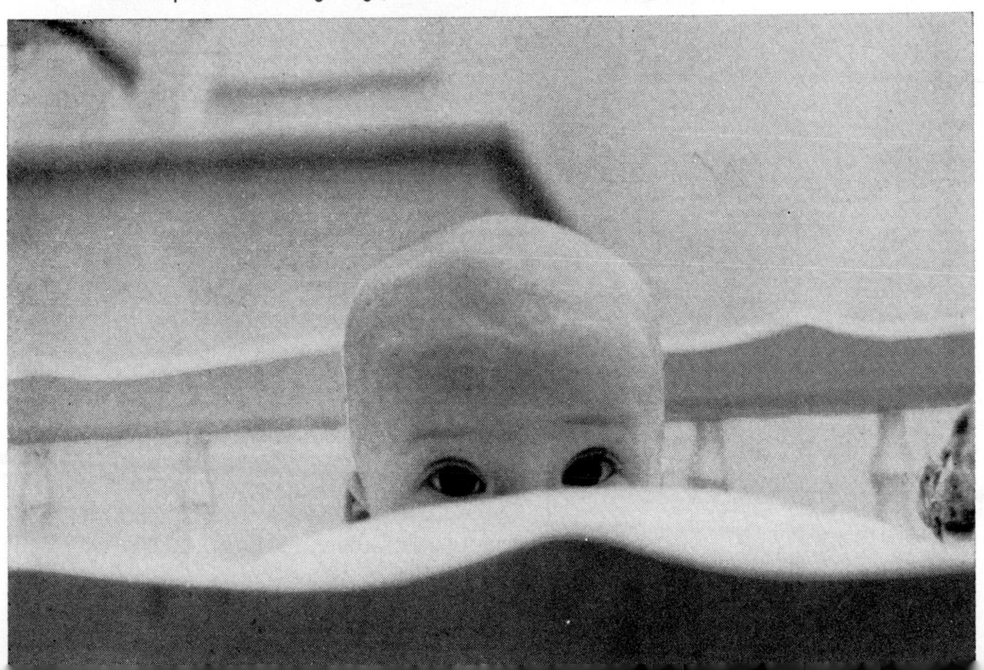

BABY IN SUN is likely to squint, scowl, or turn head away. Not a good picture.

JACQUES LOWE

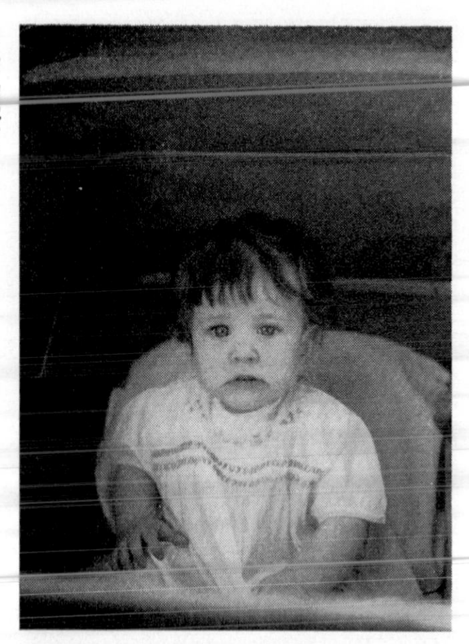

BETTER but dark. Baby is relaxed, but cutting off all sunlight has produced dull photo.

Background, angle, level: all are important.

Long before babies' backs are developed enough to permit sitting up, their arms are relatively strong. Put a tot on his tummy and almost instinctively he'll try to push up head and shoulders to look at you. This is one of the best poses. But compare these two pictures.

The near child appears to have no body; the couch covers confuse the picture; the low couch arm causes even more background confusion.

In contrast (far right) is an almost perfect example of making the best of ordinary surroundings. The draped baby blanket is simple, but the muted design adds an appropriate touch. The baby is at "eye level" (sit on the floor to take the picture), with the result that this child *seems* to be raising his head much higher than the other one. The three-quarter angle shows the rest of the little body. Quite a difference!

CONFUSING is best description of this photo, which has little to recommend it.

BACKLIGHT combines advantages of face in shade, highlights on hair, for best results.

Bright sunshine: it's a tricky light to use.

After the crib comes the carriage or stroller, and what photographic crimes are committed in the name of Vitamin D! Back 20 or 30 years ago it may have made sense to put a subject in bright sunlight. Films were slow, most snapshot cameras had small lens openings, and one shutter speed. Shade pictures were tough to make.

With Land films many times as sensitive as those old films, this "rule" no longer applies. Bright shade, backlighting, reflected light from walls and other surroundings—these are the lighting tools to work with outdoors, particularly for baby pictures. You'll get best results by the light of a hazy, overcast day.

So, next time you aim your lens at a brightly-lighted, sharply-shadowed, squinting tot, hold it until you've made a try at changing the lighting.

PETER GOWLAND

APPEALING result here comes from skillful use of elements similar to those which were present in opposite picture, but which were not properly employed.

FANCY SNOW SUIT: Overhead sun highlights nose, cheek, yet face is relaxed in shade.

◁ NELSON MORRIS ▽ PETER GOWLAND

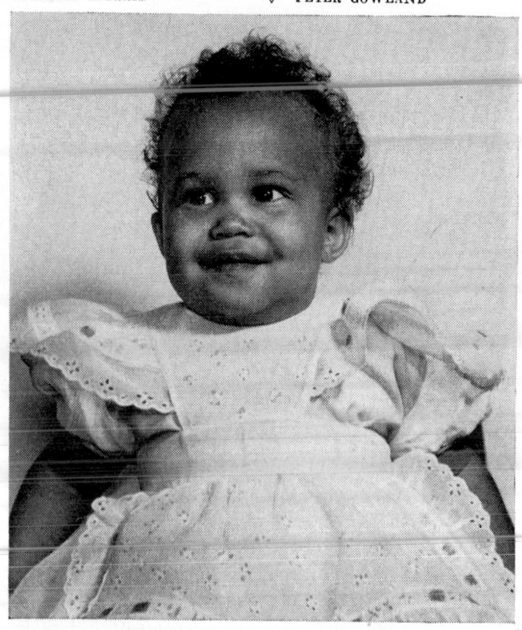

FANCY DRESS: +1 close-up lens brings you near enough to get large image full of detail.

Make a photo record of clothes, big events.

Your camera remembers better than you can. Today's snapshot is a priceless record to enjoy and cherish half a lifetime from now. One of the most rewarding snapshot projects is to take a picture of every kind of outfit a baby wears throughout the year—for baby clothes change with the seasons, too. Every time the youngster gets a new dress or other outfit, take a picture of it, record the date in the margin. Likely as not, in the process your pictures will record situations and events which might otherwise have escaped your memory completely. Here are a few examples of such photos.

Another good snapshot record idea is to take a picture on every birthday. preferably under exactly the same conditions, or as close as possible. Not many people have the gumption to stick to such a project, but when they do carry it out for many years the results are truly wonderful and amusing. Here we have the start of a birthday cake series but that's by no means the only kind.

One of the most popular is built around the child's growth. Each birthday you stand the youngster up against the same kind of background with a card carrying the date, height, and weight in large, bold letters. Of course, for the first birthday, some help may be needed to prevent toppling. Taking these pictures against a door, or next to a piece of furniture, shows graphically the actual growth in proportion to the same surroundings.

J.W.

FANCY SKIN: Babies and mudpies, surefire combination for charming pictures. Avoid directly overhead noon sun, if possible.

BIRTHDAY: Chocolate writing not only tastes good, it photographs better than plain white.

NELSON MORRIS

▽ TANA HOBAN ▷

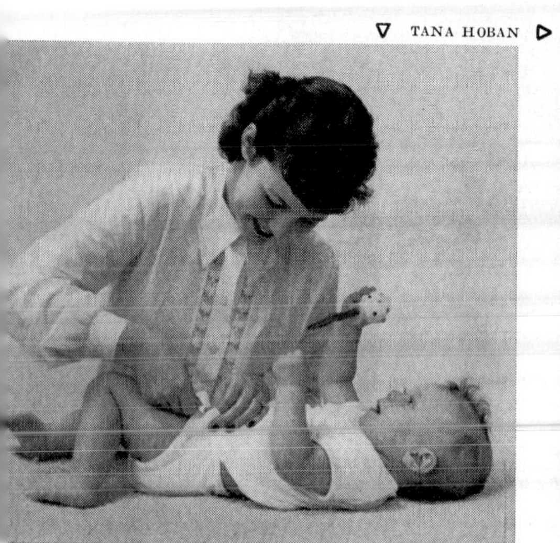

DIAPERING: Large white areas can lead exposure astray. Come close with meter, take reading off baby's skin, disregard surroundings.

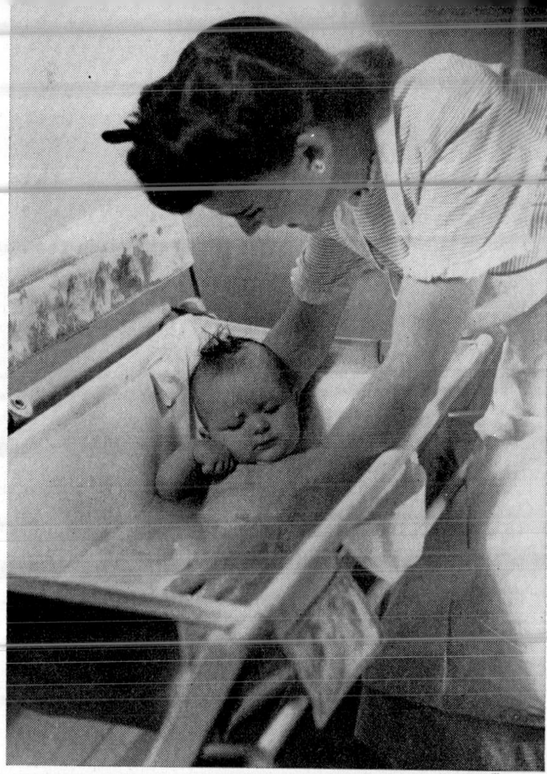

BATHING: For pictures by window light, white curtain makes a fine diffuser, softens light, hides window, prevents harsh shadows.

Mother and child: catch their daily routine.

The big picture at right symbolizes one of the most important photos you'll ever make—the first snapshot of your brand new son (or daughter). Since newborn babies are tiny and almost meaningless by themselves, why not make that first picture one of mother and child?

Every father wants a picture of his baby right away; of course, grandparents have to get one, too. For this, nothing can match pictures in a minute; there's no danger of bungling the job and not finding out until next week. So, shoot a roll or two, keep the best for yourself, mail the other good ones to important relatives right away. They'll have pictures of "mother and child doing well" with the next mail delivery.

Send one of your best prints off to Polaroid Corp. for a copy negative (see *Copies*); from this you can have your local camera store make up photographic birth announcements. Or, just order lots of copy prints and send them out with little notes.

Many hospitals forbid pictures of infants in the nursery, and arrange schedules so that visitors never see mother and child together. You may have to wait until they come home.

There used to be big arguments about the advisability of flashing bulbs at babies. With 3000 speed film, flash is almost unnecessary, but if you must use it, make sure it's bounce flash.

Once mother and child come home they start a daily round of chores which may be routine, but are the source of delightful pictures. Snap while both parties are fully absorbed in their activities.

NELSON MORRIS

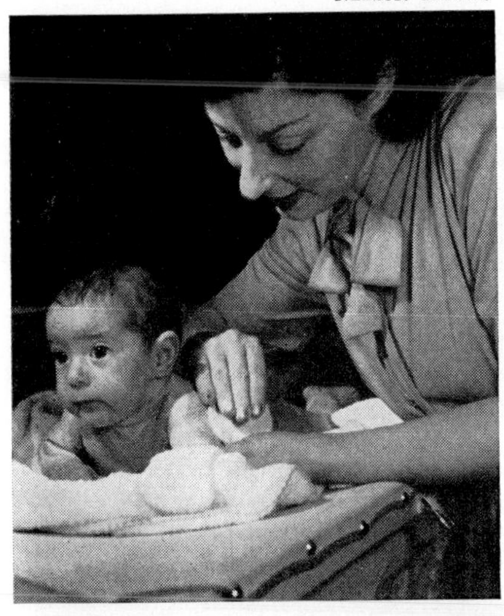

POWDERING: Even young ones have expressive faces. Wait, wait, patiently for such a look.

FEEDING: Cluttered background detracts from charm of scene. See same pair, next page.

JACQUES LOWE

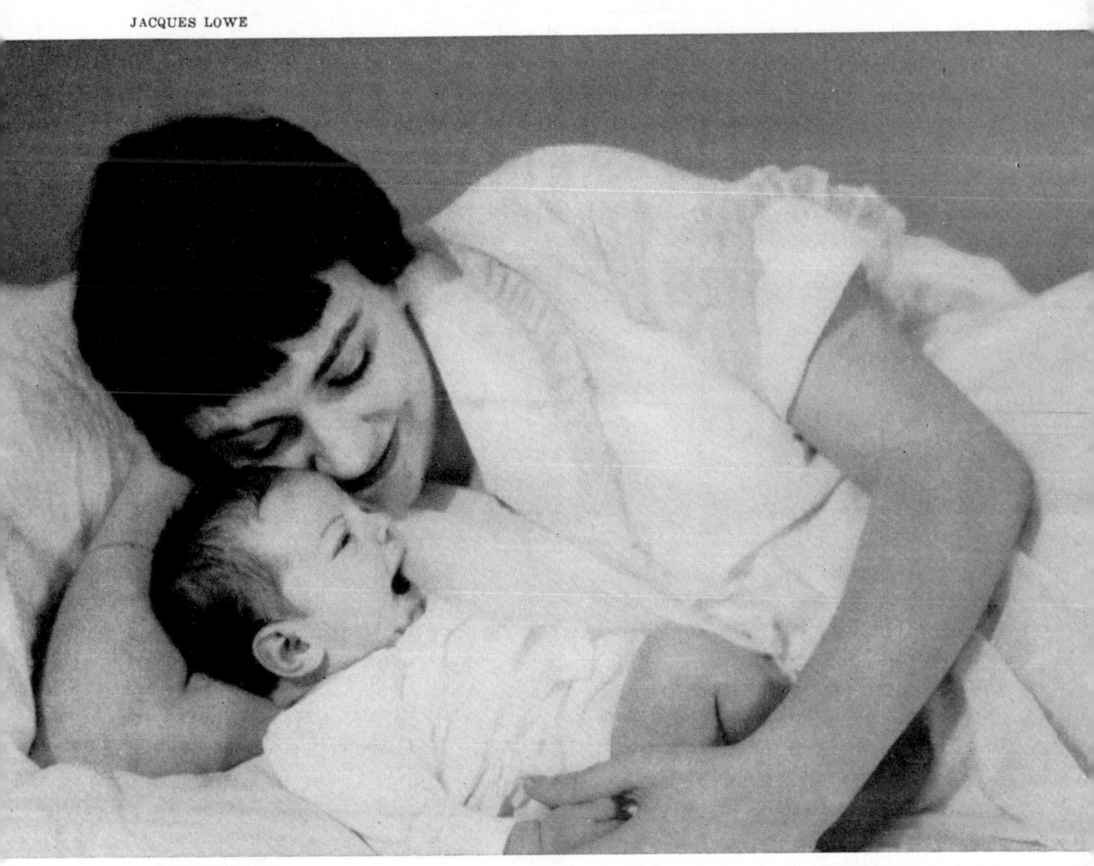

FIRST PICTURE has to be right; seeing picture in a minute lets you know it is. Mother and child make better subject than newborn infant alone. Come close to get a big image.

JACQUES LOWE

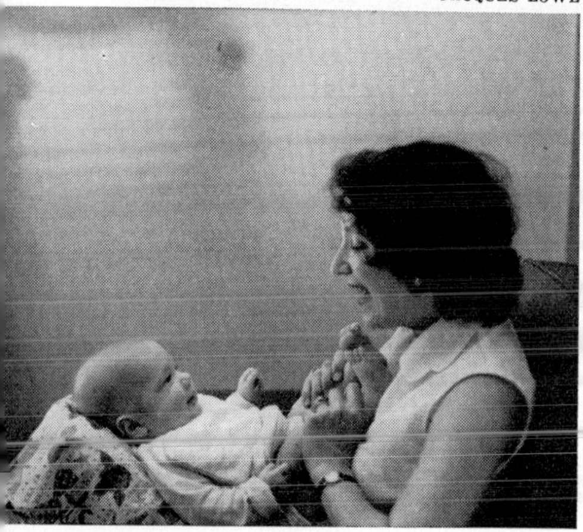

SEATED: Placing mother's feet on box, stool, or hassock, raises her knees, makes natural support for child too young to sit up, brings heads closer. Picture interest is concentrated.

USUAL: This is what most snapshooters try for, but actually it's awkward for mother to stand so she and child face camera. Result is usually static. Bounce flash, 200 speed film used here.

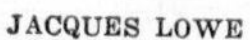

Babe in arms: most common mother and child

Mother and child will both look better if they are concentrating on each other and enjoying it instead of looking into the camera. Try to place them so that their heads are fairly close together. Then you can come nearer, get bigger images in the print; the area of picture interest will be more concentrated than if their heads are widely separated.

Try for soft, even lighting that gives full separation of heads and background, as in the four pictures above. Bounce flash or flood does this almost automatically; with window light, careful placement is necessary. Or, you can shine a lamp on the background, as described in *Floods*.

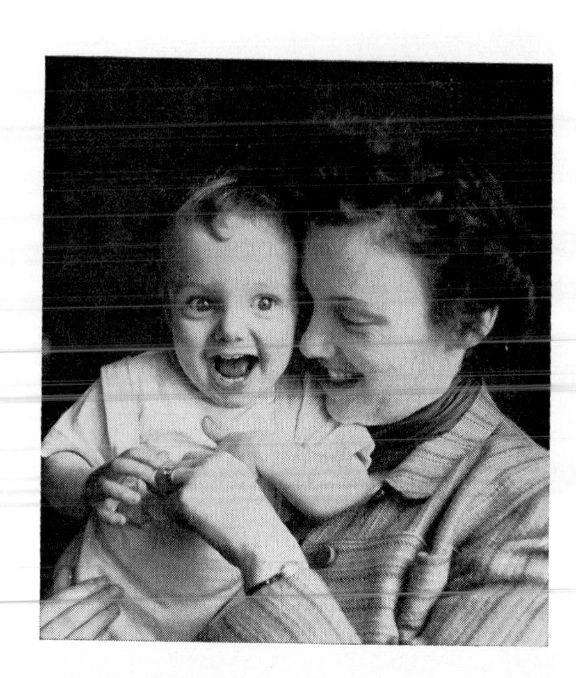

SHOOT A SERIES: This takes a few minutes with the Land camera, but time races by when mother and child play. Baby is held high—that's good. Combination of window light, dark background causes "spotlight" effect.

HAROLD FEINSTEIN

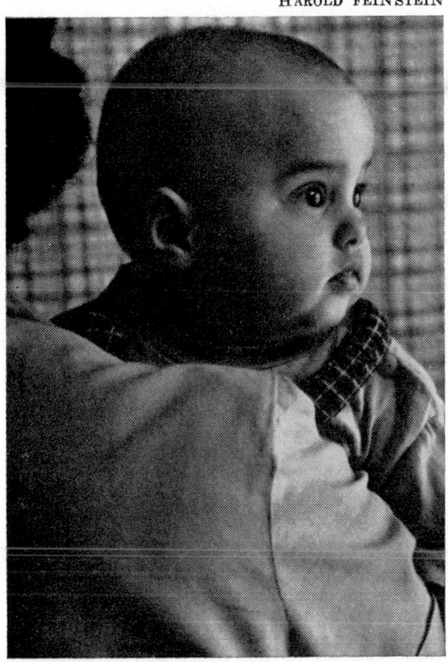

OVER SHOULDER: Comfortable for both. Good for close-up of baby alone. Or, if mother has fine profile, back up, have her turn head, look at child. This was made with window light.

J.W.

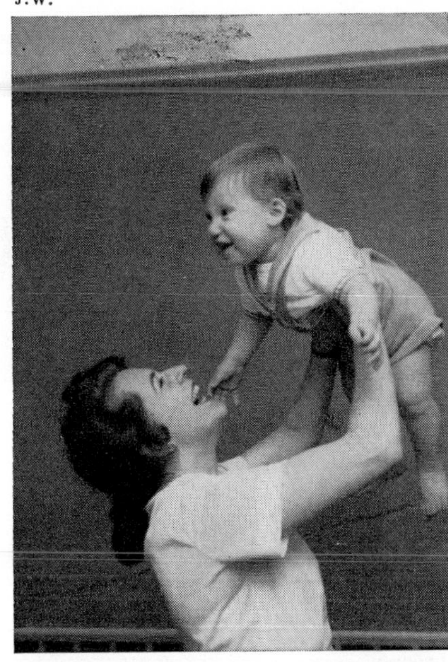

HIGH UP: This is always good for a laughing expression on both faces. Keep an eye out for pictures on wall and other high objects in background. Bounce flash provided even lighting.

photo. Here's how to make yours more successful.

JACQUES LOWE

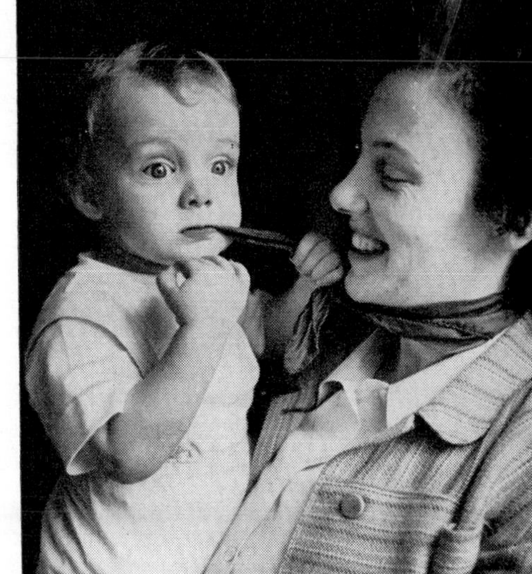

HOW IT WORKS

More details about the camera and film, plus an explanation of the picture-making process.

THE LAND SYSTEM of photography is the invention of Dr. Edwin H. Land, president and director of research of Polaroid Corp. It is based on a set of new ideas touching almost every aspect of the photographic process.

Look at the system from a mechanical viewpoint and you see: 1) a composite film that contains, within itself, all the materials necessary for making a positive picture, including the light-sensitive negative, the print paper, and the chemical reagents, and 2) a camera that incorporates the mechanical arrangements for cooperating with this composite film to perform the picture-making process. The mechanics of this setup are shown in the drawing opposite.

The design of the film and the design of the camera are intimately interwoven. For example:

1. By placing the reagent in the film, the camera is kept perfectly dry. This avoids the need for troublesome camera structures such as tanks, sponges, sprays, wet rollers, or other devices which would otherwise be needed for handling a liquid reagent.

2. Providing a separate pod of reagent, one for each picture, ensures a supply of just the right amount for each picture, of the proper type to match the type of film.

3. Because each charge of reagent is used only once, the reagent is always fresh, and as new as the film. This eliminates the problem of exhaustion and replenishment of reagents that has to be dealt with in ordinary tank or bath processing of films and prints.

4. Processing starts automatically when the film is advanced for the next exposure, and proceeds to completion within the camera itself. This ensures uniform processing, by eliminating the variations that would occur in hand-controlled separate operations.

Attached to a strong paper leader are a roll of light sensitive negative material on a spool *(bottom of drawing)*, and a bulkier roll of positive paper which is not light sensitive and not on a spool (*top of drawing*). The positive paper is the material on which your final print will appear. Crossing the long strip of positive paper at suitable intervals (one is supplied for each print to be made) are metal foil pods (small, tube-like affairs) filled with a viscous, jelly-like compound —the chemicals necessary for developing the picture.

The negative material consists of a base (paper or acetate film) on which is coated a thin layer of silver halide crystals suspended in gelatin.

An important mechanical feature of the camera is a pair of closely spaced, accurately made, heavy steel rollers. In loading the camera, the negative and positive rolls are deposited in separate chambers, and the paper leader which connects them is led through the film path, between the steel rollers, and out a slit at one end of the camera back (this is where you see the two arrows at the bottom of the drawing). The first negative is brought into position in the camera by pulling the paper leader through the slit until it stops automatically at the right spot.

Now let's assume that you have snapped a picture and wish to develop the print. The developing process begins automatically as you advance the film to the next frame. To advance the film it's merely necessary to (1) press a small release button or switch (on the Highlander you do it by raising the cutter bar) and (2) pull the paper leader straight out until it automatically stops with the next negative in position to be exposed.

If you look at the drawing you will notice that the film path is such that when the film is advanced, the exposed negative and a section of the positive paper strip are forced together between the two steel rollers. At the beginning of each section of positive paper is its foil pod full of chemicals, which is too big to fit between the rollers. So, the rollers squeeze the pod open, spreading a very thin (about three ten-thousandths of an inch—.0003 in.) layer of the viscous, jelly-like liquid evenly between the negative and positive materials, both of which must remain in firm contact with the layer of chemicals throughout the developing process.

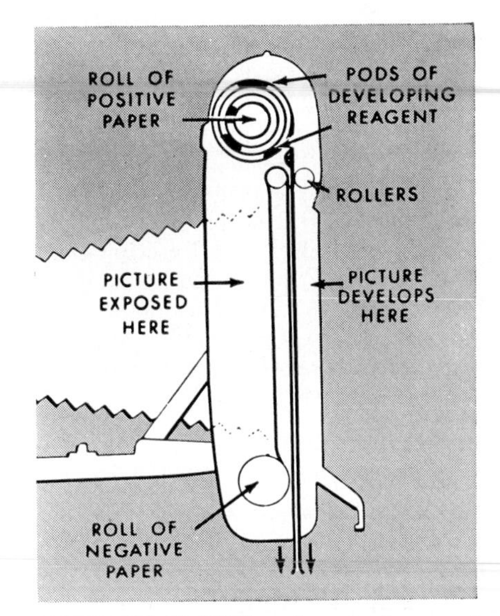

INSIDE THE CAMERA: Schematic diagram of the Land camera shows how the negative and positive materials start from different locations, come together for the developing process. Compare this with the description in the text and the photos in the chapter *Loading*.

(The author is indebted to scientists of Polaroid Corp., Cambridge, Mass., for the following technical explanation of the Land system of photography and how it produces a picture.—Ed.)

In the films described here, the Land system of photography makes use of the principle of diffusion transfer reversal, to produce a print directly on a light-insensitive paper from the exposed negative. After the exposure has been made and the processing reagent has been released, the exposed silver halide grains of the negative are developed much as they are in the conventional wet process.

The unexposed grains in the negative emulsion are dissolved by a chemical action much like the first stage of conventional fixing in a hypo bath. That is, the unexposed silver halide crystals are converted to soluble complexes. In the conventional process, these complexes would be "fixed out" in a hypo bath and discarded. In the Land process, however, the soluble silver complexes diffuse across the microscopically thin layer of the processing reagent, and are transferred to the positive paper. There the silver of the complexes is caused to precipitate as metallic silver, to form the positive image.

The processing reagent carries both the developing agent and the agent for dissolving the unexposed silver grains. Both the developing and dissolving reactions take place almost simultaneously. The positive image is forming while the development of the negative is taking place.

To harness the diffusion transfer reversal principle for use in general photography, Dr. Land had to overcome two major and apparently inescapable limitations of the principle. Earlier investigators had not been able to make it work with the faster types of emulsions required for everyday photography; it worked only for the slow emulsions of the type used in printing papers for document duplication. And it had only been made to work properly for lights and darks, not for intermediate tones. Different tonal values of gray often came out in different hues varying from yellow to brown.

In addition to creating the mechanical system, Dr. Land was the first to surmount these technical obstacles. He not only developed a process that could be performed successfully with fast, negative-type emulsions, but worked out the physics and chemistry of the silver precipitation to control the color, and at the same time to produce full tone gradations, high maximum densities, and low minimum densities. A high degree of control over the chemistry and physics of the development, dissolution, and precipitation, characterize the Land diffusion transfer reversal process. *(And that's the story of the miracle of photographic chemistry that goes on inside the Land camera each time you pull the tab. Ed.)*

Removing the print

After a suitable time for development (usually about a minute) you open the back door of the camera, lift up a little paper tab, and separate the print from the rest of the positive paper strip (a special die-cut edge makes it easy to lift out the print). All the chemicals cling to the negative—the print is clean and dry. Ordinarily the negative gets light-struck during removal of the print and is worthless, so it is discarded. The basic loading and operating steps are shown in other chapters.

Film development times vary according to the type of film being used. Also, the temperature may speed up or slow down development depending on how hot or cold it is. As a general rule the films require longer development at temperatures below 60F and decreased development when it gets above 80F.

Why the camera looks that way

The designers of the camera set out to accomplish a variety of widely divergent aims, each of which contributed something to its final appearance. We have described the reasons for the two-roll film package, the two chambers to receive the rolls, and the steel rollers. Since the print which came out of the camera was a final product, it had to be big enough to show a large image with plenty of detail. To make such a print by the Land process meant a big camera. If it were a box, it might be quite bulky, so they made it a folding camera.

It was to have the flexibility in exposure control of a camera with adjustable shutter speeds and lens openings. Yet, it had to be as simple to operate as a box camera, for most snapshooters find their worst stumbling block in the complexities of conventional f-numbers and fractional seconds in combination. Have you ever tried to explain the meaning of f/16 and 1/100 second?

The shutter is a simple device, but accurate and dependable. The one on all the large cameras but the Pathfinder has four speeds (1/13, 1/25, 1/50, 1/100 second) while the Highlander has only two speeds (1/25 and 1/100 second). The mechanism is of the self setting type—it clicks each time you press the lever, with no need to cock it before each exposure. Provision is made for a cable release and there is a control to permit time exposures. (The Pathfinder has a conventional type of shutter with a wide range of speeds.) All models are synchronized for wink-light and flash, and all but the Highlanders have synchronization for speed light. For full details about these subjects, see the chapters *The Wink-light*, *Flash*, and *Speed Light*.

The unique exposure controls

The following explanation of the exposure controls applies to all Polaroid Land cameras except the Pathfinders, which have conventional shutter and lens controls.

To control the amount of light entering the camera there is a rotatable metal disc, with holes of various sizes spaced around its rim. These come into place in the light path of the lens as the disc is turned. By itself this is not a new principle. What's new about it in the Land camera is that the lens opening and shutter speed controls have been coupled, so that by turning a single wheel to various positions identified by single "exposure value" numbers, a wide range of exposure can be had with ease and accuracy.

Although all the cameras utilize this principle, all models do not carry exactly the same set of numbers.

Current cameras are numbered from EV 10 to 17 (Models 150, 800, 95B) and EV 11 to 18 (Model 80A). Older models were numbered from 1 to 8 (all the large cameras) and 2 to 9 (Model 80).

Except that the EV numbers on the new cameras are 9 higher than the old system numbers giving equal exposure (EV 12 gives the same exposure as #3, and so on) there is no difference between the two numbering systems. And the following information applies to all camera models.

As you turn the exposure control wheel from a low number to the next higher one, exposure is cut in half; if you turn still another number higher, it is cut in half again. Going the other way, from a larger number, such as EV 16, to the next smaller one, EV 15, the exposure is doubled; go from EV 15 to EV 14 and exposure is doubled again, and so on.

The widest-lens-opening/slowest-shutter-speed combination (lowest number) gives an exposure 128 times as great as the smallest-lens-opening/fastest-shutter-speed combination (highest number).

An important part of the camera's exposure control mechanism is illustrated below. In the *Technical Facts* section there is a chart showing the conventional f-number and shutter speed equivalents of the Polaroid Land camera exposure value numbers, for all models.

This method of exposure control is certainly simple to operate and has many advantages. Exposure guides and exposure meters are reduced to the simplest elements. If you take a picture and it's underexposed (too dark), you just turn the wheel to the next lower number, knowing that by so doing exposure will be doubled. The system also has a few minor disadvantages, which have been pointed out in earlier chapters, together with information on how to overcome them without difficulty.

The following general information about lenses applies to all Polaroid Land cameras except the Model 95 and the Pathfinders; specific details about those models are given at the end of this section, on the following page.

Lenses for cameras are usually described by a few terms which have special meaning: number of elements; focal length; relative aperture.

How light entering the camera is controlled.

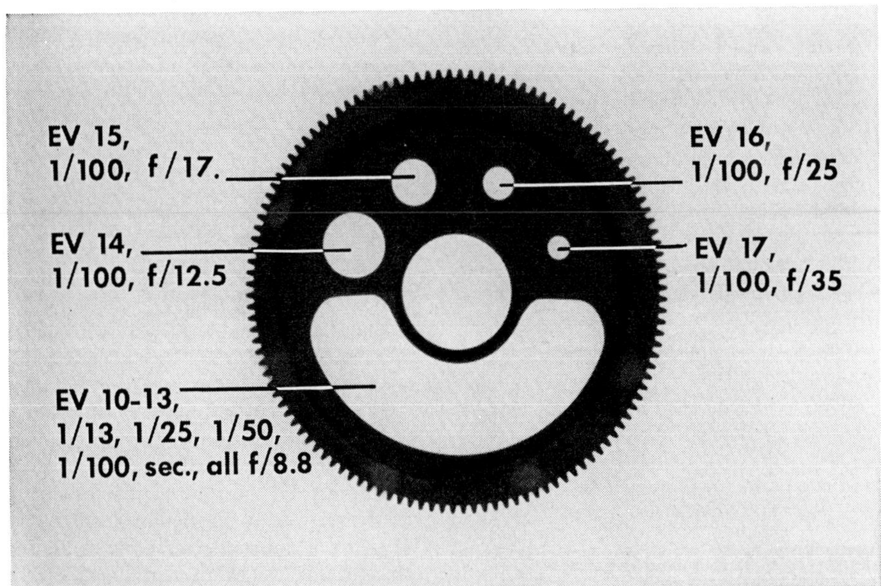

EXPOSURE CONTROL DISC is in shutter housing, mounted between lens elements on pivot that passes through center hole. Gear-tooth edge connects to control wheel on exterior of shutter housing; control wheel is also coupled to shutter mechanism. As exposure control wheel is turned to different settings, disc rotates, holes of various sizes move between lens elements to regulate amount of light which can pass through lens, and shutter speeds change automatically. This is disc for Models 150, 800, and 95B. Model 890A has different combinations of shutter speeds and lens openings.

The "number of elements" refers to the actual number of pieces of glass included in the complete optical system. All models have lenses made of three elements of rare earth optical glass which can produce very sharp pictures.

The "focal length" refers to the distance from the film, through the inside of the camera, to a central point in the lens. Lenses on the large cameras have a focal length of 130mm (about 5¼ in.); the Highlander's lens has a focal length of 100mm (about 4 in.).

The "relative aperture" of a lens is simply a measurement of the amount of light it will pass through itself in a given instant. This measurement is expressed by an f-number, which states the size of the widest lens opening in proportion to the focal length of the lens. Lenses which have a very wide opening, in proportion to their focal length, pass a great amount of light in a given instant and are generally called "fast" lenses. F-numbers such as f/2 and f/2.8 indicate very fast lenses. Lenses whose widest opening is still quite small in proportion to their focal length, don't pass much light in a given instant and are usually referred to as "slow" lenses. F-numbers such as f/22 and f/32 indicate small lens openings, and a lens with a maximum opening of f/22 would be a very slow lens indeed.

The lenses on Polaroid Land cameras have relative apertures of f/8.8 at their widest opening, indicating modest speed. However, they were designed for use with Polaroid Land films which are of very high speed (that is, extremely sensitive to light), so it is possible to take pictures with them even under adverse lighting conditions.

The Model 110A Pathfinder's lens is of a different type, made with four elements, with a focal length of 127mm and maximum aperture of f/4.7 indicating a fairly "fast" lens.

The focusing system

Polaroid Land cameras are set for distance by one of two methods. Models 150, 800, 110A, and 110 are equipped with accurate rangefinders that are coupled to the lens. You simply sight through the rangefinder at your subject and rotate the focusing knob (thus moving the lens back and forth) until the rangefinder indicates that the lens is sharply focused for that distance (see *Get Them Sharp* for full details).

All the other cameras are focused manually. That is, you carefully estimate the camera-to-subject distance in feet (from the front of the lens) and then move a control on the camera which sets the lens to the correct position to take the picture in sharp focus.

On all models but the Highlander the entire lens/shutter assembly moves back and forth as you swing the focusing lever across the distance scale. On the Highlander, you rotate the front element of the lens (which has a distance scale engraved on it) until the desired distance setting reaches the marker. The front element is mounted on a screw, and turning it moves the glass in and out slightly.

The closest focusing point with both cameras is about 3½ feet. For pictures of objects nearer than that you need the close-up kit, described in *Close-ups.*

Even though you may not be the world's best distance guesser, you have an excellent chance of getting sharp pictures every time with the Land camera. This is due to the lens design. With any lens, when you focus on a subject at a given distance from the camera, (say 10 ft.), objects somewhat nearer than the subject and further than the subject will also be in sharp focus. This is the "zone of sharp focus." Lenses used at very wide aperture, such as f/2, have a very shallow zone of sharp focus.

The Land camera lenses, with maximum aperture of f/8.8, have a remarkably deep zone of sharp focus, even when "wide open" at setting EV 10. And, if you're in bright sunlight, with the lens closed down to a small aperture, such as setting EV 17, the zone of sharp focus is really very deep, particularly on the far side of the point at which you're aiming. Despite this "focusing insurance," always try to set the distance correctly.

When using the Photoelectric Shutter #440 on your camera the zone of sharp focus increases to a remarkable degree. The #440 shutter reduces the lens aperture to f/54, a tiny hole. The result is that with the camera's focusing scale set to 6 ft., everything in the scene is in sharp focus from about 3½ ft. to as far as you can see—to infinity.

Important loading tips

There's hardly any camera easier to load than this one. Yet, just because it is such an easy, rapid operation, there are a couple of points at which a little carelessness can ruin part or all of a film roll with the result that you extract blanks from the back of the camera, not pictures.

Be sure to read *Loading* carefully, and pay special attention to page 17.

Don't forget to release

After you have put the film in the camera and closed the back, you pull the paper leader until the film stops at "No. 1. Ready to take." It stops because two metal pins automatically go into holes in the positive strip. Now suppose you have made an exposure and are ready to develop it, by pulling the paper tab projecting from the camera. There's something to do, first.

Before pulling the tab, you must get those pins out of the holes in the paper, or they will rip it (if you have a strong pulling arm). This is done with the film release. On all models but the Highlanders, it's located on the back, near the cutter bar—a little red switch to be thrown in either direction. It doesn't matter how many times the switch is thrown, it does the job the first time. (On older models, you push a button to release the film. *Don't keep the button down while pulling the tab* or you will suddenly be holding about a yard of film outside the camera.)

On the Highlander, the film is released by raising the cutter bar as far as it will go—not halfway, or nearly all the way, but all the way. Once it has been raised, the pins are released and film may be advanced. This action is like that of the switch—raise it as many times as you want, the first time does the trick.

Most important: pulling the tab

Now you can advance the film, and when doing so let the cutter bar ride on the paper until the film hits the next stop.

After the film has been released (as described above) grasp the protruding paper tab firmly and pull it straight out in a single, smooth, swift motion. Don't stop halfway and pull again—this causes white streaks across the print. Pull it all the way, until the metal stop pins engage the next pair of holes in the positive strip and stop its movement. Then lift the cutter bar and see if the next film is "Ready to take." If you don't see this phrase, pull the tab a little more until the printing appears.

Don't pull the tab as though you were hauling a heavy anchor, nor give it a sudden yank near the end of the pull—the paper will be pulled right past the automatic stop, tearing it and possibly crushing the developer pod for the next section of paper. It will also cause a black line on the bottom or right side of the next print, which indicates that the picture was pulled out of register.

If the tab won't pull after operating the film release, make these checks:

Open the picture door. In case a negative has stuck to it this will free it. Close and relatch the door, operate the film release again, and pull once more.

Perhaps the tab was not pulled all the way, the time before this. Try to inch it forward slightly (about ⅛ in.), then operate the film release again and try another pull.

If there's a piece of black tape on the inside of the door to prevent light leaks, make sure it lies completely flat and is well fastened at corners and edges.

When the camera is empty, check the rollers for free spin. If they bind or squeak, put a single drop of light oil at each end of each roller (don't oil models with permanently lubricated rollers).

Finally, always pull the tab *straight out*, parallel to the camera body. If it goes at an angle it may cause the release mechanism to get fouled up, or may tear up one side of the paper strip.

For important details on these points, see the two chapters *Let's Make a Picture* and *Pulling the Tab*.

SLIDES

You can make them on the spot with this new, special type of Polaroid Land film.

EXCELLENT black-and-white slides can be made in any of the large Polaroid Land cameras with the Polaroid Land Projection Films, which have both negative and positive materials on an acetate film base. Although these films can be used by anyone, they are intended mainly for business, science, industry and professional fields.

The film comes in two varieties: Type 46 makes 2¼ x 2¼ in. slides for use in a special Polaroid projector (opposite); Type 46-L gives a larger, rectangular picture for use with 3¼ x 4 in. lantern slide projectors. The film can produce sharp and grainless images which may be projected on the biggest screens.

In addition to projection, these slides have a wide variety of other uses. They can be reproduced on the printed page by any of the standard methods. They combine readily with certain industrial copying methods, and can of course be copied and enlarged by standard photographic means. They have been successful in commercial and closed circuit TV. For literature explaining these various applications, write to Customer Service, Polaroid Corp., Cambridge 39, Mass.

The film is mighty fast—daylight exposure index is 800. Thus, it can be used where there is little light. The high speed also introduces the danger of tab slot light leaks. The cutter bar must always be kept closed, except when pulling the tab, and then the cutter bar should "ride" the film. Older model cameras which have shiny black paint inside must be fitted with a black tape light trap, supplied with the Field Kits (photo below). *Every picture must be developed for two minutes.*

Since the Type 46 slide format is a 2¼ in. square, the camera's viewfinder does not match this field of view. For cameras with wire finders, a mask is provided (photo below). Some newer camera models with enclosed viewfinders have four small arrows outlining the edges of the field of view for Type 46 film. As new models appear, this may change. If you are in any doubt as to how to use your camera with Type 46 film, write to Customer Service.

The photos opposite give a brief summary of the operating steps.

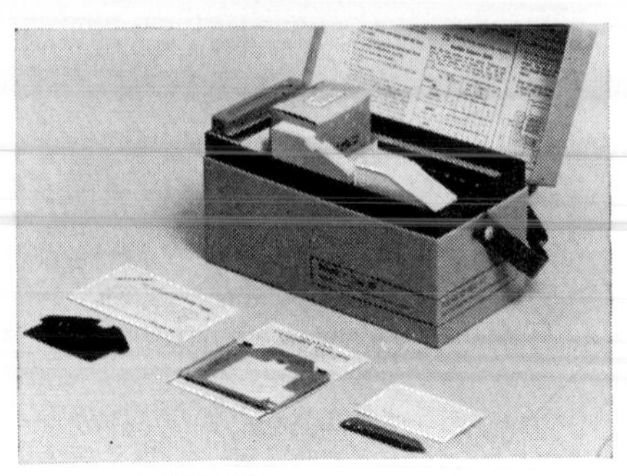

CONVENIENT KIT: Everything needed to make slides is included in Field Kits. They come in sizes for Type 46 or Type 46-L films, with matching components and complete instructions inside lid.

VIEWFINDER MASK: Of light metal, it clips onto wire viewfinders to show field of view for Type 46 film (2¼ x 2¼ in. slides). Text explains setup for cameras with other than wire finders.

1. REMOVE PICTURE: You snap picture, pull tab, develop for two minutes. As acetate film is stiffer than paper prints, metal pick is supplied to help separate "print" from rest of film.

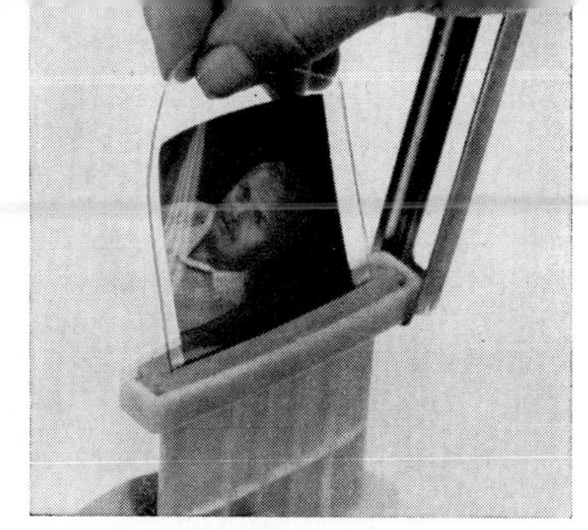

2. INTO DIPPIT: After brief air drying, picture is inserted in Dippit for hardening bath. Film should be curved slightly and inserted with great care to avoid scratching delicate image.

3. SEAL IT AND INVERT: Metal frame clamps soft lips of plastic Dippit closed. When it is inverted, liquid in bottom reservoir fills narrow part of Dippit, surrounds film, hardens image.

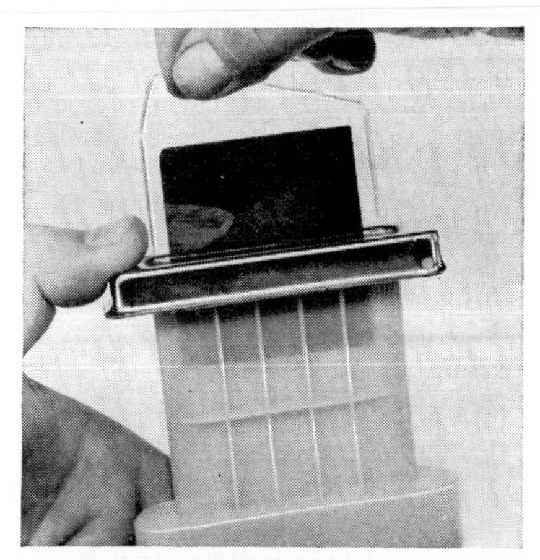

4. REMOVE, SQUEEGEE: After 10 seconds Dippit is turned right side up. Holding metal frame closed, film is pulled out between lips of Dippit, which squeegee it dry. It's ready to mount.

5. MOUNT IT: White plastic mounts clip together. Design makes it impossible to mount or project Type 46 slide incorrectly. Mount for Type 46-L is rectangle with visual projection guides.

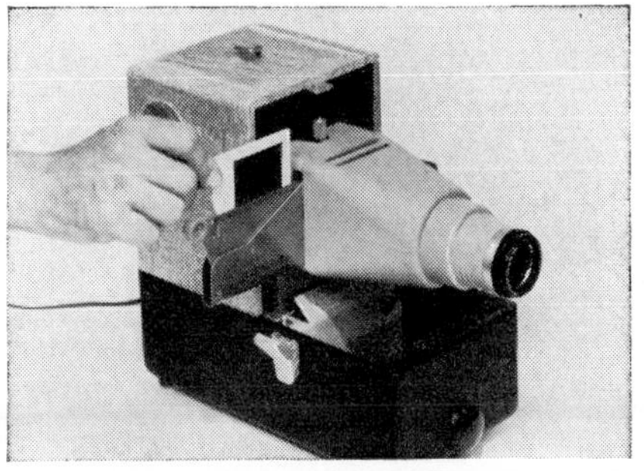

6. PROJECT IT: Polaroid slide projector has special carrier for Type 46 slides. Lens tube disconnects for compact storage. Type 46-L slides are for use in 3¼ x 4 in. lantern slide projectors.

THE COPYMAKER

Use it for slides, titles, and record close-ups of documents, photographs, and small objects.

NO GADGET, the Polaroid Copymaker #208 is an effective tool for use in preparing slides and titles for audio-visual and other purposes, or for making record copies in a hurry. You mount your own camera (any model but the Highlander) on it for this kind of work.

Although any film type may be used, the Copymaker does its best work with Polaroid Land Projection Films, Types 46 and 46-L, described in *Slides* .

Two fluorescent lamps provide even, shadowless, glareless light on the easel. Camera Setting Charts (right) carry all the data necessary to set the device and the camera properly. The Copymaker instruction booklet gives exposure guides for various film types when used to copy photographs or documents.

To reduce the chance of timing error all pictures are time exposures, made fairly lengthy (2 to 20 seconds) by means of a neutral density copy filter placed over the copy lens on the camera.

If your camera is a Model 110A or 110, the copy lenses supplied with the Copymaker will not fit on the camera. Return the copy lenses to Customer Service, Polaroid Corp., Cambridge 39, Mass., for free replacement lenses.

Opposite is a brief operating summary. For more details about the Copymaker, write to Customer Service, Polaroid Corp., Cambridge 39, Mass.

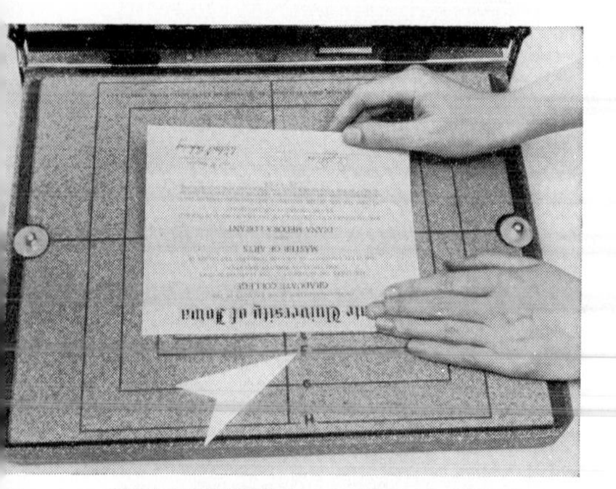

PICK A FRAME: Key to the data on the Camera Setting Chart is the frame (arrow) which will enclose the copy material. One easel side (for Type 46 film) has square frames with identifying letters; other side (for Type 46-L and all other films) has numbered rectangular frames. Once the copy has been positioned it is framed and held in place by metal margins, as shown in the photograph on the opposite page.

FOR EXTRA LARGE copy material, with Type 46 film only, the camera lens must be repositioned. To do this, insert the Refocus Plate in the bed before extending the bellows. It must fit behind two metal tabs near the front end of the bed. Then extend the bellows until the shutter housing brace rests on two white metal prongs at the rear of the Refocus Plate. Need for the plate is indicated on the chart by R*.

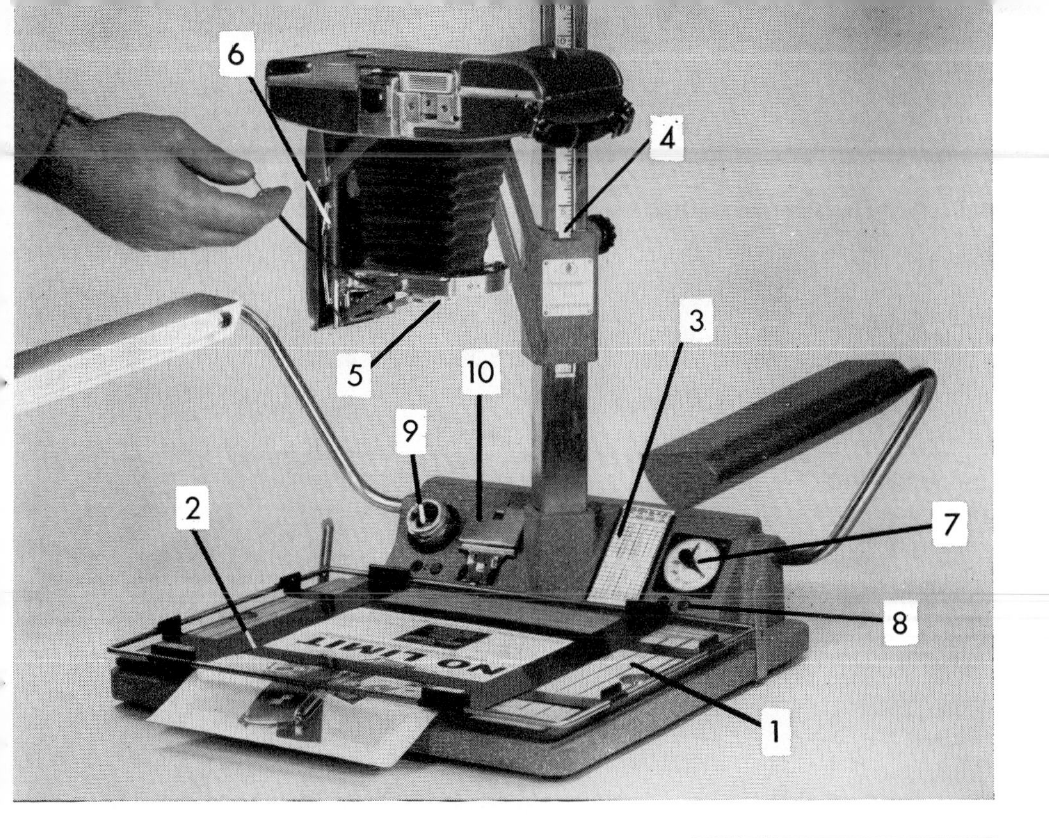

HOW THE COPYMAKER WORKS

Set the material to be copied on the easel and note the number or letter of the smallest easel frame (1) which will enclose it. Move the metal margins (2) in to frame and hold down the copy material.

On the camera setting chart (3, and at right) find the number of the frame enclosing your copy material. Next to this frame number the chart shows which copy lens to use, how high the camera should be, and where to set the camera's focus scale.

Raise the camera to the height (4) specified on the chart. Slip over the lens (5) the copy filter and the copy lens recommended by the chart. Set the camera's footage scale (6) to the distance given on the chart. Set the black hand of the timer (7) to the desired exposure time and start the red hand moving by pressing a button (8).

Copy lenses are stored on a mount (9). For extra large copy material (with Type 46 film only) the Refocus Plate (10, and at left) is needed. The left lamp is turned on and off by buttons next to the copy lens storage mount. The right one is operated by the buttons which control the timer.

CHART II			
FRAME NO.	CAM. FOCUS	CAM. HEIGHT	COPY LENS
FOR RECTANGULAR FORMAT 3¼" x 4"			
1	3½	¾	2+4
2	4	2⅞	4
3	50	3⅞	4
4	3½	8⅜	2
5	5	9½	2
6	8	10⅞	2
7	15	12⅛	2
8	50	13⅜	2
FOR SQUARE FORMAT 2¼" x 2¼"—TYPE 46			
A	3½	¾	2+4
B	4	2⅞	4
C	50	3⅞	4
D	3½	8⅜	2
E	8	10⅞	2
F	25	12⅞	2
G	4	12⅞	4+R*
H	5	16¼	4+R*

*REFOCUS PLATE

CAMERA SETTING CHARTS similar to this supply vital data for operating Copymaker. Use the right chart for your camera model. If you don't, the settings will be wrong and the results unsatisfactory.

THE PRINT COPIER

If you can't wait to get copy prints from Polaroid Corp., this is the gadget.

WITH THIS device and your own Polaroid Land camera you can make copy prints in a minute as easily as you made the original pictures in a minute.

The Print Copier/camera combination can turn out copies showing amazing fidelity to the originals. In fact, a too dark original can even be lightened and improved somewhat in copying.

The original print should be correctly exposed and *must* have clear, sharp details. If not, the copy will be at least as unsharp, and it may look much worse.

You may use any type of Polaroid Land film in the camera. However, if it's loaded with 3000 speed film you must install in the Print Copier lamp houses (photo 5, page 184) two light reducing filters which are in a holder underneath the bottom of the Print Copier. Instructions for use come with the filters.

There are three types of Print Copiers. Model 240, shown, is for all large cameras except Pathfinders. Model 2401 for Pathfinders, and Model 230 for Highlanders differ only in details.

The following pages explain some of the operating procedures.

COPY AND ORIGINAL: Well-made Print Copier product (left) is amazingly faithful copy of original.

READY TO SHOOT: This is how the camera and Print Copier look when the units are fitted together.

LOOKING IT OVER

1. On-Off push button for lamps and electric timer.

2. Timer hand rotates once a minute over second markings.

3. Rim of timer can be turned to any position; pointer on it aids in timing for exposure and development.

4. Cable release storage.

5. Front lock; must be lifted to close front.

6. Doors to lamp houses.

7. Print Copier lens turret; camera lens rests on ledge.

8. Locating pin fits in camera's tripod socket.

9. Lock screw to hold locating pin in proper position.

10. Exposure guide.

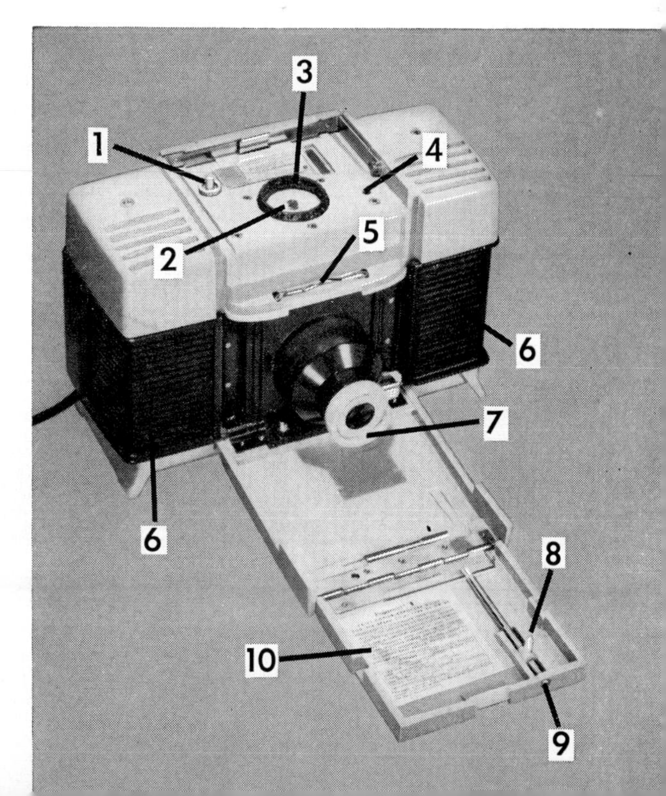

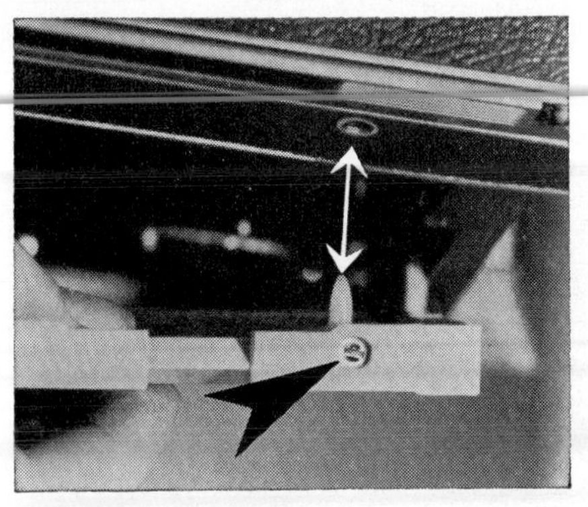

1. LOCATING PIN: It fits into the tripod socket on the side of the camera, keeps the camera body in proper relation to the Print Copier (#8, photo page 167). A ¼ left turn of the locking screw (arrow) lets the pin slide on a rod; lock it in the desired position by turning the screw to the right. Text explains how to position the pin.

2. PRINT TO BE COPIED: Open the door in the back of the Print Copier, insert the print in the black metal holder. Hinged wire frame comes down around edge of the print, holds it in place. Close the door—the print's ready to be copied.

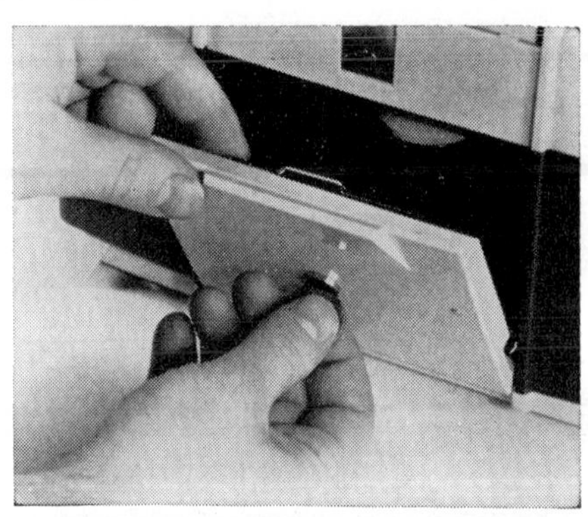

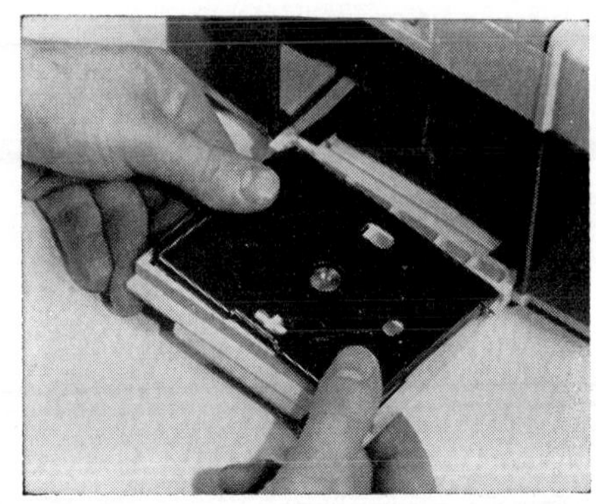

3 & 4. GETTING EXACT ALIGNMENT: Usually, the film in the camera and the print in the Print Copier are automatically aligned correctly. But some Print Copiers may need an exact alignment. To do so, loosen the screw in the back door (left) until the metal frame can be moved (right). Often, just centering it is sufficient. Then tighten the screw. For perfect alignment, guide lines on a test picture can be lined up with lines on the metal frame. This procedure is described in the Print Copier instruction booklet. Text at right explains symptoms of and cures for misalignment.

5. THE LAMPS: Doors to lamp house at each side of Print Copier swing open, can easily be lifted off. Midget lamps are 115/125-volt, 25-watt, double contact bayonet base type.

6. CLOSED FOR CARRYING: With front closed, the Print Copier resembles a medium-sized portable radio. Novel clip on rubber plug keeps cord securely wrapped around base.

Following are brief notes on Print Copier operations. For more details see the instruction booklet for each model.

Before placing your camera on the Print Copier, set it as follows:

Turn the exposure control to EV 17, #8, f/4.7, or f/4.5, depending upon the camera model. Set the shutter to "B" for a time exposure. Attach the cable release. Set the distance to 3½ ft. (Exceptions: set Models 80, 80A to Infinity; set original Model 95 to 4 ft.)

The camera is held on the Print Copier at two points. The lens mount is supported on the ledge of the Print Copier lens turret, against which it should rest snugly. *Caution: Never force the lens into place if the fit is tight.* A locating pin fits into the tripod socket (photo 1).

If the camera lens fits against the turret too tightly or too loosely, the locating pin must be moved. Use the metal key supplied with the Print Copier to unlock the screw with a ¼ turn to the left. With the pin in the tripod socket, slide the camera back and forth slightly until it fits just right. Lock the screw with a right turn.

You should be able to remove and replace the camera without trouble. Once the pin is set for your camera you need not adjust it again.

Highlanders are fitted to the Model 230 Print Copier in a different manner, described in the instruction booklet for that Print Copier. In 1959, the print borders of the Series 30 films (for the Highlander) were narrowed slightly. The smaller prints will not fit correctly in the #230 Print Copier. A simple metal adapter designed to hold the prints correctly in the back door of the Print Copier may be had free by writing to Customer Service, Polaroid Corp., Cambridge 39, Mass. This adapter is now supplied with currently manufactured #230 Print Copiers.

Exposure and development

Connect the Print Copier to a 110-volt AC outlet. Press the On-Off button —lights should go on and the timer hand should start to revolve.

Open the back door of the Print Copier and insert the print to be copied as in photo 2. Close the door.

Each copy requires a time exposure of several seconds. On all cameras but Pathfinders and Highlanders the shutter automatically returns to "snapshot" after a time exposure. Be sure to reset it to B for every copy.

For "average" prints, 7 seconds is a suggested exposure. The copy on page 182 was made with 5 seconds exposure. For prints in which important details are on the light side, expose for 2-3 seconds less than the "normal" 7 seconds. If important details are mainly dark gray, expose 10-12 seconds.

If the original is full of detail but is much too dark, it may be improved in copying. Set the exposure control one number lower (to EV 16 or #7) or double the exposure time, or both.

It's best to lift the camera off the Print Copier to develop the print. Pull the tab and immediately turn the timer rim to line up the pointer with the second hand. This saves having to remember when you pulled the tab.

Ordinarily, copy prints should be developed for a full minute. In some cases the final result may be too contrasty—blacks and whites predominate, with few delicate middle tones. This is most likely when the original is very contrasty. Copy contrast may be reduced by developing for only 45 seconds—but no less.

When developing time is up, open the back door of the camera, remove, straighten, and coat the print. If the copy is too light, cut exposure by one to three seconds. If the copy is too dark, increase exposure a bit.

Don't use the Print Copier in direct sunlight or near any other strong light source. Light leaks can cause streaks on the copy prints.

The Print Copier magnifies the original about 4% to allow for slight centering errors. If you get an occasional black margin of varying size, on a narrow side of the copy, it's probably due to not pulling the tab all the way each time.

If copies consistently show a gray margin in one area, the back door may need alignment (see photos 3 & 4).

TECHNICAL FACTS

CONVENTIONAL EQUIVALENTS OF THE EXPOSURE NUMBERS

THE CHARTS below show the conventional f-number and shutter speed equivalents of the exposure numbers used on Polaroid Land cameras. This information has mainly a curiosity value. Because of the unique shutter and lens controls of Polaroid Land cameras (except the Pathfinders), correct exposure is most easily determined with a Polaroid exposure meter.

If it should be necessary to determine exposure with a meter lacking Polaroid Land camera exposure number calibrations, these charts will be of help. You must set the meter for the exposure index of the Land film type you are using. This information is on the instruction sheet in the film package.

It's unlikely that your meter will be marked with such divisions as f/8.8 or f/12.5. Just set it to the nearest f-number—the error, if any, will be minor.

MODELS 95A, 95B, 100, 150, 700 and 800		
EXPOSURE NUMBER	GIVES LENS OPENING OF	AND SHUTTER SPEED OF
EV 10 or 1	f/8.8	1/13 SEC.
EV 11 or 2	f/8.8	1/25 SEC.
EV 12 or 3	f/8.8	1/50 SEC.
EV 13 or 4	f/8.8	1/100 SEC.
EV 14 or 5	f/12.5	1/100 SEC.
EV 15 or 6	f/17.5	1/100 SEC.
EV 16 or 7	f/25	1/100 SEC.
EV 17 or 8	f/35	1/100 SEC.

MODEL 95		
EXPOSURE NUMBER	GIVES LENS OPENING OF	AND SHUTTER SPEED OF
1	f/11	1/8 SEC.
2	f/11	1/15 SEC.
3	f/11	1/30 SEC.
4	f/11	1/60 SEC.
5	f/16	1/60 SEC.
6	f/22	1/60 SEC.
7	f/32	1/60 SEC.
8	f/45	1/60 SEC.

MODELS 80 and 80A		
EXPOSURE NUMBER	GIVES LENS OPENING OF	AND SHUTTER SPEED OF
EV 11 or 2	f/8.8	1/25 SEC.
EV 12 or 3	f/12.5	1/25 SEC.
EV 13 or 4	f/8.8	1/100 SEC.
EV 14 or 5	f/12.5	1/100 SEC.
EV 15 or 6	f/17.5	1/100 SEC.
EV 16 or 7	f/25	1/100 SEC.
EV 17 or 8	f/35	1/100 SEC.
EV 18 or 9	f/50	1/100 SEC.

ADAPTING CONVENTIONAL CAMERAS FOR USE WITH LAND FILMS

Polaroid Land films cannot be used in conventional roll film cameras, nor can Land cameras be adapted to use conventional roll films. However, several manufacturers of press and view type cameras are now making available specially adapted Polaroid Land backs, which fit right onto the back of the conventional camera.

In effect, the backs are the rear halves of Land cameras, fitted with light-tight flanges to secure them to conventional cameras.

For complete information about the availability of Land backs, and the technical problems connected with their use, write to Customer Service, Polaroid Corp., Cambridge 39, Mass.

LAND BACK: It consists of rear half of Polaroid Land camera, with special flanges for attachment to certain conventional press and view cameras.

FILTER FACTORS FOR POLAROID LAND FILMS

When you put a filter over the lens, it cuts down the amount of light which will reach the film. Therefore, exposure must be increased. The amount of exposure increase necessary is called the *filter factor*. A 4X filter factor means that exposure must be four times as great as if no filter were used. This chart also tells you how to adjust all models of the Land camera to get correct exposure.

Filter Type	Types 42, 44, 47, 37 — All Models Except Pathfinders	Types 42, 44, 47, 37 — Pathfinders and Cameras With Backs		Type 32-400 — Models 80A, 80	
	Set exposure control	Open diaphragm	Filter factor	Set exposure control	Filter factor
Yellow (Polaroid)	1# lower	1 f-number	2X	1# lower	2X
Orange (Polaroid)	2# lower	2 f-numbers	4X	2# lower	4X
Polarizer	2# lower	2 f-numbers	4X	2# lower	4X
Wratten K2 (#8)	1# lower	1 f-number	2X	1# lower	2X
Wratten X1 (#11) light green	2# lower	2 f-numbers	4X	2# lower	4X
Wratten B (#58) green	3# lower	3 f-numbers	8X	3# lower	8X
Wratten C5 (#47) blue	3# lower	3 f-numbers	8X	2# lower	4X
Wratten A (#25) red	4# lower	4 f-numbers	16X	5# lower	32X

THIS CHART LISTS ALL POLAROID LAND CAMERA MODELS

CAMERA	Photo-electric Shutter	Wink-light	Flash	Bounce Flash Bracket	Meter
80A Highlander	None	#250	#281	#292	PR-23A #620 #625
95B Speedliner	#440	#252	#202	#290	PR-23B #620 #625
150	#440	#250	#281	#292	PR-23A #620 #625
800	#440	#250	#281	#292	PR-23A #620 #625
110A Pathfinder	None	#250	#281	#292	PR-23A #620 #625
95	None	None	#202	#290	#620 #625
95A Speedliner	#440	#252	#202	#290	#620 #625
110 Pathfinder	None	#251	#222	#290	#620 #625
80 Highlander	None	#250	#281	#292	#620 #625
700	#440	#252	#202	#290	#620 #625
100	#440	#252	#202	#290	#620 #625

Note: Cameras below the double line are not now in production, but second hand models are on the market.

AND THE FILM TYPES AND ACCESSORIES WHICH FIT THEM

Filter Kit	Orange Filter	Close-up Kit	Compart-ment Case	Shoulder Case	Lens Shade	Film
#541	#546	#540	#383	#381	#545	32-400 37
#541	#546	#540	#310	#306A	#545	42, 44, 46, 46L, 47
#541	#546	#540	#310	#306A	#545	42, 44, 46, 46L, 47
#541	#546	#540	#310	#306A	#545	42, 44, 46, 46L, 47
#551	#551	#550	#310	#306A	#550	42, 44, 46, 46L, 47
#541	#546	#540	#310	#306A	#545	42, 44, 46, 46L (47 not recommended)
#541	#546	#540	#310	#306A	#545	42, 44, 46, 46L, 47
#551	#551	#550	#310	#306A	#550	42, 44, 46, 46L, 47
#541	#546	#540	#383	#381	#545	32-400 37
#541	#546	#540	#310	#306A	#545	42, 44, 46, 46L, 47
#541	#546	#540	#310	#306A	#545	42, 44, 46, 46L, 47

INDEX

ACKNOWLEDGEMENTS

I wish to express my appreciation and thanks to a number of people, without whose help it would have been impossible to produce the third edition of this book.

To members of the scientific staff of Polaroid Corp., who have once again supplied much important information and checked the text for technical accuracy.

To Miss Lois Feick and Stanford Calderwood of Polaroid Corp., for maintaining smooth and rapid liaison between the author and the sources of technical information, and for many helpful suggestions.

To Ernest G. Scarfone, Art Director of Amphoto, who designed the layouts for the picture sections, and Anthony Palagonia, who did other art work.

To my wife, who helped me greatly with the photographs, and the editing, and offered much useful criticism of the text.

To Harold Feinstein and Peter Gowland, for their remarkably creative work with the Polaroid Land camera.

To friends who posed patiently for functional photos.

To all the photographers whose beautiful pictures are reproduced in the book.

To many friends and associates, for their worthwhile suggestions in planning text and pictures, and for their help in securing suitable material. J.W.

The cover photograph was supplied by Polaroid Corp.